KEEPING
HOUSE

Women's Lives in
Western Pennsylvania

1 7 9 0 — 1 8 5 0

KEEPING HOUSE

Women's Lives in Western Pennsylvania

1790–1850

by Virginia K. Bartlett

with an Introduction by Jack D. Warren

HISTORICAL SOCIETY OF WESTERN PENNSYLVANIA

UNIVERSITY OF PITTSBURGH PRESS

Published by the Historical Society of Western Pennsylvania
and the University of Pittsburgh Press, Pittsburgh, Pa.
Editor: Fannia Weingartner
Designer: Jo Butz
Manufactured in the United States of America
by BookCrafters, Chelsea, Michigan

Library of Congress Cataloging-in-Publication Data

Bartlett, Virginia K.
    Keeping house : women's lives in western Pennsylvania, 1790–1850
by Virginia K. Bartlett : with an introduction by Jack D. Warren.
       p. cm.
    Includes bibliographical references and index.
    ISBN 0-8229-3854-5 (alk. paper).—ISBN 0-8229-5538-5 (pbk. : alk. paper)
    1. Women—Pennsylvania—History—19th century. 2. Women—
Pennsylvania—Pittsburgh Region—History—19th century. 3. Women—
Pennsylvania—Social conditions. 4. Women—Pennsylvania—
Pittsburgh Region—Social conditions. I. Title.
HQ1438.P4B37 1994
305.4'09748—dc20
                                         94–22983
                                          CIP

CREDITS

Illustrations and photographed objects from the Collections of the Historical Society of Western Pennsylvania are identified in the text, as are quotation sources. Credits for all other illustrations, as well as for large blocks of quoted material, are listed by page number in the order in which they appear in the text. Any omissions or misattributions are entirely inadvertent.

ILLUSTRATIONS

INSTITUTIONS

Page 2 (top), Shelburne Museum, Shelburne, Vt.

Pages 3, 7, 9, Dunbar Collection, Henry Ford Museum & Greenfield Village, Mich.

Page 12, Courtesy of Westmoreland Museum of Art, Greensburg, Pa.

Page 49, Courtesy of Erie County Historical Society, Erie, Pa.

Pages 56, 59, Courtesy of Westmoreland County Historical Society, Greensburg, Pa.

Pages 57, 131, 132, 164, Courtesy of The Carnegie Library of Pittsburgh, Pa.

Page 93, Courtesy of The Historical Society of York County, York, Pa.

Pages 101, 135, 161, Courtesy of Henry Ford Museum & Greenfield Village, Pa.

INDIVIDUAL COLLECTIONS

Pages 22, 28 (top), 107, Courtesy of Jo Butz, Ligonier, Pa.

Page 44, from *Historical Collections of the State of Pennsylvania,* by Sherman Day. Courtesy of Rina Youngner, Pittsburgh, Pa.

Pages 52 (bottom), 60, 134 (bottom), 137, from Godey's *The Lady's Book,* 1833 and 1837. Courtesy of Virginia K. Bartlett, Hingham, Mass.

PUBLICATIONS

Page iii, from *Treasury of American Design,* by Clarence P. Hornung, Vol. 2, Harry N. Abrams, Inc., N.Y., 1950.

Page xii, from *The History of an Expedition against Fort Du Quesne in 1755: Under Major-General Braddock,* by Winthrop Sargent, Lippincott, Grambo & Co., Philadelphia, Pa., 1855.

Pages xiii, 14, from *Old-Fashioned Illustrations of Books, Reading & Writing,* Carol Belanger Grafton, ed., Dover Publications, Inc., Mineola, N.Y., 1992.

Page 5, from *The National Road, Most Historic Thoroughfare in the United States, and Eastern Division of the National Old Trails Ocean-to-Ocean Highway,* by Robert Bruce, co-published by author and National Highway Association, Washington, D.C., 1916.

Page 18 (bottom), from *A Geography of Pennsylvania,* by Charles B. Trego, Edward C. Biddle, Philadelphia, Pa., 1843.

Pages 19, 27, 39, 85, 87, 166, from *Good Olde Days, Graphic Source Clip Art,* Graphic Products Corporation, Rolling Meadows, Il., 1986.

Pages 21, 35, 143, from *Liwwät Böke, Pioneer, 1807-1882,* Luke B. Knapke, ed., Minster Historical Society, Minster, Ohio, 1987. Copyright © 1987 by Minster Historical Society.

Pages 28 (bottom), 158, from *All Sorts of Good Sufficient Cloth: Linen-Making in New England 1640-1860,* Merrimack Valley Textile Museum, Mass., 1980, Museum of American Textile History, North Andover, Mass.

Pages 38, 40, 41, 127, 154 (top), from *Historical Collections of the State of Pennsylvania,* by Sherman Day, 1843. Re-issued by Ira J. Friedman, Inc., Keystone State Historical Publications Series No. 1, N.Y., 1969.

Pages 53, 75, 117, 121, from *Trades and Occupations: A Pictorial Archive from Early Sources,* Carol Belanger Grafton, ed., Dover Publications, Inc., Mineola, N.Y., 1990.

Pages 54, 148-49, from *Old Westmoreland,* Vol. 4, No. 1, Southwest Pennsylvania Genealogical Services, Laughlintown, Pa., 1983.

Page 106 (top), from *Landscapes and Gardens for Historic Buildings,* by Rudy J. Favretti and Joy Putman Favretti, American Association for State and Local History, Nashville, Tenn., 1978.

Page 109, from *The Indian Physician,* by Dr. Jonas Rishel, 1828. Reprinted by Friends of the Libraries of The Ohio State University, Columbus, Ohio, 1987.

Pages 110, 123, 124, from *Old-Time Schools and School-Books,* by Clifton Johnson, Dover Publications, Inc., Mineola, N.Y., 1963.

Pages 120, 128, from *Old Redstone: Historical Sketches of Western Presbyterianism, Its Early Ministers, Its Perilous Times, and Its First Records,* by Joseph Smith, D.D., Lippincott, Grambo & Co., Philadelphia, Pa., 1854.

Pages 134 (top), 169, from *Harper's New Monthly Magazine,* Vol. I, Harper & Brothers, N.Y., 1850.

Page 154 (bottom), from *An Old-Fashioned Christmas in Illustration & Decoration*, Clarence P. Hornung, ed., Dover Publications, Inc., Mineola, N.Y., 1970.

Page 155, from *McCall's Magazine*, December 1930.

Page 159, from *Harper's New Monthly Magazine*, Vol. II, Harper & Brothers, N.Y., 1851.

QUOTED MATERIALS

Page 14, from THE TREES, by Conrad Richter, 1940. Reprinted by permission of Random House, Inc.

Pages 18, 77, 90, 128, 144, from THE FIELDS, by Conrad Richter. Copyright 1945, 1946 by Conrad Richter and renewed 1973, 1974 by Harvena Richter. Reprinted by permission of Alfred A. Knopf, Inc.

Page 58, excerpt from THE KING'S ORCHARD, by Agnes Sligh Turnbull. Copyright © 1963 by Agnes Sligh Turnbull. Copyright © renewed 1991 by Martha Turnbull O'Hearn. Reprinted by permission of Houghton Mifflin Company. All rights reserved.

Page 65, research for the Historical Society of Western Pennsylvania, prepared by Matrix Communications Associates, 1993.

Page 101, temperance song reprinted from *America's Families, A Documentary History*, by Donald M. Scott and Bernard Wishy, eds., Harper and Row, N.Y., 1982.

Page 101, temperance poem, Henry Ford Museum & Greenfield Village, Mich.

Page 106, herbs list from *Landscapes and Gardens for Historic Buildings,* by Rudy J. Favretti and Joy Putman Favretti, American Association for State and Local History, Nashville, Tenn., 1978.

Excerpts from *Liwwät Böke, Pioneer, 1807-1882*, Luke B. Knapke, ed., published by the Minster Historical Society, Ohio, 1987. Copyright © 1987 Minster Historical Society. Reprinted by permission of Minster Historical Society.

Selected quotations from LeMoyne Papers, Washington County Historical Society, Washington, Pa. Reprinted by permission of Washington County Historical Society.

Selected quotations from letters of Nancy Swearingen to her family, 1813-1829, from Bedinger-Dandridge Family Papers, Special Collections Library, Duke University, N.C. Reprinted by permission of Special Collections Library, Duke University.

Selected quotations from Professional Diary of Jacob Zimmerman, 1841-1899, Westmoreland County Historical Society, Greensburg, Pa. Reprinted by permission of Westmoreland County Historical Society.

TABLE OF CONTENTS

FOREWORD

The idea for this book was prompted by several handwritten books of recipes and remedies, dating from the 18th and early 19th centuries, in the archival collections of the Historical Society of Western Pennsylvania. When these manuscripts were shown to Virginia K. Bartlett, author of *Pickles and Pretzels: Pennsylvania's World of Food* (1980), also known for her television programs on WQED Pittsburgh and WGBH Boston, they inspired her to embark on the research that resulted in this book.

As have others before her, the author discovered that materials dealing specifically with the lives of women settlers in this region were relatively sparse. However, by using published reminiscences of settlers and travelers of both genders, family papers in archival collections, newspapers, and other contemporary publications, she was able to develop a vivid picture of women's lives and conditions both on the frontier and in the fledgling Western Pennsylvania towns of the post-Revolutionary era.

Historian Jack D. Warren of the University of Virginia, a contributor to the Society's quarterly magazine *Pittsburgh History*, was invited to introduce this book, both because of his extensive knowledge of early immigration into this region and his interest in women's history.

A generous grant from the H. J. Heinz Company Foundation, which chose this project, in part, as a way of recognizing its own 125th anniversary, made this publication possible. Founded in Pittsburgh in 1869 by Henry J. Heinz, son of German immigrants, at a time when commercially prepared foods were not available, the company has grown into a world-wide producer and distributor of prepared foods of many kinds. Intrigued by the Historical Society's holdings of domestic recipes used by Western Pennsylvanians of an earlier era, H. J. Heinz Company gave its enthusiastic support to the development and publication of this book. Further linking the Heinz family name with the Pittsburgh region's history, the Historical Society announced this year that in 1996 it would open The Senator John Heinz Pittsburgh Regional History Center, a new 160,000-square-foot museum facility in the city's Strip District. The H. J. Heinz Company's commitment to history has found expression, as well, in the recent donation of its collection of 35,000 artifacts and photographs to the Historical Society of Western Pennsylvania.

The publication of *KEEPING HOUSE* offered an ideal opportunity to introduce some results of the intensive collection effort initiated in 1986 by John Herbst, Executive Director of the Historical Society of Western Pennsylvania, in preparation for the opening of The Senator John Heinz Pittsburgh Regional History Center in 1996. Many of the illustrations for *KEEPING HOUSE* are paintings and engravings, or newly created photographs of artifacts of the period, from the Society's collections. Building collections of artifacts and archival materials will remain a central goal of the institution, since these authentic materials form the basis of exhibitions, publications, and educational programs.

Like all museum projects, this was a collaborative enterprise, involving archivists, curators, librarians, and numerous other staff members, as well as the collective resources of the Museum Programs, Collections and Research, and Library and Archives divisions. Working in concert, Collections and Publications staff organized the identification, selection, and photographing of artifacts which yielded many of the illustrations for this book, as well as creating a visual record that will serve researchers for years to come. Meanwhile, public programming sponsored by the Historical Society of Western Pennsylvania and supported, in part, by IKEA, will ensure that the insights offered by this book will reach a broad popular audience.

Another joint effort of note involves the co-publishers of this book—the Historical Society of Western Pennsylvania and the University of Pittsburgh Press, two institutions with a distinguished record of cooperation in the publication of local history. Working together in the 1930s and early 1940s, they helped sponsor a great burst of research, the Western Pennsylvania Historical Survey, which resulted in a string of books that included Leland D. Baldwin's local classics *Pittsburgh, The Story of a City* and *The Keel-boat Age on Western Waters* and Randolph C. Downes's *Council Fires on the Upper Ohio*.

The publication of *KEEPING HOUSE* marks a renewal of this alliance, established with the guidance and expertise of Frederick A. Hetzel, retired Director of the University of Pittsburgh Press, and Acting Director Peter Oresick.

In the same way that the objects and papers that were part of people's everyday lives constitute the collections of the Historical Society of Western Pennsylvania, this publication brings readers a sense of many of the common experiences that marked the lives of the courageous, adaptable—and often eloquent—women who settled in this region.

Historical Society of Western Pennsylvania
Pittsburgh, Pennsylvania, Fall 1994

PREFACE

A woman born in 1780 and turning 70 in 1850 would have seen her world turned up-side down by the dizzying pace of change. After years of struggling to raise a family in the wilderness, she could buy almost anything she wanted in her local store, from readymade clothing to kitchen stoves. Trains, canal boats, and fast stages made travel easier. Women had begun to attend colleges, form literary societies, and found charitable organizations. But in spite of this a woman's role as wife and mother remained essentially the same, as did her anxieties and uncertainties. The endless household and farm chores, the con-cerns about marriage and children, about disease, crop failure, and death are common threads in accounts by women from New England to California. Ironically, as technology helped to change women's lives for the better, attitudes towards women's roles showed little change.

Although women living in New England and the far West left numerous diaries and letters, most accounts of frontier life in Western Pennsylvania were written by men, so that our knowledge of that period is shaped by their views and their prejudices. For whatever reasons—lack of time and opportunity, loss of family records, illiteracy—the experiences of women in Western Pennsylvania are sparsely documented.

One resource for learning more about these women's lives is the collection of manu-script recipe and remedy books in the Historical Society of Western Pennsylvania. Each one is a very personal document, a collection of recipes, remedies, and household advice growing out of a woman's experience or that of friends and relatives.

When men wrote of life on the frontier, the children were all rosy-cheeked and healthy; the men strong, stalwart, and invincible; the women stoic, loving, indefatigable, radiating health and strength. On Route 40, the old National Road, just east of Washington, Pennsylvania, the traveler will find a monument dedicated to pioneer mothers, erected by the Daughters of the American Revolution. Called "Madonna of the Trail," it portrays a pioneer woman, a baby in her arms, another clutching at her skirts. In her long dress and sunbonnet, she is striding forward, a determined yet serene expression on her face. It is a highly romantic image of what we all long to believe about our ancestors. There is, of course, a great deal of truth in it. These women were indeed intrepid and determined. But it is well to remember that they were also angry, exhausted, irritable, joyful, shy, impatient, anxious, greedy, ill, curious, gossipy, mean-spirited, generous, loving, and frightened. Just like us.

§ § §

I am indebted to the many people who helped make this book possible, in particular the staff of the library at the Historical Society of Western Pennsylvania. Three people deserve special appreciation: my editor, Fannia Weingartner, who is talented, patient, and lots of fun; my good friend and research associate, Josie Stanton, who brought her intelligence and enthusiasm to this project; and book designer, Jo Butz, whose concern for the right illustration in the right place made an invaluable contribution to the book.

Virginia K. Bartlett

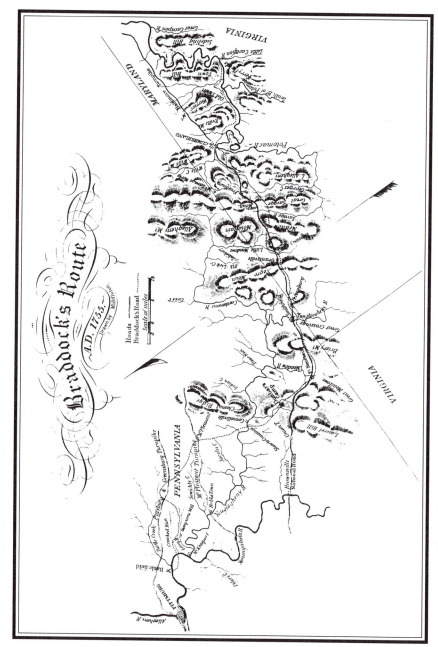

Most settlers moving into Western Pennsylvania from Virginia in the 18th century followed the military road constructed by Braddock's army in 1755.

INTRODUCTION

THE EARLY PEOPLING OF WESTERN PENNSYLVANIA

This book is about the experience of ordinary women in Western Pennsyl-vania during the decades in which it was transformed from an isolated and dangerous area on the fringes of Anglo-American settlement into a stable farming country in the center of the new American nation. In 1755 a disgusted British army officer, William Johnston, described Western Pennsylvania as "a desolate coun-try uninhabited by anything but wild Indians, bears and rattlesnakes."[1] In 1842 Mary Corwin, a young New Jersey woman who passed through Western Pennsyl-vania, described it as "a beatifull country" peopled by "first rate farmers" living in fine houses as well as desperately poor families who lived "in some of the most wretched looking hovels that I ever saw."[2]

Women shared in this transformation, but their experience has never been fully understood or appreciated. In part this is due to the nature of the sources, which make the lives of ordinary women on the early trans-Appalachian frontier particularly difficult to reconstruct. Unlike their counterparts in the older com-munities of the East, few women in early Western Pennsylvania seem to have kept diaries or maintained regular correspondence with friends and relations—or if they did, fewer of these documents survive. Due to the legal limitations on women's rights to own and convey property or otherwise maintain a social, economic, or legal identity distinct from that of their husbands, women tended to make a faint impression on the kinds of documents—newspapers, court proceedings, business papers, and church records—upon which historians generally rely; often they vanish altogether. Not the least important factor in the failure of historians to treat the experience of women on the early trans-Appalachian frontier is the fact that many of them have been inclined to regard women's lives as peripheral or even irrelevant to the central story of American history—a story dominated by politics and war, in which the common man shrinks to insignificance and the common woman to oblivion.

KEEPING HOUSE is an attempt to redress this imbalance by focusing on the experience of ordinary women in the first several decades of European settle-ment in Western Pennsylvania. Women came there as daughters, wives, and mothers, their status almost completely dependent on men. Yet their social experiences were not exclusively dependent on men. Like their counterparts in the East, they established social spheres in which they enjoyed a certain degree of autonomy. They established patterns of household management, child-rearing, and interaction within the family and with neighbors over which men exercised limited influence. *KEEPING HOUSE* explores these patterns, as well as the other ways in which women responded to the experience of life on a changing frontier.

§ § §

The social experiences of women described in this book worked themselves out within the broader context of European settlement in the region—a great movement of people shaped by impersonal demographic and economic pressures, imperial competition, the acquisitiveness of wealthy men, and the ceaseless ambition of ordinary people to acquire land for themselves and to provide a better life for their families. In the beginning this movement of people was guided by the speculative designs of men who sought to make fortunes out of the land beyond the limits of British colonial settlement.

The prevailing systems of land distribution at the end of the 18th and the beginning of the 19th centuries generally favored the ambitions of speculators and often crushed the hopes of ordinary people. The settlers of Western Pennsylvania were mostly the sons and daughters of Eastern farmers or recent immigrants from Ireland or Germany. Most were landless, and saw little prospect of acquiring sufficient land to support themselves in the long-settled areas east of the Appalachians; they moved into Western Pennsylvania intending to establish farms of their own. Often they found that the best land had already been claimed by speculators. Large numbers squatted on the land of absentee owners, hoping to establish title through possession and improvement, only to find themselves forced off the land by legal action. By necessity many became tenants or moved to unclaimed but less productive land, where they were barely able to work a living out of the soil. Others were forced to become landless laborers. By the second quarter of the 19th century the distribution of land and wealth in Western Pennsylvania mirrored that of the many long-settled parts of the East, with land-ownership concentrated in the hands of an ever-smaller percentage of the population. The region boasted many prosperous farms and rapidly growing towns, but many of its people—perhaps the majority—lived in circumstances of desperate poverty.

The rich bottom lands along the Ohio and its tributaries began to attract the attention of speculators and settlers alike in the early 1750s. Most of the settlers came, not from Pennsylvania at all, but from Virginia. On the basis of the vague provisions of their colonial charter, Virginia authorities claimed title to the entire Ohio Valley. Nature favored Virginia's claim. The easiest route into the region from the seaboard was up the Potomac River and its tributaries and into the valleys of the Youghiogheny and Monongahela. In 1747 a group of enterprising Virginians intent on exploiting this route organized the Ohio Company of Virginia, and two years later they received a grant of 200,000 acres to be surveyed south of the Ohio River. The partners in this venture planned to establish a trading monopoly with the Indians of the region and to sell land to potential settlers as soon as the Indians could be pushed out or bought out. The Ohio Company's ambitious plans proved premature. The company's early settlements in the Monongahela Valley were destroyed during the French and Indian War and the company subsequently became mired in political and legal struggles, losing its central role in the development of the region. Rival companies, foreign investors, and other speculators, as well as ordinary settlers took its place in the scramble for land.[3]

The permanent settlement of Western Pennsylvania began after 1758, when the capture of Fort Duquesne assured British control of the upper Ohio. After wresting control from the French, the British government declared the land west of the mountains reserved for the Indians and closed to settlers except by military permit. Permits were granted for settlement near the new forts at Bedford, Ligonier, Pittsburgh, and Redstone, and for farms established along roads leading to the forts. These permits hardly began to satisfy the desire of ordinary settlers for land. Squatters without military permits soon began taking up land in the backcountry away from the forts and main roads. Colonel Henry Bouquet complained to Virginia Governor Francis Fauquier that as early as 1760 the Monongahela Valley was "over run by a Number of Vagabonds, who under pretense of hunting, were making settlements." Pennsylvania authorities made repeated efforts to expel the squatters in the 1760s, mostly to no avail. In 1766 a force was dispatched down the Monongahela to order "Lawless and Licentious" settlers to leave at once, threatening that if they did not comply, "the Commander-in-Chief, will order an armed force to drive you from the Lands." Threats and intimidation did little to persuade backcountry settlers to move on. "Not withstanding all the trouble that has been taken [to] moove the People settled on Redstone Creek, & Cheat [River]," George Croghan complained in 1767, "I am well assured there are double the Number of Inhabi[tants] in those two Settlements that ever was before."[4]

In 1768 British authorities lifted the restriction on settlement west of the mountains, and settlers began moving into the area in unprecedented numbers. A contemporary estimated that between 4,000 and 5,000 families settled in Western Pennsylvania between 1768 and 1770, and noted that the roads into the region were filled with wagons heading toward the Ohio. Settlers from Virginia and Maryland were most numerous, but they were joined by a steady stream of settlers from Pennsylvania and recent immigrants from Britain and Germany.

Speculators competed with ordinary settlers for the most valuable farmland. The dispute between Virginia and Pennsylvania over the region tended to encourage speculators, since both colonies were anxious to validate their claim to the region by granting title to the land. Virginia law permitted settlers to patent tracts of 1,000 acres or more for a trifling sum per acre, and Virginia authorities issued patents to scores of absentee landowners. Virginia had issued bounty certificates redeemable in land to soldiers at the end of the French and Indian War; wartime officers like George Washington bought up many of these certificates and had extensive tracts surveyed in the Ohio Valley. Washington himself visited the area in the fall of 1770 and found the entire region consumed with land fever. "People from Virginia & elsewhere," he recorded in his diary, "are exploring and Marking all the Lands that are valuable not only on the Redstone & other Waters of the Monongahela but along down the Ohio as low as the little Kanawha."[5]

Virginians vied for land with Pennsylvanians, who usually occupied the land as squatters. Pennsylvania law actually encouraged squatters by making it fairly easy for them to obtain legal title to their property after settlement. Settlers who could certify improvement of unwarranted land could apply to have the land surveyed and would subsequently be granted a patent in return for purchase price of the land—set at £5 per 100 acres—with back interest. Those who could not afford the price either kept squatting on the land and risked being ejected by a future patent holder, or sold their improvements to another squatter family and moved farther west. Those who could afford to pay the purchase price for their claims usually took advantage of this policy. Such squatters were not necessarily poor people; many well-off families took physical possession of new land before obtaining legal title. When George Washington was forced to file a lawsuit to eject squatters from his claims on Millers Creek in 1784, the defendants included several prominent and fairly well-to-do settlers.[6]

By the eve of the Revolution perhaps as many as 40,000 people were living in what became the southwestern corner of Pennsylvania west of the Allegheny Ridge. Most lived in distinct religious or ethnic communities rather than on isolated farms far from friends, relatives, and co-religionists. The Uniontown area was settled initially by Quakers in 1767, and served as a nucleus for Quaker settlement until after the Revolution. The early settlers of Brownsville were mostly Virginians, with a large number of Quakers among them. Germans settled in large numbers around Ligonier. Even the Scots-Irish—famous for their fierce independence—tended to settle in groups. By 1775 Southwestern Pennsylvania was a patchwork of ethnic and religious enclaves, each with an active community life of its own.

Such communities served many functions: all but the smallest seem to have supported a few rudimentary craftsmen, midwives, and other part-time specialists. Established by people of common background and with common interests, these communities—after the family—were the basic organizing structures of society in early Western Pennsylvania. For women in particular, such communities provided a network of kin and friends with which to share the most difficult or demanding household tasks. In good times they built churches and towns and in bad times they built blockhouses to protect their members against Indians and made common cause against rival land claimants.[7]

Life in these communities was apparently extremely difficult. Primitive living conditions, isolation from markets, and confusion over political and legal jurisdiction compounded the widespread insecurity over land ownership. The Revolution added to this turmoil but did not halt the flow of settlers. From 1774 to 1782 the region suffered from repeated Indian attacks. At times whole settlements were destroyed and settlers were frequently forced to take refuge in blockhouse forts to avoid being killed or taken prisoner. The Revolution also added to the complications and uncertainties over land titles. Pennsylvania's land office, located in distant Philadelphia, was closed for the duration of the war. Squatters continued to occupy the land, but with no certainty that they would be granted title to the land they cleared once the war was over.

The settlement of the boundary dispute between Pennsylvania and Virginia in 1780 did not end the confusion. Pennsylvania assumed authority over the region, but agreed to respect the prior land claims of Virginians over the claims of Pennsylvanians. Since many of the Virginia claims were held by absentee owners, large numbers of Pennsylvania settlers were forced off the land or became tenants as a result of this agreement. In the decade between 1780 and 1790, the proportion of settlers with clear title to land seems to have dropped precipitously. In 1780 perhaps one-third of the population of Western Pennsylvania was landless, and economic conditions in the region seem to have gotten worse as the decade passed.

Southwestern Pennsylvania boasted a population of about 75,000 people when the first census was taken in 1790. About 60,000 of these inhabitants were settled in the fertile, fairly level land west of Chestnut Ridge; the rest were scattered in the valleys to the east. A third of the population was of English background, and another third was Scots or Scots-Irish. The rest was made up of Welsh, German, and other ethnic groups. Nearly all lived in farm families. Surviving evidence suggests that many—perhaps even most—lived at a bare subsistence level or even below.

Travelers were frequently struck by the poverty of the settlers and appalled at the primitive conditions in which they lived. Mary Dewees, a young woman traveling through Western Pennsylvania in 1787, described spending the night in a log cabin that passed as ordinary. "The people [were] very kind but amazing dirty," she wrote. "There was between twenty and thirty of us; all lay on the floor, except Mr. Rees, the children and your Maria, who…were favored with a bed, and I assure you that we thought ourselves lucky to escape being fleaed alive." Others were less charitable, describing the inhabitants of the region as "a parcel of abandoned wretches" living "like so many pigs in a sty." Economic circumstances apparently got worse rather than better in the generation after the Revolution. Life in the towns was apparently not much better. Few people lived in towns in 1790—Pittsburgh was the largest and boasted only 376 people—and the majority of them were apparently poor laborers, widows, servants, and other dependent and usually propertyless people. Artisans made up about 16 percent of the population, and merchants, lawyers, and other professionals about 7 percent.[8]

The opening of the region north of the Ohio and west of the Allegheny rivers to purchase and settlement was delayed until 1792. It set off an unprecedented speculative boom. Between 1792 and 1794, the state land office issued over 5,000 warrants. Many of these warrants were obtained by speculative land companies: the Holland Land Company obtained warrants on over 1.5 million acres in Pennsylvania; the Pennsylvania Population Company acquired warrants to some 450,000 acres in Northwestern Pennsylvania alone. Settlers moving north up the Allegheny Valley frequently occupied and improved tracts previously warranted by Eastern speculators, who might later file suits to eject them. Settlers soon became wary of speculators, and settlement of the region west of the Allegheny was apparently slowed as a consequence.

The peopling of Northwestern Pennsylvania proceeded slowly for other reasons as well. The region was a considerable distance from established travel and trade routes between the East and the growing Ohio Valley and much farther from the New Orleans market than the contemporary settlements in Ohio and Kentucky. Local outlets for farm produce developed slowly. Many of the most industrious early settlers soon moved on to Ohio, and living conditions for those who remained were difficult. Their cabins were typically smaller and more poorly furnished than those of other frontier areas, their diet more limited, their clothing more meager. In the early years draft animals were uncommon, and most settlers could only farm as many acres as they could cultivate with a hoe. The Moravian agent and missionary John Heckewelder visited such a family in 1800; the couple had five children, were in debt to the Holland Land Company for nearly $600 for provisions, and lived in complete destitution and despair.[9]

Harm Jan Huidekoper, an agent for the Holland Land Company in Meadville, wrote in 1805 that the local settlements presented "a picture of wretchedness I have never seen equalled in America." Particularly distressing were the circumstances of the hundreds of recent Irish immigrants sent out by the company. Mostly penniless and lacking any practical experience in clearing new land, many of them seem to have lived in the coarsest conditions, soon giving up any idea of land ownership and accepting menial labor of any kind merely to survive. Not surprisingly, Huidekoper noted that the people were moving out in a steady stream.[10]

Not until the decade between 1810 and 1820 did a degree of social stability finally begin to touch the lives of ordinary people in Western Pennsylvania. Population growth, which had long exceeded the national average, slowed considerably. Between 1810 and 1820 the population of Western Pennsylvania grew from 210,000 to 271,000, or about 29 percent. Most of this growth probably came from natural increase, as births in the region surpassed migration as the principal source of population growth. Unfortunately the economic prospects of ordinary farmers did not improve at the same time. After increasing briefly, prices for farm commodities collapsed in the economic depression that followed the War of 1812. A measure of prosperity was slow in returning, and not until the mid-1820s was the economic recovery complete. By that time frontier conditions had given way to settled community life in all but the most remote parts of Western Pennsylvania, and social conditions in the region had begun to approximate those in the more stable and ordered communities of the East.[11]

§ § §

Recent historical research suggests that the social experience of settlement on the early trans-Appalachian frontier was characterized by poverty, unrest, and disorder and that these conditions gave way only slowly to ordered community life in the decades after 1800. If this research is correct, women on the Western Pennsylvania frontier underwent a harrowing experience that included a prolonged decline in living standards, economic uncertainty, and hard labor. The primary social consequence of this experience seems to have been a relative decline in status.

One hundred years ago, historian Frederick Jackson Turner argued that frontier experience tended to level social distinctions and liberate settlers from the constraints imposed by the traditional order of Eastern society, encouraging the development of political and social equality, democracy, and economic individualism. Turner's famous thesis has long dominated the way Americans think about the frontier, yet it seems to have no application to the experience of women. Rather than liberating women from the constraints imposed by Eastern society, the experience of the early trans-Appalachian frontier actually seems to have deepened their subordination and limited their sphere of independent action. The women's movement that began in earnest in the second third of the 19th century was most active in the well-established cities of the East; it had little discernible effect in the upper Ohio Valley until much later. Nor were women in early 19th-century Western Pennsylvania able to exercise as much influence in other aspects of public life as their Eastern counterparts. In the East women played an important public role through their work in religious and charitable institutions, but such institutions—more characteristic of towns than rural areas—developed slowly on the sparsely settled and economically backward trans-Appalachian frontier.

More importantly, the frontier experience failed to lead to an increase in personal autonomy for women. As American society became more commercially oriented in the early decades of the 19th century, ordinary women established a broader sphere of personal independence through their involvement in the marketplace. The development of manufacturing in the Northeast offered women the opportunity to become independent wage earners. Even if they were unable to free themselves from the control of men—some early factories employed only unmarried women, and imposed strict control over their income and activities— the growth of manufacturing employment offered some women a chance to establish a limited degree of personal economic autonomy.

For the much larger number of rural women, the growth of domestic production for the marketplace was the basis for enlarging the sphere of personal independence and control. In Southeastern Pennsylvania, for example, butter-making developed from a traditional domestic art into an important commercial enterprise dominated by farm women. Farm women had long made butter for home consumption. Some of this butter made its way into local markets— sometimes in cash transactions, more often through barter. Increasingly during the early 19th century, however, domestic butter manufacturing served a growing regional and foreign export market. Butter-making and similar domestic manufacturing enterprises offered farm families a way to diversify their production and to cushion themselves against fluctuations in the price of staple crops. They also offered a means of providing a steady cash income with which to buy household goods. The production of a regular cash income—even if husbands and fathers ultimately controlled its disposition—gave women an increasingly important and independent role in the family economy at a time when the ability to buy an increasing array of consumer goods—everything from lace tablecloths to china dishware and imported cloth—was beginning to define the American middle class.[12]

On the Appalachian frontier the growth of this sort of economic autonomy for women was severely retarded. The demands of establishing a farm in the wilderness and the need to produce a broad array of household goods at home rather than purchasing them in the marketplace, subordinated wives to their husbands and limited women's opportunities to play a role in the market economy apart from them. Most frontier settlers were cash poor, and remained so at a time when their Eastern counterparts were enjoying a widening array of consumer goods. To meet their cash needs, Western Pennsylvania settlers frequently turned to lumbering, saw-milling, and a variety of craft employments. Salt-making, for example, was a common commercial employment in Crawford and adjacent counties in Northwestern Pennsylvania.[13] Most of this rural commercial activity in Western Pennsylvania was dominated by men; women had few opportunities to engage in market-oriented activities. Their labor consequently continued to be considered subordinate, and probably inferior, to that of their husbands.

Economic conditions in early Western Pennsylvania constrained women's autonomy in other ways as well. Suzanne Lesbock, in her study of late 18th- and early 19th-century Petersburg, Virginia, argues that women managed to increase their autonomy and free themselves from subordination to particular men by remaining unmarried, by working for wages, and acquiring separate estates beyond the reach of men. These opportunities were not available to women on the early trans-Appalachian frontier. Unmarried women and widows who chose not to remarry faced a life of poverty on the Pennsylvania frontier; frequently they were forced to become domestic servants simply to survive. Wage labor for women remained a scarce and uncertain source of income.[14]

While women on the early trans-Appalachian frontier seem to have remained more completely subordinate to their husbands than women in other regions of the country, they also seem to have been just as successful as women in other rural areas in establishing a separate social sphere. *KEEPING HOUSE* attempts, in part, to define this "woman's sphere," describing how women managed their households, reared their children, and interacted within the family and with neighbors.

The idea that women and men naturally occupied "separate spheres" became widespread early in the 19th century, and was rooted mainly in the experience of the urban middle class. It embodied the practical distinctions between workplace and household, and more specifically between the income-producing labor of men and the household labor of women. It also embodied the more subjective distinction between the male and female character. Naturally given to greater selflessness, piety, and virtue, women were expected to enjoy considerable autonomy and power in the home, while their husbands, who were more decisive, aggressive, and practical were to represent the family in the marketplace and in public.[15]

The nature of the "woman's sphere" in farming areas and on the 19th-century frontier has been one of the most widely contested problems in women's history in the last several years. Some historians have argued that the idea of "separate spheres," whatever its value for analyzing the social life of the urban middle class, is of limited utility for understanding the role of women and the relationship between husbands and wives in farming areas. There the distinction between the spheres was blurred, and the work of men and women was not as clearly divided into separate work routines. In her study of 19th-century farm women in New York, Nancy Grey Osterud argues that while women tended to be responsible for household labor, they often shared responsibility with their husbands for farming tasks. Women and men worked together in dairying, for example, and set aside their normal household work at planting and harvest time. Others argue that a strong attachment to distinct gender roles and segregated work patterns characterized rural communities in the West throughout the 19th century.[16]

In addition to treating the patterns of household management, child-rearing, and other aspects of the "woman's sphere," *KEEPING HOUSE* seeks to evoke the personal responses of women to the difficult and often dangerous experience of living in early Western Pennsylvania and to suggest how that experience forced changes in their diet, manners, and habits, as well as in the way they interacted with one another. In doing so, *KEEPING HOUSE* compels us to remember that history happens to everyone, and that the great movements of the past, like the settlement of the trans-Appalachian West, worked themselves out in the ambitions, struggles, and accomplishments, great and small, of countless ordinary men and women. [Endnotes page 176]

Jack D. Warren, University of Virginia

KEEPING
HOUSE

Women's Lives in
Western Pennsylvania

1 7 9 0 — 1 8 5 0

Conestoga Wagon on the Pennsylvania Turnpike, *painting by Thomas Birch, 1816.*
Shelburne Museum, Shelburne, Vermont, photography by Ken Burris.

Lithograph by Pittsburgh Lithography Company, late 19th century. HSWP Collection.

GETTING THERE

If you were 18 years old in 1790 and recently married to a strong and hand-some young Philadelphian, the prospect of setting forth to make a home in the wilderness of Western Pennsylvania might have seemed daunting but also exciting. If you were 30, with four children needing your attention, you might reasonably have doubted the wisdom of a decision to leave family, friends, and a comfortable home for the frightening uncertainties of the frontier. And if you were 50, with a dozen grandchildren and often painful rheumatism, the idea of a month's journey over the Allegheny Mountains on foot or in a bouncing wagon would have been fearful to contemplate.

There are no records to show us how many wives were consulted about their desire to make the Western journey, but we know that generally women went where their men went. The reasons families emigrated were usually uncompli-cated—the chance for a better life for everyone and a brighter future for one's children; land of one's own; a productive farm; escape from undesirable situations, such as debt or punishment for criminal behavior; the opportunity to pursue one's religious convictions; and, surmounting all of these reasons, for men at least, the thirst for adventure.

"Set out for Chestnut Ridge, horrid roads and the stoniest land in the world I believe; every few hundred yards, rocks big enough to build a small house upon." —Mary Dewees

Although there have indeed always been women with a strong sense of adventure, it is probably safe to say that most women were conservative, primarily con-cerned with feeding, housing, nurturing, and above all preserving their families. The expectation of new experiences may have added some spice to their otherwise routine lives, but it was undoubtedly fairly low on their priority list.

How did women feel, then, about leaving family and friends and departing for the unknown West? Margaret Van Horn Dwight, writing in 1810, noted:

Shall I commence my journal, my dear Elizabeth, with a description of the pain I felt at taking leave of all my friends or shall I leave you to imagine—The afternoon has been spent by me in the most painful reflections & in almost total silence by my companions....I did not imagine parting with any friend could be so distressing

as I found leaving your Mama. I did not know till then, how much I loved her &
and could I at that moment have retraced my steps! but it was too late to repent.
[Dwight, p. 1]

A foreign lady visitor to the Pittsburgh area in the 1840s commenting on
American women wrote:

> While descanting on the singular freedom which is allowed American ladies,
> I cannot resist paying my tribute to their strength of mind and energy of purpose,
> in which qualities they certainly stand pre-eminent....[A woman will] if neccesary,
> throw aside her silks and satins, and accompany her husband into the half-formed
> settlement of the far west. There she will endure without a murmur or a word of
> repining, the toils and the dangers, and often sickness attending this new mode
> of life; and when, (as too frequently happens) their husbands are reduced by one
> unfortunate speculation from wealth and ease, to poverty and privation, then it is
> that their fortitude smooths the path of misfortune, and their courageous exer-
> tions lessen the force of the blow. [Houston, p. 136]

In 1807 Elizabeth Van Horne set out over the Alleghenies with her family,
including a very sick father. "I already think it a great undertaking," she wrote,
"to remove a family from Jersey State to the State of Ohio. Was there no Invalids
among us it would be something easier. Yet for any family—*Strength, fortitude,
resolution,* and a good share of *Patience* is absolutely necessary."

Whatever their destination, women were loath to leave their family and
friends. When Christiana Tillson left for the West, her family was in despair.

> In 1822 it was still a great event to undertake a journey to Illinois, and many were
> the direful remarks and conclusions about my going. Your grandmother dreaded
> my starting without any lady companion....Your Great-grandmother Briggs had
> seen the carriage pass her house, and in telling how she felt at parting with her
> eldest granddaughter, and the sadness it had given her to see the carriage that
> was to take me away, was not aware that she said "hearse" instead of carriage....
> the sad forebodings I was constantly hearing at that time of the fearful journey,
> and the dismal backwoods life which awaited me were not calculated to dispel
> the clouds that would sometimes come over me. [Tillson, pp. 31-32]

If travelers were coming from Boston, Philadelphia, or New York, they would
take the Pennsylvania road that General Forbes had hacked across the Alleghenies
in 1758. Scarcely more than a path in places, the road was often impassable, even
after the Revolution, but the state assembly began setting aside funds for its
improvement in 1785. Work on another thoroughfare following the course of
the old Braddock Road was begun in 1811 and this became the National Road, a
service to travelers from Cumberland, Maryland, to Uniontown and Washington,
Pennsylvania, and, eventually, into West Virginia.

Few travelers would have agreed that this official attention to road building
and improvement made any noticeable difference. Most had detailed complaints
about the abysmal state of the roads and the lack of repairs being made. John
May, in his 1788 *Journal*, lamented the difficulty of the trip over a mountain out-

side of Mercersburg, noting "this mountain is 10 miles over. [I]t took us 3 hours and a half to cross it. I can truly say this is the worst mountain to climb I have yet attempted, and is one of the four capital ranges of mountains which belong to the Alleghana [*sic*] family, and strike such a terror on travellers." Mary Dewees wrote, "Set out for Chestnut Ridge, horrid roads and the stoniest land in the world I believe; every few hundred yards, rocks big enough to build a small house upon." [Harpster, p. 178]

Travelers complained that little was being done to improve the roads. In 1816 David Thomas noted:

> We descended a very long and steep hill, by a shocking road....we then ascended another hill by an equally bad and dangerous road. It is astonishing that in so fine and improving a country more attention is not paid to the roads. A turnpike is projected from Pittsburgh to Harrisburg, which I am clearly of opinion, might be kept in repair by a reasonable toll. [Harpster, p. 273]

Travelers bound for the West had few choices for transportation. The poorer migrants walked, usually in family groups, no matter what their ages. Elderly men and women walked slowly, leaning on their canes, often with a young grandchild strapped to their backs. Because of the poor condition of most roads, wagons were impractical and pack horses more widely used. The opportunity to take one's household goods over the mountains to the new home was, therefore, severely limited, usually to what each person could carry for him or herself. Cherished pieces of furniture and china or glass had to be left at home, and only the absolute necessities of life could be taken along. The Reverend David McClure, traveling from Eastern Pennsylvania toward Pittsburgh in 1773, wrote of a family he encountered on the trail:

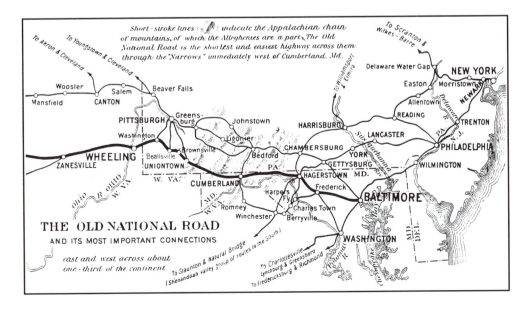

THE OLD NATIONAL ROAD AND ITS MOST IMPORTANT CONNECTIONS

> I noticed particularly, one family of about 8 in number. The man carried an ax and gun on his shoulders—the Wife the rim of a spinning wheel in one hand, and a loaf of bread in the other. Several little boys and girls, each with a bundle according to their size. Two poor horses, each heavily loaded with some poor necessities, on top of the baggage of one was an infant rocked to sleep in a kind of wicker cage, lashed securely to the horse. A Cow formed one of the company, and she was destined to bear her portion of service, a bed cord was wound round her horns, and a bag of meal on her back. [Bausman, p. 175]

In 1817 an English gentleman traveling to Illinois through Pennsylvania observed:

> The waggon has a tilt or cover, made of a sheet, or perhaps a blanket. The family are seen before, behind, or within the vehicle, according to the road, or the weather, or perhaps the spirits of the party. The New Englanders, they say, may be known by the cheerful air of the women advancing in front of the vehicle; the Jersey people by their being fixed steadily within it; while the Pennsylvanians creep lingering behind, as though regretting the homes they have left. [Harpster, pp. 274-75]

Judge Samuel Wilkeson described his family's journey in 1784, as one of 20 groups that emigrated from Carlisle to the West. His father and mother, three children, and an indentured lad of 14 crossed the mountains on three pack horses:

> …[O]n one of [them] my mother rode, carrying her infant, with all the table furniture and cooking utensils. On another were packed the stores of provisions, the plough irons, and other agricultural tools. The third horse was rigged out with a pack saddle, and two large creels, made of hickory withs [boards] in the fashion of a crate, one over each side, in which were stored the beds and bedding, and the wearing apparel of the family. [Wilkeson, p. 139]

Wilkeson and his sister were laced in between the creels, "so that only our heads appeared." Each family took one or more cows, whose milk furnished the morning and evening meal for the children.

Liwwät Böke traveled from Germany to the Ohio frontier to join her husband in 1835. Landing in Baltimore, she continued by wagon on the turnpike road. Her sketches of the journey show what look like modified Conestoga wagons driven by a team of horses; other wagons in their group were pulled by oxen. "There was a dispute between the travelers and the wagoners. They thought the trip too slow …city people don't realize the weaknesses of and the difficult pulling for the horses. Their patience is thin, too many days, and people are tired." Despite the alleged "good" road, she found the journey "perilous" and the mountain storms frightening. "Up and down, sideways, bouncing…my behind is ruined and sore!" While climbing the mountains, they had fresh teams every day, and "they grease the axles two times a day." [Böke, p. 45]

The uneven terrain made for journeys that were not only uncomfortable but dangerous as well. "This afternoon my Father & Mother & Mary was in the carriage descending a hill very much rutted—and overset. My Fathers ear was cut a little—My Mothers shoulder and arm hurt but no bones broke nor any serious effects I believe to be apprehended," wrote Elizabeth Van Horne.

Judge Wilkeson described the perils of traveling by pack horse. "In many places the path lay along the edge of a precipice where, if the horse had stumbled, or lost his balance, he would have been precipitated several hundred feet below." Streams swollen from melting snow, deep ravines and swift currents made crossing the water incredibly dangerous, as there was rarely a bridge or a ferry and rivers had to be forded.

The more affluent rode horses, or engaged a seat on a stagecoach. One step up from a wagon, these stages were really boxes on wheels, usually with nine uncomfortable seats offering little shelter from the clouds of thick dust, rain and snow. As stages rocked along on their leather thorough-braces, passengers felt, in Frederick Marryat's words, as if they were "being tossed in a blanket, often throwing you up to the top of the coach, as to flatten your hat, if not your head." [Larkin, p. 208] Mrs. Frances Trollope, the indefatigable English visitor, found the stages more comfortable when full, since when only a few passengers were aboard, they were "tossed about like a few potatoes in a wheelbarrow. Our knees, elbows and heads required too much care for their protection to allow us leisure to look out the windows."

Old-time reminiscences of the Concord coach, however, would have us believe they were impressive vehicles indeed:

> To see it ascending a long hill, increasing speed, when nearing the summit, then moving rapidly over the intervening level to the top of the next hill, and dashing down it, a driver like the stately Redding Bunting wielding the whip and handling the reins, revealed a scene that will never be forgotten....Their arrival in the towns was the leading event of each day, and they were so regular in transit that farmers along the road knew the exact hour by their coming, without the aid of clock or watch. [Swetnam, pp. 15-16]

People were amazed at the speed with which they traveled. The record for the 8 miles between Uniontown and Brownsville was 44 minutes; the 222 miles from Frederick, Maryland, to Wheeling, West Virginia, 23 1/2 hours.

The condition of the roads and the limited amount of clothing and goods the traveler could carry were great levelers. Those with cash could afford somewhat better accommodations, if they existed. But the mud, the rocks, the rain, the snow, the mosquitos, snakes, and summer heat were there for everyone to endure, no matter what his or her station in life might be.

At the foot of steep hills, passengers were often asked to get out and walk so that the horses pulling stages or wagons would have an easier climb. Elizabeth Van Horne noted that her mother and sisters had walked 7 miles one day, with "snow and shine" alternately the whole day. On another day she estimated 15 miles. After more than two weeks of travel, Margaret Dwight walked 3 1/2 miles over a mountain. "I did not stop at all to rest till I reach'd the top. ...It is not a little fatiguing to walk up a long mountain I find." The following day she noted, "I have walked about 8 miles today and feel as much fatigued as I have almost ever been in my life." And the next day she wrote, "We had a good night's rest, but I am so lame I can scarcely walk this morning—I have a mountain to walk over, notwithstanding." That night she added, "All this afternoon we have been walking over young mountains…I was so lame and so tired that for an hour I did not know but I must set down and die—I could not ride—the road was so bad, it was worse than walking."

Sally Hastings crossed the Alleghenies in 1800 with her sister and brother-in-law's family.

> Yesterday we crossed the Laurel-hill; which is very steep, and so rocky that no one could venture to ride over it. The rain and snow began to fall in great abundance; which, freezing, formed a crust on the rocks, and rendered them so slippery, that the utmost Caution was insufficient to prevent our receiving some severe Falls. The Cold was intense; Night came on with pitchy darkness; and my sister, unaccustomed to Difficulty, and totally exhausted with Fatigue, was obliged to sit down with her Children on a rock; where she wept. [Harpster, pp. 236-37]

Judge Wilkeson acknowledged the special burden such a trip put on the women.

> It was the mothers who suffered; they could not, after the toils of the day enjoy the rest they needed at night. The wants of their suffering children must be attended to. After preparing their simple meal, they lay down with scanty covering in a miserable cabin, or as it sometimes happened, in the open air, and often unrefreshed, were obliged to rise early, to encounter the fatigues and dangers of another day. [Wilkeson, p. 141]

Perhaps the most disconcerting part of the long journey over the Alleghenies was the uneven quality of the accommodations available to travelers. Virtually every journal, diary, and letter details good and bad inns, jolly and dour landlords, drunken waggoners and gentlemen of breeding and education, many of whom had to share their beds with uncouth and dirty compatriots. After a long and arduous day on the road, travelers looked forward to a good bed, a satisfying meal, and a little peace and quiet. Too often they found exactly the opposite. Mrs. Trollope, traveling near Laurel Hill, complained:

> Arrived at our inn, a forlorn parlour, filled with the blended fumes of tobacco and whiskey, received us; and chilled as we began to feel ourselves with the mountain air, we preferred going to our cold bedrooms rather than sup in such an atmosphere. We found linen on the beds they assured us had only been used *a few nights;* every kind of refreshment we asked for we were answered, "We do not happen to have that article." [Trollope, p. 150]

Joshua Gilpin, on an extended tour in 1809, found:

> a great farmer having several farms in this country and a very decent kind of man —appearances were in favor of its being a good Inn as we were shown into a large room with a good bed in it, & had a decent supper.—we soon found however, that this was the family eating, & bedroom and were obliged to give way to a host of people to have their supper—consisting of the Landlord his wife children, workmen, a number of travellers, waggoners and Minists [Mennonites] or Dunkards, a species of Moravians with long beards—we found also that we must lodge in another room upstairs not above 10 feet square with a bed made up of blanketts for Henry & our own a very small one which stunk intolerably. [Gilpin, pp. 62-63]

In 1817 another English visitor, Morris Birkbeck, noted the disconcerting lack of privacy in American inns.

> Everything is public by day and night; for even night, in an American inn, affords no privacy. Whatever may be the number of guests they must receive their entertainment *en masse*, and they must sleep *en masse*. Three times a day the great bell rings, and a hundred persons collect from all quarters to eat a hurried meal, composed of almost as many dishes. At breakfast you may have fish, flesh or fowl; bread of every shape and kind; butter, eggs, coffee, tea; everything and more than you can think of. Dinner is much like breakfast, omitting the tea and coffee; and supper is the breakfast repeated. Soon after this last meal you assemble once more

A NEW BERTH.

Candid Landlady. "THE FIRST FROM THE TOP, SIR, IS THE ONLY BED VACANT; BUT YOU HAVE GOT VERY NICE NEIGHBORS—ONE GENTLEMAN CHEWS, BUT THE OTHERS ONLY SMOKE!"

Cartoon, c. 1845. "Candid Landlady, 'The first from the top, Sir, is the only bed vacant; but you have got very nice neighbors—one gentleman chews, but the others only smoke!'"

in rooms crowded with beds, something like the wards of a hospital; where, after
undressing in public, you are fortunate if you escape a partner in your bed, in
addition to the myriads of bugs which you cannot hope to escape. [Harpster, pp.
275-76]

Mary Dewees reported that the family "put up at a little hut on the Mountain,
which was so small that we prefferred lodging in our waggon to be crowded with
Frenchmen and negroes on an earthern floor." She also reported on a log cabin
inn, "Perhaps a dozen logs upon one another, with a few slabs for a roof, and the
earth for a floor, and a Wooden Chimney constituted this extraordinary ordinary." Despite her reservations, however, she admitted that "the sight of a log
house on these Mountains after a fatiguing days Journey affords more real
pleasure than all the magnificent buildings your city contains."

Arthur Lee, in 1784, related his dismay when "ourselves, our servants, several waggoners, his wife, and eight children, and a young daughter, all undressed
and went to bed on the floor together, in a miserable log house."[Harpster, p. 153]
Many travelers commented on the ever-present dirt and bugs. Margaret Dwight
complained that "the house is very small and very dirty—it serves for a tavern,
a store, & I should imagine hog's pen stable & everything else—The air is so
impure I have scarcely been able to swallow since I enter'd the house—The
landlady is a fat, dirty, ugly looking creature...." A few days later, "We were put
in an old garret that had holes in the roof big enough to crawl through. Our bed
was on the floor, harder it appear'd to me, than boards could be—& dirty as
possible—a dirty feather bed our only covering." After leaving Pittsburgh, they
put up at a house with only one room, one bed and many travelers. "The
pillowcase had been on 5 or 6 years I reckon, so I pin'd over my handkerchief—
& put night gown over my frock."

Elizabeth Van Horne took matters into her own hands, somehow acquiring
a broom on the road, because some of the taverns, she thought, "use a broom
more frequent in their barns than houses." She and her sister Ann often went on
ahead of their party in order to sweep out the bedroom before her ailing father
arrived. Often accommodation of any kind was lacking, and the travelers were
thrown on their own resources, as Mary Dewees discovered.

> We in Company with another waggon were obliged to Encamp in the woods....
> Our men went to give refreshment to the Horses, we Females having had a good
> fire made up, set about preparing Supper, which consisted of an Excellent dish of
> Coffee, having milk with us, those who chose had a dish of cold ham and pickled
> beets with the addition of Bread, Butter, Biscuit and Cheese, made up our repast.
> After Supper, Sister, the children, and myself took up our lodging in the waggon,
> the men with their Blankets lay down at the fire side. [Harpster, p. 178]

Traveling with one's family or a party of friends was no guarantee that one's
companions would all be agreeable and friendly. The journey made for strange
bedfellows in every sense of the word, and often the most genteel of ladies were

forced to share their suppers and bedrooms with men and women far beneath them on the social scale.

Conversation with fellow travelers could be entertaining as well as exasperating. Margaret Dwight was especially irritated by the Dutch, and found a dozen or so talking at once "really intolerable....How can I live among them 3 weeks?" Later she describes "The woman who is with Mr. Beach....such a foolish old creature that we are all out of patience with her." Near Laurel Hill their party overtook:

> [A] young doctor—who is going with his father to Mad river in the state of Ohio —He has been studying physic in New Jersey,—but appears to be an uneducated man from the language he makes use of....He thinks of himself as a gentleman of the *first chop,* and takes the liberty of coining words for himself—Speaking of the people of this state, he said they were very ignorant & very *superstitionary* — perhaps you have heard the word before—I never did. [Dwight, pp. 48-49]

Inquiries about Dwight's marital status were frequent, and the idea of a single lady traveling west was hard for the settlers along the way to accept. At one tavern, a man asked where they were going, "& he at once concluded it was to get husbands. He said winter was coming on & and he wanted a wife....I concluded of course the next thing would be, a proposal to Miss W or me to stay behind and save trouble for us both; but nothing would suit him but a rich widow." Dwight's dry sense of humor served her well on more than one occasion. One of her fellow travelers with an eligible son "has cast her eyes on Susan or me for a daughter in law—for my part, though I feel very well disposed toward the young man, I had not thought of *making a bargain* with him, but I have jolted off most of my high notions, & perhaps I may be willing to descend from a judge to a blacksmith." Later she notes, "There is a curiosity in the house—a young lady who has come from N Connecticut *unmarried,* a thing I never before heard of, & had begun to think impossible. I feel quite encouraged by it...." She was not impressed by the cross, complaining gentleman who traveled with them. "If I were going to be married I would give my *intended*, a gentle emetic, or some such thing to see how he would bear being sick a little."

Accommodations could be especially trying for women travelers, who sometimes were subject to the unwelcome attentions of fellow tavern guests. Margaret Dwight related her frightening experiences with waggoners:

> I took off my frock & boots, & had scarcely lain down, when one of the wretches came into the room & lay down by me on the outside of the bed—I was frighten'd almost to death & clung to Mrs. Jackson who did not appear to mind it—& I lay for a quarter of an hour crying and scolding and trembling, begging of him to leave me. At last, when persuaded I was in earnest, he begg'd of me not to take it amiss, as he intended no harm & only wished to become acquainted with me—A good for nothing brute, I wonder what he suppos'd I was. [Dwight, p. 40]

Liwwät Böke's usual good spirits were sorely tried on the road. "A long, cruel day, eighteen hours on the way....The night place was small. All the women slept in one room with the children. I was tired and a little afraid with these strangers, so I hid my money and papers in my underwear. I brought with me a little club which perhaps I must use if there is a fight."

The quality of the taverns was very uneven, and although the bright spots seemed few and far between, there are documented instances of good food and peaceful nights. "We have tonight a comfortable room and good fire," wrote Elizabeth Van Horne. "I am astonished at the excellent supper provided by this Landlady." Mrs. Trollope found little good about America, but she had a few positive experiences in Pennsylvania, including a stay at an inn near Brownsville.

> We were regaled luxuriously on wild turkey and mountain venison....The vegetables were also extremely fine....We fared much better than the night before, for they gave us clean sheets, a good fire, and no scolding. [Trollope, pp. 151-53]

As the roads improved and traffic increased, inns proliferated and some even improved. Along the National Road, food was plentiful, with even the most penurious landlord setting out a variety of biscuits and cornbread, bacon and eggs, chicken, fried squirrel, and venison. "I must not, in the enumeration of 'the delicacies of the season,'" commented a tourist, "forget to mention with respect a sort of pancake, which we had at Brownsville, in the greatest perfection; it is made of Indian corn, and is brought in very *hot* and in *relays*. It is, I fancy, called a 'Johnny cake,' and is generally eaten with molasses; but it is excellent, and is, I believe, one of the causes of the brevity of human existence here."

The rosy glow which surrounds the harsher memories of the past is well illustrated in this paean to inns on the National Road from a settler who watched the coaches go by as a young boy.

> On the mountain division, every mile had its tavern. Many of them with inviting seats for idlers, and all with cheerful fronts toward the weary travelers. The signboards were elevated on high and heavy posts, and their golden letters twinkling in the sun, ogled the wayfarers from the hot roadbed, and gave promise of good cheer, while the big trough, overflowing with clear, fresh water and the ground below it sprinkled with fragrant peppermint, lent a charm to the scene that was well-nigh enchanting. [Swetnam, p. 19]

On the Monongahela, *painting (detail) by William Coventry Wall, 1860.*

Despite the intense discomforts, the beauty of the new land was noted by many travelers, particularly women. "The views from the *mountains* of the surrounding *Hills & Mountains* are really charming—such prospects I never beheld, all the tops of the surrounding Hills covered with lofty Pines interspersed with Chestnut and Oak. The chilling blasts of Autumn cause them to look varieagated Pictureque and grand." Mary Dewees wrote, "The Monogahela, with the many colored woods on each side, is Beautiful, and in the Spring must be delightful." Even the acerbic Mrs. Trollope was in awe of the countryside she passed through west of Laurel Ridge.

> The whole of this mountain region...is a garden. The almost incredible variety of plants, and the lavish profusion of their growth, produce an effect perfectly enchanting....The magnificent rhododenron first caught our eyes; it fringes every cliff, nestles beneath every rock and blooms around every tree...oak and beech, with innumerable roses and wild vines, hanging in beautiful confusion among their branches, were in many places scattered among the evergreens....all that is noblest in nature was joined to all that is sweetest. [Trollope, p. 149]

Our image of wilderness travel is of lonely travelers, and days of isolation with the occasional inn an oasis of socialization. But by 1780 the roads were well traveled. "You would be surprised to see the number of pack horses which travel these roads, ten or twelve in a drove," wrote Mary Dewees, while Margaret Dwight commented, "There is another impassable creek ahead & a hundred waggons waiting to cross it.... From what I have seen and heard, I think the State of Ohio will be well fill'd before winter, Waggons without number, every day go on.... We almost every day see them with 18 or 20." On the National Road:

> Up to twenty four-horse coaches have been counted in line in one time on the road: and large, broadwheeled wagons, covered with white canvas stretched over bows, laden with merchandise, and drawn by six Conestoga horses, were visible all day long at every point, and many times until late in the evening, besides innumerable caravans of horses, mules, cattle, hogs and sheep. [Swetnam, p. 16]

Who were all these people on the road? Fortescue Cuming, writing in 1810, called the numbers of travelers "truly astonishing" and went on to describe them:

> [W]agonners, carrying produce to and bringing back foreign goods from the different shipping ports on the shores of the Atlantick, particularly Philadelphia & Baltimore;—Packers with from one to twenty horses, selling or trucking their wares through the country;—country men, sometimes alone, sometimes in large companies, carrying salt from M'Connelstown, and other points of navigation on the Potomack and Susquehanah, for the curing of their beef, pork, venison, etc; —Families removing further back into the country; some with cows, oxen, horses, sheep, and pigs, and all their farming implements and domestic utensils, and some without; some with wagons, some with carts and some on foot, according to their abilities;—The residue who make use of the best accommodations on the roads, country merchants, judges and lawyers attending the courts, members of the legislature, and the better class of settlers removing back. [Cuming, pp. 46-47]

 Conrad Richter won a Pulitzer Prize in 1951 for *The Town*, the third volume of his remarkable trilogy, *The Awakening Land: The Trees* (1940), *The Fields* (1945), *The Town* (1950), published by Alfred A. Knopf, New York. In his fictional treatment of Western Pennsylvania and Ohio, he gives his characters life and vigor, detailing the relentless repetitiveness of their daily lives, their sorrows and joys, their fears and anxieties, the strengths and weaknesses of ordinary people who become extraordinary through his skill in depicting them.

In *The Trees*, Jary's footloose husband Worth begins dropping hints about moving on from Pennsylvania to Ohio. The game, he explains, is leaving the forests, and only famine can result. Jary is reluctant to move once again:

> *Jary sat quiet on her homemade hickory rocker. Oh, she knew how bad Worth wanted an excuse to get away from here. Her eyes slanted down toward the clay floor. Her mouth rounded a bit as if she took all these things, good, bad and indifferent and was running them quietly around inside her lips. Her mouth was so gentle and yet could shut like a mussel shell.... "You're aimin' to cross the Ohio?" she asked, and her eyes glinted a moment dangerously at her man. He gave a nod....He took out his clay pipe and made to fill it, but his eyes never stopped watching her face.... "I told you I'd never go way back there."...She dropped her eyes and stared a long time across the doorsill, then around the cabin room at the familiar slab stools and puncheon table, the hand-whittled loom and wheel, and across the doorsill again to the mite of a grave in the clearing.... "And yit," back in her mouth she complained, "what's a body to do if the game's left the country?"*

Englishman Morris Birkbeck noted in 1817, "Old America seems to be breaking up, and moving westward." And move they did, whenever the traffic seemed a little too heavy, the neighborhood a little too crowded. Johann David Schoepf noted as early as 1777, when stopping at a modest tavern near Laurel Hill:

> The Captain was not at all pleased that the neighborhood was beginning to be so thickly settled. "It spoils the hunting," he said, "makes quarrels; and then they come and want to collect taxes; it is time some of us were leaving and getting deeper into the country." Hence we supposed we should find a thickly settled region, but had to go not less than seven miles before we came to the next neighbor. [Harpster, p. 133]

Men who made their living as hunters and trappers, however, watched with dismay as the game disappeared and the endless waves of new settlers continued to come. Contemporary Americans tend to romanticize the abundance of wildlife in pioneer days, but as early as 1763 writers were bemoaning the scarcity of meat. Very few panthers, wild cats, bear, and deer remained and buffalo and elk had disappeared entirely. The wild turkey and woodcock were rarely seen and the scarcity of game was a major factor in the decision of many settlers to move on as well.

A large number of those bound for the West made at least part of the journey by boat. Approaching from the north, the town of Olean, New York, at the head of the Allegheny River, was a popular point of embarkation. It was possible to bring one's family and household goods there over the mountains from the East, sell the wagon, buy a flatboat or keelboat, and head for the Ohio River. In 1817 one traveler wrote that he counted 1,200 immigrants of all ages and sexes waiting for the ice to break and permit navigation. Some had been there two months waiting for their opportunity.

Historian Leland Baldwin speculates about the immigrant camps which grew up on the river banks waiting for the water to become navigable. Some families pulled their flatboats on to the shore and lived in them. Because they had fireplaces and modest shelters on deck, this was a reasonably comfortable way to pass the winter. Less prosperous travelers lived in their wagons, or used tents and lean-tos. In these camps they were crowded together; children, dogs, and livestock ran wild, and local merchants could and did exploit them, charging whatever they pleased. Once conditions became favorable, the rush to get started was chaotic. Traveler Tilly Buttrick, Jr., described the plight of 1,200 immigrants waiting at the headwaters of the Allegheny to go downriver.

> On Saturday night sat up late, heard some cracking of the ice, several of us observing that we should soon be on our way went to bed. Next morning at daylight found the river nearly clear, and at eight o'clock it was completely so. The place now presented a curious sight; the men conveying their goods on board the boats and rafts, the women scolding, and children crying, some clothed and some half clothed, all in haste, filled with anxiety, as if a few minutes were lost their passage would be lost also. By ten o'clock the whole river for one mile appeared to be one solid body of boats and rafts. [Harpster, p. 266]

The same problem could arise in Pittsburgh. If spring rains were inadequate or the traveler missed the raised water level after the winter ice broke up, he might be doomed to a long, uncomfortable wait until the autumn rains arrived. Then the resulting river traffic could be astonishingly heavy. In 1787 the *Pittsburgh Gazette* announced:

> Since Sunday evening last, upwards of one hundred and twenty boats have passed by this town on their way to Kentucky, which at an average of 15 persons each, will add 1800 persons to that young settlement. This excessive immigration, it is said, is owing to the badness of the crops of corn in old Virginia: which have not, in general, provided more than one-fourth of the quantities that are expected. There are more than the above number now up Mon river nearly in readiness to depart for the same country. [*Pittsburgh Gazette*, November 17, 1787]

Eight years later, the migration to the West continued unabated.

> The Emigration to this country this fall surpasses that of any other season—
> and we are informed, that the banks of the Monongahela, from M'kees Port to
> Redstone, are lined with people intending for the settlement on the Ohio, and
> Kentucky. [*Pittsburgh Gazette*, November 21, 1795]

For the more well-to-do, waiting around for the water to rise could be just as
tedious and boring as for the less fortunate.

> Sewing and reading, and when the weather is fine, walking, are the amusements
> we enjoy. The gentlemen pass their time in hunting deer, turkeys, ducks, and
> every other kind of wild fowl, with which this country abounds....This is the most
> tedious part of our Journey as we still continue in one place....Mrs. Hamilton and
> Miss Conrad from the Island called on us to take a walk up the hill to gather
> grapes, which we got a great abundance of. [Harpster, p. 183]

In order to move down the rivers, migrants could hardly do better than to
follow Zadok Cramer's advice in his popular book *The Navigator.* "The first thing
to be attended to by emigrants or traders wanting to descend the river, is to
procure a boat...." One must be careful, he warned, because "many of the acci-
dents that happen in navigating the Ohio and Mississippi, are owing to the
unpardonable carelessness or penuriousness of the boat builder."

Passengers had limited choices in boat transportation. One possibility was
a flatboat, consisting of an oblong platform with a slightly curved roof over part
of it, built of massive timbers and designed to carry heavy loads of barrels, livestock, and families. The good news was that they could be fitted out with stoves
and comfortable beds, and could provide a modicum of privacy. The bad news

Monongahela Wharf in Keel Boat Days, *painting by Leander McCandless, c. 1840, showing
wooden bridge at Smithfield Street destroyed in 1845. HSWP Collection.*

was that there was no possibility of steering the barge, so that passengers were at the mercy of the currents and weather. Flatboats were also unwieldy to maneuver, requiring enormous effort to land and float again, to say nothing of getting stuck on a sandbar. In 1818 an English traveler set off down the Ohio:

> [W]e all six of us set sail in as clumsy a contrivance for navigation as can well be conceived. We all agreed it was in shape more like an orange box than anything else we could compare it to.... Such a thing as a plane had never been used at all in its construction. In this machine we floated with the current, not caring which side foremost, using a couple of planks as oars to keep her from striking against obstacles. [Cramer, *The Navigator*, pp. xxvii-xxviii]

Since flatboats had no rudders and were unable to make their way upstream, passengers had no use for their barges once they reached their destination. It was common practice to break up the timbers and re-use them or sell them. Despite these disadvantages, after the settlers' long trek over the mountains, the flatboats often seemed like home, and Mary Dewees was well satisfied.

> Our boat is 40 foot long; our room 16 by 8 with a Comfortable fire place; our Bed room partitioned off with blankets, and fare preferable to the Cabins we met after we crossed the mountains. We are clear of fleas, which I assure you is a great relief, for we were almost devoured on Shore. [Harpster, p. 180]

The keelboat was a distinct improvement on the flatboat, since a rudder made it possible to pole the boat upstream as well as float downstream. However, keelboats required as many as seven pair of tough, hard-working polesmen to move a large boat against the current.

The women who crossed the Alleghenies with their families were subject to the same rigors as the men, but to these physically exhausting trips were added the usual responsibilities of keeping house on the trail or aboard the boat. The men supplied the meat by hunting; the women cleaned the game, cooked it, washed up afterwards, meanwhile seeing to the needs of the children and elderly. They were expected to be cheerful, brave, uncomplaining, and supportive of their husbands. "We are praised and commended by all travelers for our courage and cheerful dexterity—no Women that go the road that excel us in activity," wrote Van Horne.

We have no way of knowing how many families became discouraged and turned back, or how many, bound for Pittsburgh or Ohio, decided to stop and seek their fortune in Greensburg or Bedford instead. Despite the hardships visited on all travelers, to the modern reader both the men and women who recorded their reactions seem to have been amazingly cheerful and ready for new experience. Margaret Dwight reported, "We have concluded the reason so few are willing to return from the Western country, is not that the country is so good, but because the journey is so bad....I have learn'd, Elizabeth, to eat raw *pork* & drink whiskey—don't you think I shall do for a new country?" §

 In Conrad Richter's *The Fields*, the Luckett family moves on to Ohio, where the wilderness is still virtually untouched by civilization.

For a moment Sayward reckoned that her father had fetched them unbeknownst to the Western ocean and what lay beneath was the late sun glittering on green-black water. Then she saw that what they looked down on was a dark, illimitable expanse of wilderness. It was a sea of solid treetops broken only by some gash where deep beneath the foliage an unknown stream made its way. As far as the eye could reach, this lonely forest sea rolled on and on till its faint blue billows broke against an incredibly distant horizon.

(above) Evening After Braddock's Defeat, *painting (detail) by William Coventry Wall, 1856. HSWP Collection. (left) Engraving of the Ligonier Valley, 1843.*

A WILDERNESS HOUSEHOLD

When Margaret Bunyan left New Jersey for Washington, Pennsylvania, one of the things she took with her was her cookbook. Dated 1790, it was apparently used for something else prior to the recipe entries, since pages have been torn out of the front. We don't know much about her, only the bare genealogical facts. She married John Morgan in 1795, five years after the first recipe entry, and the next year the couple moved to Pennsylvania with her father-in-law George Morgan and his family. Colonel Morgan had been an Indian trader at Fort Pitt in 1767, then a troop commander, then an Indian agent, and later a colonel in the Commissary Department of the army.

We don't know exactly why the Morgans left New Jersey for Pennsylvania. One could speculate that Colonel Morgan's service at Fort Pitt and as an Indian agent was rewarded with land grants in lieu of money, as was the case with many Revolutionary soldiers, or Morgan may have seen Washington as the city of the future, or he may simply have wanted to retire and pursue his interests in scientific farming. Whatever the reasons, the Morgans appear to have been well educated and probably affluent. However, they had to make the same treacherous wagon journey across the Alleghenies as their contemporaries of whatever class.

"If a rest is given to the arm the candles become too hard and break, or the tallow in the pot gets too cool, so dip, dip, dip, six candles at a time..."

—Christiana Tillson

It is interesting to speculate about Margaret's thoughts as the family wagons pulled up to the local tavern after a long and exhausting trip across the mountains and she had her first glimpse of the town that would be her future home. In 1796 Washington was larger than Pittsburgh, and its neat houses and bustling activity must have reassured her.

Colonel Morgan built his family an impressive house which he named "Morganza," on a site now marked by a monument built with stones from the foundation of the house. Most settlers were not as fortunate as the Morgan family, however, as their homes were built in the midst of the wilderness. Just a short distance from any of the towns in Pennsylvania the land was undeveloped and heavily wooded. The prospect of living there could be frightening, as Liwwät Böke recalled:

> Of the *forest*, my first impression was: I am imprisoned, swallowed deep in its gloomy throat. In these wooded depths there is no dimension or direction, so dreadfully quiet, so damp, dark, cool. Behind, below, above, in front are the brush, the weeds, and two million unbending trees. Their branches, their boughs clutch at me at each step, and there is no path except by the old branchless trees.
> [Böke, p. 101]

When the pioneering family arrived at its chosen tract of land, the first order of business was a temporary shelter. Usually a half-faced camp was erected, a three-sided arrangement of poles and brush, one side sloping to the ground to protect the occupants from rain and wind. A fire was built just outside the lean-to so that the women could prepare food for the family, using the kettle or two they had packed in the wagon. Most families brought along a bag of corn meal, the basis for johnny cake and mush, and since game was still plentiful, the men provided meat, pegging the skins for later use as blankets, clothing, or for trade.

Depending on the weather, a farmer might choose to clear some land before building a cabin in order to prepare for planting next year's crops. Trees were girdled—a deep strip cut around their trunks to hasten their demise—and thick stands of vine and brush cleared, a seemingly endless task. Liwwät Böke wrote:

> We must constantly fight against nature in order to coax her to become our ally. To that end, we always deceive her and play with her and trick her. And then, often enough, she drowns us with water, or makes us thirsty with no water.
> [Böke, p. 73]

A cabin site was always chosen close to a spring, and some settlers built their home directly over water. This was handy for the housewife and useful in case of Indian attacks. The log cabins were simple structures, with one or two windows and a loft which could be used as sleeping space for children or guests. Floors were made of puncheons—split logs smooth on one side, rough on the other—or of hard-packed dirt. Windows were covered with a piece of oiled paper and could be barricaded with wooden shutters against animals or in case of attacks by Indians. Chinks and cracks between the logs were filled, and if this was done properly, the cabin could be a warm and cozy place. "In the holes we stuck chinking of clay, sand and hair from many different animals," wrote Liwwät Böke. "That mixture sets itself up hard and strong. The cold wind, the snow are forced to stay outside....they cannot blow through."

The farmer could cut his cabin logs by himself, but unless he had several strong young sons, he had to rely on neighbors to help him raise the logs in place. The frontier virtue of independence was all well and good, but settlers soon found that cooperative efforts on big tasks were a necessity. When the call for help went out, the response was generally excellent, since isolated settlers looked forward to any opportunity to socialize, and they never knew when they might need help

"We help one another, wives too."

"Natz is strong, as when he had to build our house today. He struck the axe deep into the tree so that it resounded at St. John."

Illustrations by Liwwät Böke, from Pioneer.

themselves. At these gatherings, the women, as always, were charged with providing food and drink, not an easy task with only a small fire and one or two kettles at hand.

Each community usually had several skilled craftsmen, and to them was left the expert work of clapboarding the roof, laying out a smooth floor, and making simple furniture—a slab table, benches, and three-legged stools, since four-legged ones wiggled on uneven ground. A bedstead was constructed by driving forked sticks into the floor, extending poles across them to fit into cracks in the wall, then laying boards across the poles and covering them with skins and blankets. Pegs driven into the cabin walls provided hanging space for a modest wardrobe, and shelves held the household's small supply of plates and bowls.

A simple cabin did not necessarily mean that a settler was poor. In 1803 F.A. Michaux stopped overnight with a prosperous farmer whom he would have expected to live in the greatest comfort:

> [Y]et he resides in a miserable log house about twenty feet long....Four large beds [including trundle beds] receive the whole family, composed of ten persons, and at times strangers who occasionally entreat to have a bed. This mode of living, which would announce poverty in Europe, is by no means a sign of it here. [Fletcher, p. 375]

A log house built by George Miller, a Scots-Irish immigrant who settled in Washington County in 1794. It has been moved to Meadowcroft Museum of Rural Life near Avella, which is jointly administered by the Meadowcroft Foundation and the Historical Society of Western Pennsylvania.

The pioneer housewife could organize her belongings and her work to suit her own style, but even on the young frontier there were prescribed ways of accomplishing the long list of tasks required to keep the family fed, clothed, and healthy. If a young woman was newly married and inexperienced, she either had to learn the hard way—and with limited resources this could prove wasteful— or rely on her distant neighbors for help. Fortunately no one on the frontier expected gourmet meals, so plain food simply cooked was the order of the day.

Christiana Tillson helped her businessman husband by keeping his accounts and writing his letters, and in order to have time for that she hired a young girl to do some of the household chores. The neighbors weren't sure how to deal with this pampered wife:

> She didn't spin nor weave, and had that little Dutch girl, and the men helped her to milk. They had hearn that she sot up nights to help Tillson write, but that wasn't much no how; never seed her in the "truck patch;" didn't believe she knowed how to hoe. [Tillson, p. 102]

For some reason, we assume that all backwoodsmen and farmers were experts at whatever they turned their hands to. This was clearly not so, as pioneers of every size, shape, and social condition set out for the West, and some of them were inept. Whatever their professional credentials might be, they proved of little use to lawyers and businessmen who opted for the wilderness life and had to build houses and hunt for and grow food for their families. And some simply proved incapable of feeling comfortable in the woods.

> In building our cabin it was set to front the north and south....we had no idea of living in a house that did not stand square with the earth itself. This argued our ignorance of the comforts and convenience of a pioneer life....The position of the house added much to the airiness of the domicile, particularly after the green ash puncheons had shrunk so as to have cracks in the floor and doors from one to two inches wide. ["Our Cabin," p. 444]

Rebecca Burland and her husband tried to make furniture for their cabin, with limited success. Her husband, "though no joiner," made a substantial table from a log, but its upper surface was far too short to be useful. They nailed a few boards on it and covered it with a cloth "to conceal its roughness," and since they had been weeks without a table of any sort, "it was far from contemptible."

Burland had no rifle and consequently was unable to shoot deer, but finally he managed to capture what he assumed to be a turkey and "brought home his game with as much apparent consciousness of triumph, as if he had slain some champion hydra of the forest." The couple dressed and boiled their prize and happily presented it to a guest. Surprised by their feast, he asked to see the head and feet. "But the moment he saw them, he exclaimed, 'it's a buzzard,' a bird which, we subsequently learnt, gourmandizes any kind of filth or carrion, and consequently is not fit to be eaten." They tossed out the offending bird and dined on a little bacon and coarse Indian meal pudding.

Liwwät Böke believed that most of the European immigrants were perplexed by this new country, confused and totally unprepared for such a wilderness. "It is impossible to describe how dense, dull and clumsy, how pitifully bewildered we and our neighbors were," she wrote. "The farmers did not have the right grasp of the how, where and what for taking over this forest, for dealing with the forest or plants. All of the routine was new and went contrary to our previous ideas and skills....In Europe we understood the weather, the land, its uses; here we dared not speculate."

Liwwät's husband was skillful, however, and his talent was important to the whole community. When he built a sundial for her, she wrote:

> He has the skill, patience and interest to figure it out. With so many needed tools and handmade things, he must think it out himself with minimum help from me. The neighbors are too far away and are not inventive. They are not interested until the time Natz has finished, built or made something...and then they praise him greatly so that he will lend the item. [Böke, pp. 99-101, 115]

The burden of adjustment was the heaviest for older people, some of whom had lived far easier lives before their western trek. An anonymous author's mother "was raised in the most delicate manner in and near London, and lived most of her time in affluence, and always comfortable." The family was building its cabin at Christmastime in weather too cold to chink cracks or daub mud between the logs.

> She was now in the wilderness, surrounded by wild beasts; in a cabin with about half a floor, no door, no ceiling overhead, not even a tolerable sign for a fireplace, the light of day and the chilling winds of night passing between every two logs in the building, the cabin so high from the ground that a bear, wolf, panther, or any animal less in size than a cow, could enter without even a squeeze. ["Our Cabin," p. 443]

There is no question that the settlers worked very hard indeed. And it is also certain that there were very specific tasks for men and women. Larkin tells us that "the farmyard, garden, house, kitchen and hearth, in diminishing concentric circles, enclosed and bounded women's daily realm." Men's tasks went outward, beginning with the farmyard, but then reaching out to the barn, the workshop, the fences, fields, pastures, woods and roads, leading away from the farm. Men's work was tied inevitably to the seasons, as was much of women's, but the latter also had a relentless series of daily tasks which had no regard for the weather, the seasons, or their state of physical or mental health—cooking, clearing up, cleaning, mending, washing, spinning, and caring for a brood of children.

Caroline Kirkland, who wrote about frontier life in Michigan in the 1830s, took issue with this arbitrary division of labor, observing that life in the woods required women to be their "own cook, chambermaid and waiter, nurse, seamstress and school ma'am, not to mention various occasional callings to any one of which she must be able to turn her hand at a moment's notice." But her husband must also be ready to take up any task called for, including tending the baby and cutting wood so she could cook his dinner. "If he has good sense, good nature, and a little spice of practical philosophy, all this goes exceedingly well. He will find neither his mind less cheerful, nor his body less vigorous for these little sacrifices."

In her autobiography, Jane Swisshelm expressed her distaste for the Pennsylvania customs against which she had rebelled:

> [W]hich made it unmanly for a man or boy to aid any woman, even mother or wife, in any hard work with which farms abounded at that time [1830s]. Dairy work, candle and sausage making were done by women, and any innovation was met with sneers. I stubbornly refused to yield altogether to a time-honored code, which required women to perform out-of-door drudgery, often while men sat in the house. [Swisshelm, p. 78]

Her young brother defied that same code and "He brought water from the cellar, and did other chores which Pennsylvania rules assigned to women, and when boys ridiculed him, he flogged them, and did it quite as effectually as he rendered them the same service when they were rude to a girl."

In 1798 Dr. Increase Matthews stopped overnight near Washington, Pennsylvania, and wrote, "I endeavored to persuade them that they put too much hardship on their women. In excuse, they plead that their business at certain seasons of the year is very urgent. This is truly the case, but it is not in my mind a sufficient excuse."[Buck, p. 330]

Phrases like "the fair sex" and "the weaker vessel" are sprinkled throughout 18th- and 19th-century American literature, but these appellations were hardly appropriate for the wilderness woman who lugged heavy cooking pots, chopped wood, built fires, stirred ponderous kettles of wet clothing, bent over the garden—and in harvest time, the fields—and carried a heavy infant, often while pregnant with another.

The realm of the men was more obviously linked with physical exertion, since it included dealing with animals and farm implements. Men and boys undertook the first steps in processing raw materials, then handed the job over to women and girls to finish. Perhaps most important of all, men made the decisions and women carried them out.

What, then, was a typical day in the life of a pioneer woman? She rose early, usually before dawn and the rest of the family, and stirred up the fire so that she could make breakfast. If the fire had gone out during the night, a youngster might be dispatched to a neighbor to borrow live coals. If there were no neighbors, the only solution was to undertake the tedious task of striking a spark with flint and tinder. When the fire was under control, water must be fetched and put on to boil; a cow must be milked to provide milk for the morning mush, which was made from the previous night's johnny cake. Bacon or salt pork must be fried and, depending on family tastes, buckwheat cakes prepared or hominy warmed or fresh johnny cake baked. In some households, the Sunday morning routine was different, as one author recalled from the days when he was 11 years old.

> My sister every Sunday morning, and at *no other time*, made short biscuit for breakfast....made out one by one, in her fair hands, placed in neat juxtaposition in a skillet or spider, pricked with a fork to prevent blistering, and baked before an open fire—not half baked and half stewed in a cooking stove.

Never mind that his *sister* might be half-baked and stewed from the open fire, his memory of the delicious biscuits prompted him to wax poetic.

> I do not believe that bankers, brokers and misers, could, from the sight of gold, experience such feelings of delight as I felt at the sight of the first skillet full piled on a plate by the fire awaiting the cooking of the second. To attempt to describe the felicity of eating those breakfasts is useless, when I cannot convey even a tolerable idea of the happiness of anticipation. ["Our Cabin," pp. 447-48]

Unfortunately, most of the recollections and reminiscences of pioneer days are written by men. More first-hand accounts by women would tell us whether the recollections of women were equally rose-colored and sentimental.

After breakfast there was clearing up to do, shaking out bedding, and sweeping the dirt or plank floor with a twig broom. But before these routines were established an earlier set of tasks had to be carried out: tablewear had to be carved from wood or horn or purchased from a peddler or village store; bedding had to be made—linen woven and bed ticks stitched, then filled with hay or feathers, if there was poultry. ("From ducks and geese we get the best feathers, to sell and for our own use to make bed covers and feather dusters and pens," To sweep, "the settlers first had to make a broom," wrote Liwwät Böke.)

Cleanliness could not be a high priority on the frontier. Simply boiling water was a major undertaking, since it first had to be carried from the spring to the house, then heated over the open fire in a heavy kettle. Most settlers went barefoot in the summer. A visiting New England physician while on a trip to Pennsylvania commented about the women he saw that, "Their feet are from twelve to eighteen inches long and from four to six inches wide; they might be made much smaller by washing."[Fletcher, p. 392] It appeared that aside from the Swedish settlers, who built bath houses as soon as their cabins were completed, most families bathed rarely or not at all. Liwwät's midwife training helped her to understand the importance of cleanliness, but her advice frequently fell on deaf ears. "People in the forest can be filthy and live untidily and think nothing of it. To sweat is good, to wash is better."

There was no way to keep rats, small animals, and insects out of the house, and since the fur hides used as bed covers could not be washed, they offered warm havens for scores of fleas and other bugs. Travelers made the same complaint about the sorry state of the inns where they stayed. "[W]e were tormented both nights with bugs, whose bites were as severe as those of mosquitoes," wrote English visitor John Pearson, describing his hotel. As a remedy against the ubiquitous bed bugs, one of the handwritten cookbooks in the collection of the Historical Society of Western Pennsylvania suggested that the housewife "take a solution of camphor and rub the bedsteads and other places affected with them—[it] will certainly dispell them."

The Housekeepers Book, published in Philadelphia in 1837, suggested beating together quicksilver and the whites of eggs and applying the mixture with a feather to "the crevices and holes in your bedsteads." The author stressed that a great deal of care and attention should be taken to rid the house of these pests, and went on to recommend taking the bedsteads "entirely assunder and washing every part of them with a strong solution of corrosive sublimate," a strong poison which the housewife should take care to mark well so that the children wouldn't get into it. Arsenic was recommended for ridding the house of cockroaches, more likely to be an urban pest, but in this regard the author noted that "It is pleasant, indeed, to hear the cricket 'chirping on the hearth,' but the cockroach ought to be expelled."

The heavily wooded forests and thick "wild herbage" were blamed for some of the insects. "It produced innumerable swarms of gnats, mosquitoes and horseflies. They must be justly ranked among the early plagues of the country." Another settler regarded the housefly, bedbug, and louse as the most common pests inside the cabin, while outside the gnat, wood tick, and horsefly were the worst. But the flea, he announced, was the all-around pest, both inside and out. Since at the time people in general had little or no awareness of the need for basic sanitary precautions, the presence of bugs and swarms of flies on the food was taken for granted.

No matter how much acreage was in corn, flax, or grain, housewives always cultivated a small truck patch of vegetables and, sometimes, flowers for the family's use. Liwwät's packing list for the journey from Germany to America included numerous seed packets—spinach, rhubarb, several kinds of peas, beans and turnips, carrots, cabbage, and cucumbers. She also included seeds from peach, apricot, apple, plum, and cherry trees, as well as seeds from snapdragons, peonies, morning glories, and tulip bulbs.

The garden patch needed tending every day. Except in the dead of winter, crops had to be planted, weeded, and picked regularly, and toward summer's end when the garden was filled with produce, there was preserving and drying to be done. Herbs used in cooking and for home remedies had to be tied and hung from the rafters. Apples and pears were cut and dried for winter use. Vegetables were salted and pickled; fruits preserved and made into jams and jellies. Chickens, though fed some table scraps, were truly free-range poultry and, like the hogs, tended to forage for themselves.

In addition to these basic tasks, there was a long list of other jobs that had to be done, but not every day. Making butter and cheese was high on the list of priorities. Good butter could only be made with good milk, and unless the cows were adequately fed, the milk was not good. "A cow pasture without grass, clover or timothy is nothing," wrote Liwwät. "It is a certainty that cattle must eat grain and root crops besides grass." She emphasized that cattle must be undercover in both hot summer and cold winter weather because "if they are not, they will gradually degenerate," their milk will be skimpy and they will die.

Churning could take a long time, and women could turn some of this chore over to their daughters or young helpers. When the butter "came," however, it needed a skilled hand to pat and shape it into molds and crocks. In the summer, butter could be salted, packed into pots and kept in a cool cellar or spring house for the following winter.

Baking was a regular chore to be undertaken, if not daily, then several times a week. The most primitive cabins lacked bake ovens, so bread, biscuits, pies, and cookies had to be baked on the open hearth in a Dutch oven or a spider, a long-handled cast iron pan. This task did not require constant watching, however, so that the housewife could turn her attention to other things while the bread was baking. Similarly, the noontime meal, which also had to be prepared, could be left on its own or under the supervision of a reliable child who could stir the kettle or turn the spit as needed.

Lunch—or dinner, as the midday meal was designated—varied with the season and the family's needs and tastes. Reading the menu of a typical dinner, one is tempted to speculate on the amount of time and energy expended for each item: cabbages, potatoes, turnips, bean or peas, sometimes cooked together, sometimes separately (picked from the garden, trimmed and cleaned, a wait for the water to boil, a wait for the vegetables to cook); wheat, corn, or rye bread with butter and cheese (meal to be ground, bread mixed and left to rise, then baked; butter churned and molded; cheese processed); salt pork and gravy, squirrel pot-pie, or venison stew (animals cleaned and cut, then cooked); pie or pudding (fillings to be picked, processed, and peeled, pastry to be made, pies baked, puddings baked or steamed, requiring ovens to be heated, water boiled for steaming). Clearly, each of these dishes required a substantial amount of time to prepare, but it was part of the expected routine. Supper was light, usually mush and milk once again.

(left) Flax plant. (below) Scutching flax, engraving, 1831.

Until the early 19th century, every piece of clothing had to be manufactured at home. If the family kept sheep, men sheared the animals and washed the wool. Women carded it, combing the mass of wool as straight as possible between two "cards" with leather backs and wire teeth. When the wool came off the cards, it was in a long, fleecy roll ready for spinning, then weaving or knitting.

Knitting was an important skill which little girls began to acquire at the age of five or six. Women manufactured caps, mittens, and scarves for the family, and on the rare occasions when there was time to sit down, the knitting needles were always busy.

Linen, the lighter weight alternative to wool, was spun from flax. "Linsey-woolsey" combined the two fibers on the loom—a linen warp and a woolen weft. Growing and processing flax was intensely difficult work. It was an important crop in Pennsylvania, but aside from growing it for commercial use, most families cultivated a patch for their own use. It was estimated that one acre of flax provided enough linen for summer clothing for a family of seven, but it was a labor-intensive crop, requiring the work of both men and women. Plants were pulled in late July, tied in small bundles, and dried for several days, then threshed to remove seed bolls. Stalks were retied and spread on the grass to rot, softening the fibers. Finally the flax was raked, tied again, but in large bundles, and the fibers separated by scutching, a task that required great strength and usually had to be repeated a second time.

When the fibers were thoroughly dry, families usually came together for a flax-scutching frolic, an all-day affair which involved removing small particles of bark, then separating the fibers. The final process before spinning the thread was called "hackling" or "hetcheling," when the fibers were drawn slowly through a hackle, consisting of long steel teeth fixed in a board. This process was repeated as often as 20 times to ensure that the fibers had been properly separated, and the reward was three products—oakum, used to caulk boats; tow, which was made into rough clothing; and fine linen for bedding, towels, and clothing.

Men generally took the process up to the hetcheling step, when the women took over. But Eastern Pennslvania women were known for their ability to perform the entire process, which amazed people like Timothy Dwight, who professed to be "struck by the Strangeness" of white women involved in such back-breaking labor. Another visitor commented that "It is a kind of work, which in New England, is always done by the men, but in the German part of Pennsylvania, tho, much out of doors work, is invariably done by females."

Spinning could be undertaken whenever there was a spare moment by girls and women of any age. Until the early 19th century and even later, farm women made all the clothes for their family, from flax planting and sheep tending to sewing the finished garment. One observer remarked, "From every farm home came the hum of the spinning wheel and the crack of the loom—these were the only instruments of music heard then." It has been estimated that one woman

Flax Spinning Wheel, c. 1779. This oak spinning wheel belonged to Thomas and Agnes Wilson, early settlers in Pitt Township, who built their log cabin in 1776. (below) Margaret Bunyan Morgan's "Recipe Book," 1790. HSWP Collection.

could spin six skeins in a day, as long as she didn't do anything else. In the process, she walked the equivalent of 20 miles at a "walking" wheel, which requires constant movement across the floor to keep the thread properly in line. Little girls began learning to spin at age five or six, and every girl's dowry included a spinning wheel. The lighter ones were often carried to another woman's house for an afternoon of neighborly work and conversation. Even today, an unmarried woman is often called a "spinster."

Weaving was one of the few non-gender-specific tasks. Both boys and girls learned this tedious job at an early age, and many villages had male weavers who worked for a percentage of the final product, sometimes carrying their looms from house to house. Much larger than a spinning wheel, looms required so much space that they were frequently placed in an attic or special weaving shed. Producing a piece of cloth required endless repetitions, the shuttle thrown and treadles pressed often more than 3,000 times in the course of a day.

Dyeing was usually done after weaving and the cloth first had to be bleached. Spread out in the sun, yards of linen lined the river banks, slowly turning pure white. Most dyes came from natural products: yellow and brown from butternut bark, as well as red oak hickory and boiled walnut hulls; yellow and orange from sassafras or the smartweed plant; a reddish-wine shade from pokeberry juice, and a bright red from the madder root. Indigo had to be purchased and was expensive, but produced a beautiful bright blue, a very popular color, and could be mixed with natural dyes to get various shades of green.

Most of the handwritten cookbooks have a recipe or two for the writer's favorite dye. Margaret Bunyan Morgan's book provides the instructions for making red lavender dye, which sounds expensive:

> Take a pint of the tops of green lavendar when seaded—one ounce cloves a littel mace a littel English saffron a littel cochinel 1/4 gallon best brandy—shaking it up well—and sett it in the sun for a few days. It will bair filling up again.

Alice Morse Earle describes an idyllic family scene where each family member is gainfully employed of an evening in various stages of wool manufacture. Even though this paints a romantic picture, the fact of the matter is that everyone was indeed involved.

> The old grandmother, seated next to the fire, is carding the wool into fleecy rolls. The mother, stepping as lightly as one of her girls, spins the rolls into woolen yarn on the great wheel. The oldest daughter sits at the clock reel, whose continuous buzz and occasional click mingle with the rise and fall of the wool-wheel and the irritating scratch, scratch of the cards. A little girl at a small wheel is filling quills with woolen yarn for the loom; the irregular sound shows her intermittent industry. The father is setting fresh teeth in a wool card and the boys are whittling hand-reels and loom-spools. [Earle, pp. 203-4]

After spinning, weaving, and dyeing, the housewife had to convert the fabric into clothes. Frontier fashions were understandably simple and serviceable. Family clothing, especially in the earliest days, was made of readily available materials—animal skins and hides and roughly woven wool or tow. Despite the romantic picture of a stalwart pioneer dressed in deerskin from head to foot, the wearer soon discovered that deerskin became cold and clammy in wind and snow, stiffening and cracking and leaving the person inside cold and very uncomfortable. Moccasins also did not stand up to wet weather and often had to be stuffed with animal hair or leaves to keep the wearer's feet warm. Men wore leather hunting shirts until well after the Revolution, but when sheep and flax-raising became common, the switch was made to breeches and shirts of rough tow cloth, woven from the short fibers of the flax or linsey-woolsey during the winter, sometimes worn with an outer jacket of deerskin. The collars of the shirts were large, often four inches wide, turned back to form a small cape which added an extra layer of warmth. The most practical and comfortable male garment was the loose hunting shirt, hanging almost to the knees, which was lapped over and secured with a belt, creating a small pouch where meat and bread could be carried while on the trail.

Women's dresses were practical, without the faintest hint of fashionable touches. Linsey-woolsey petticoats were covered by a "bed gown," a smock-like dress gathered at the waist with a belt, an apron around the waist, a kerchief around the neck. Another popular style was the "short gown," a long blouse worn over a petticoat. In the 1830s when calico and other manufactured yard goods became available, farm and frontier wives wore "the frontier classic," long-sleeved, tied at the waist, with a high round neck, the dress beloved by all costume designers for their pioneer heroines. Indigo dyed cloth was widely used, so much so "that it was said that when the minister prayed at town meeting, a square acre of blue frocking rose up to greet him."[McKnight, p. 30]

Women of refinement all wore caps day and night. Their bonnets were sun-bonnets, or made of beaver, gimp (a ribbon-like fabric), and leghorn, a finely plaited straw. Men wore coon or other fur hats in winter, chip or oat-straw hats in summer.

All garments were, of course, sewn by hand, another time-consuming task when multiplied by the number of people in the family requiring clothing. Liwwät Böke described the additional tasks necessary to keep wardrobes in shape.

> In the evening I make *buttons* out of *bones*, with rough and fine files. One files a little piece of bone into a round and thin shape finally drilling 2 holes, first with a little drill and then with a hammer and punch. I make a dozen in one evening of various sizes, thick and thin, in proper sets for their future use. [Böke, p. 71]

Animal skins, whether used for a garment or a bedcover, had to be dressed and tanned, and although Margaret Bunyan Morgan lived in the fairly sophisticated town of Washington in 1795, the fact that her cookbook provides instructions for the first part of this process shows that some importance was given to this housewifely chore even there.

> To Dress Scins with fur on Take the scin in Salt and water 24 hours than with a dul nife scrape all the flesh and blud of then take water enuf to cover it well and make it strong with rock salt and allum—lett it lay 24 hours—than ring it well—and rub it till dry.

It was a long and sometimes distasteful task involving hours of scrubbing, soaking, scraping, and pounding using lye made from wood ashes; tannin made from bark; lard, tallow, and soot. By 1790, however, tanneries were appearing all over the state and farmers could take their skins to the local tanner, who usually took half of them in payment. If the settlers didn't have the skill to make their own shoes, they paid for that service as well, and since cash was scarce or non-existent, many families resorted to wearing shoe packs. These were a simpler version of a moccasin and not beyond the skill of a handy farmer.

Even if standards of cleanliness in the wilderness were lower than those of contemporary housewives elsewhere, clothes eventually had to be washed. Making soap was the first step. Every old recipe begins with wood ashes cooked in water several times to produce a residue of potash or lye. This was boiled with tallow, fat, or the entrails of hogs to the proper consistency for soft soap, as thick as molasses or syrup, "and with peppermint in it" for "a better fragrance." If the soap was left to stiffen, it could be cut up into bars in a few days. More fastidious housewives produced three kinds: a white bathing soap made of white pearl ash and sheep tallow; a hard brown soap for washing and housecleaning; and an all-purpose soft brown soap. They were careful to wash out the containers for lye at once so that it didn't eat directly through the receptacle. One young man remembers using hardened cakes of soap "that not only removed the several layers of dirt that usually encased a country boy's hands, but, it appeared to us, always carried away one or more layers of skin with it."

Eliza Leslie, in 1840, instructed women to have a large fireplace so that several kettles of water could be put on to boil at once. She also gave detailed instructions for making lye ("hickory ashes is the best, but good oak ashes will do very well") and suggested a separate lye barrel be kept in the cellar, along with a special receptacle for fat of all kinds.

Lydia Maria Child, author of *The American Frugal Housewife*, published in 1843, counseled young women who lived in the country to make their own soap. She gave complicated directions for making lye, but cautioned them about making it strong enough. "One rule may be safely trusted—If your lye will bear up an egg, or a potato, so that you can see a piece of the surface as big as a ninepence, it is just strong enough."

Washday itself was dreaded by everyone in the family. At least once a month, the housewife rose before dawn to carry sufficient water to fill the large wooden or metal wash tub, set it to boil, plunged her arms into the hot water and soap suds, and got to the unpleasant work of ridding the clothes of forest dirt and mud. If washboards were wanted, they had to be made, wrote Liwwät. "The new washboard that Natz made is all of wood. One (that is I!) can rub clothes vigorously up and down against the ridges with soap. This will completely bring out the dirt, especially the grease." After repeated washes and rinses, the laundry had to be wrung and spread to dry on the grass or over the rail fences. One lady from the East used clothespins, after she found someone to whittle them for her, and it became the talk of the neighborhood.

> The first time they were used I was attracted to the window to see what was the source of such jollification as was being shown by two of our backwoods neighbors. They were looking at the clothes yard, and calling to the third, who was on his way to join them, "See here, ain't that jest the last Yankee fixin'? just see them ar little boys ridin' on a rope." [Tillson, p. 148]

However, most women thought that washday was a day of leisure compared to candle-making day. Harriet Beecher Stowe noted that it was "seven-fold worse in its way than even washday" when women worked from "day-dawn" to late at night dipping candles. Long strings had to be prepared, the tallow melted, and a rack made ready; then began the tedious chore of dipping each string and laying it across the rack, repeating the dipping again and again until the candles had attained sufficient thickness. Christiana Tillson described the process graphically.

> I used to dip sixteen dozen in the fall and twenty dozen in the spring. For the spring candles I boiled the tallow in alum water to harden it for summer....I can fancy my poor tired shoulder and strained arm are now in sympathy with the toil of tallow. Not like practicing two hours on the piano, which when you are tired you can stop, but from three to four mortal hours the right arm must be in constant movement. If a rest is given to the arm the candles become too hard and break, or the tallow in the pot gets too cool, so dip, dip, dip, six candles at a time; each time the candles grow heavier, and the shoulder more rebellious. [Tillson, p. 150]

Candles could also be molded, a somewhat easier process, but the molds had to be obtained from a store or a peddler, and some people thought that the light they gave off was not as clear as light from dipped candles.

Some light was obtained from the fireplace, and many settlers supplemented this with pine knot torches, the knots cut from the heart of a tree, lighted and placed in cracks in the wall or on the floor between the boards. The "betty" lamp widely used on the frontier consisted of a shallow receptacle with a projecting nose or spout filled with grease in which an old rag was inserted to serve as a wick. It gave basic light but smelled foul and usually smoked as well. A simple dish of grease did almost as well but had the same disadvantages.

If there were any time left in the day, the women and their menfolk could make various household articles to make their lives easier, as Liwwät and her husband Natz did. From bone they made combs and needles, as well as "handles, wheels, butter paddles, awls, buckles, quilting needles, needles for knitting work; also clothes pins, hooks for clothes and coats, and many other things." From wood they made soup and cooking spoons, meat forks and a rolling pin, butter and flour scoops. "Also a wooden dough board for kneading dough for bread baking. It gets no other use, so that it always remains clean, and no dirt or foreign growth can get on it." They created wooden pans for cooking, wooden buckets, a vat for the lye used to make soap, a sieve from the sinews of a deer, glued on with horsehoof glue. "We make the glue from the hooves of animals by very slowly boiling them in water until the last little bit is dissolved and that is the glue. The best. One can also make it from fishes; the smell is fearsome and horrible. No! No!"

Margaret Bunyan Morgan's cookbook includes a more expensive recipe for glue. She recommended "60 grains Isinglass 9 sponfulls brandy—desolved on a gentel fier till the isinglass is quite desolved." (Isinglass is a form of gelatin made from fish bladders.) Other recipe-remedy books include instructions for making cement, liquid foil for silvering glass, for paint, for the preservation of small birds, and for treatments for the ailments of horses, oxen, calves, and sheep.

In addition to the myriad daily, weekly, and seasonal tasks required to care for their family, housewives were often forced to drop everything and help in the fields. When the Burlands were newly arrived on the frontier, they faced the important planting season with few implements and no help.

> We had land and seed, but no plough, nor any team, except an old mare, that we feared would scarcely live while she foaled, and consequently we could not yoke her....We set to work with our hoes; I, husband, and son, the latter under ten years of age, and day after day, for three succesive weeks, did we toil with unwearied diligence till we had sown and covered in nearly four acres. [Burland, pp. 79-80]

The next year, when their wheat crop was ready for harvesting, Burland cut himself and the wound became badly infected. They had no means to hire reapers, so his wife was obliged to do it herself.

smell for sleep. (Perhaps now, Natz will not snore so much when he is tired. But only perhaps!)

In the evening I make <u>buttons</u> out of <u>bones</u> (<u>bone</u> makes the best buttons, <u>needles</u> and <u>combs</u>) with rough and fine files. One files a little piece of bone into a round and thin shape finally drilling 2 holes, first with a little drill and then with a hammer and punch. I make a dozen in one evening of various sizes, thick and thin, in proper sets for their future use.

The <u>needles</u> vary, some with pointed ends, others half pointed.

Handel handle *Gornelul*   Schuff scoop *safuff.*

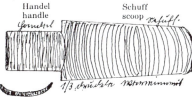

1/3 *deriulele mstormimumil*

The end view. It is curved a little.

<u>Boot</u> <u>horns</u> and shoe horns of bone and also of wood which we recently made in the winter.

<u>Combs</u> are made from <u>bone</u> with saw and file.

End view

From <u>bones</u> we also made: handles, wheels, butter paddles, <u>awls</u>, buckles, quilting needles, needles for knitting work and needles for making stockings; also clothes pins, hooks for clothes and coats, and many other things.

From <u>wood</u> Natz and I have made many things for household use, such as: pancake rack, soup cooking spoon, other sizes of wooden spoons; of elm wood, meat forks and garden stakes for climbing grape vines and such.

We also made a wooden rolling pin (1) with handles at each end, butter scoops (2) and flour scoops (3). Also a wooden dough board (4) for kneading the dough for bread baking. (One uses it only for rolling and kneading dough. It gets no other use, so that it always remains clean, and no dirt or foreign growth can get on it.)

Also various wooden pans (5) in which to set anything for cooking, baking or broiling.

Wooden <u>buckets</u> (6) with leather handles and hoops. Also we made one or two vats to use with lye water for making soap.

A <u>sieve</u> (7) for sifting flour and other things. The mesh in the sieve is from the sinews of a deer glued on with horse hoof glue. We make the glue from the hooves of animals by very slowly boiling them in water until the last little bit is dissolved, and that is the glue. The best. One can also make it from fishes; the smell is fearsome and horrible. No! No!

We made <u>brooms</u> (8), about a half dozen, from young birch trees, the stem not over 2 inches thick. First from the bottom of the stem upwards make splits, hundreds, and wind them around with corn husks.

Natz uses a log roller (9) many times.

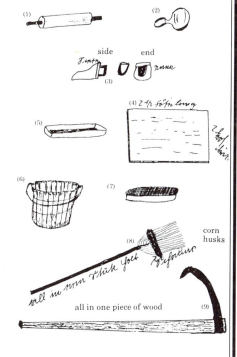

From **Pioneer,** *Liwwät Böke's account of her experiences in making a home in the wilderness. Her candid memoirs are richly illustrated by her own hand.*

I took my eldest child into the field to assist me, and left the next in age to attend
to their father and take care of the youngest, who was still unweaned. I worked
as hard as my strength would allow; the weather was intolerably hot, so that
I almost melted. In little more than a week, however, we had it all cut down.
[Burland, p. 91]

Until the 1780s working in the fields courted a special danger—Indian attacks. John Boucher observed, "Every acre, every rod of ground had to be cleared
with the ax and held with the rifle." Early settlers never ventured outside the
cabin without a gun, and children were carefully watched to make certain they
did not wander off and fall into the hands of hostile Indians. Stories of attacks on
isolated cabins as well as on small communities kept settlers in a constant state
of anxiety and watchfulness. DeCrèvecoeur, the French diplomat and writer who
spent some years as a farmer in America, wrote:

We never go to our fields but we are seized with an involuntary fear which lessens
our strength and weakens our labor....We never sit down either to dinner or supper but the least noise immediately spreads a general alarm and prevents us from
enjoying the comfort of our meals....At night the howling of our dogs seems to
announce the arrival of the enemy; we leap out of bed and run to arms....At last,
finding that it was a false alarm, we return once more to our beds; but what good
can the kind of sleep of nature do us when interrrupted by such scenes?
[Fletcher, p. 76]

Native American tribes watched as white settlers usurped their lands and
retaliated by burning cabins, and taking captives as well as scalps. Hanna's Town
in Westmoreland County was burned to the ground in 1782 by Senecas, who,
along with the Shawnee and Lenni Lenape tribes, comprised the majority of
Native Americans in Western Pennsylvania. By the close of the Revolutionary
War, raids had begun to decline, and by 1784 a series of treaties had been ne-
gotiated between the American government and the Indian nations. Sporadic
resistance to the relentless tide of settlers continued, however, and in 1784
General Anthony Wayne mounted a fierce campaign.

He met the Indians in force...and in a hard fought battle, completely crushed
the power and spirit of the savage foes....After this there were no further Indian
troubles about Pittsburgh or Indian raids into Allegheny county, and the tide of
emigration began to flow with constantly increasing volume into the rich valleys
north of the rivers. [Lambing, p. 73]

The federal census of 1790 noted that there were but 1,300 Indians on the
northwest branch of the Susquehanna River, with "probably" some roving bands
of Iroquois in the northwest corner of the state. When the Treaty of Grenville was
signed in 1795, settlers breathed a collective sigh of relief as Native American
boundaries were pushed far beyond the borders of Western Pennsylvania.

Fear of Indian attack was just one in a litany of worries for the frontier
housewife—disease, wild animals, snakebite, crop failure, starvation, death, and

*Fowling Rifle, c. 1780. Though fowling pieces were intended for hunting wild birds, family
history indicates that this gun was used by David Shaw on July 13, 1782, in the defense
of Hanna's Town, an early settlement on Forbes Road. HSWP Collection.*

loneliness. Much of her burden had to be borne without the warmth and aid of a
friendly neighbor, however, since houses in rural Pennsylvania were frequently
widely scattered.Villages were scarcely worthy of the name, sometimes distinguished by only one store and a blacksmith, not even a church. Women often
longed for the companionship of a like-minded female. "It was a very rare but
pleasing thing," one wrote, "to hear a neighbor's cock crow."[Fletcher, p. 437]
The sound of an axe ringing in the forest or the sight of a plume of smoke rising
from a newcomer's cabin could be an occasion for much excitement and
anticipation. New neighbors meant the beginning of a community with all that
implied—quilting parties, cabin raisings, weddings, births, and deaths, the
shared experiences of community life, and the mutual aid so important to family
life in the wilderness. All of these longings, however, had to be sublimated to the
daily tasks required to sustain the family. In 1755 a country minister's wife wrote
in her diary that she had so much to do that she had no leisure for complaining.

> So much did it press upon me that I could scarcely divert my thoughts from its
> demands even during the family prayers, which both amazed and displeased
> me, for during that hour, at least I should have been sending all my thoughts to
> Heaven for the safety of my beloved Husband and the salvation of our hapless
> Country; instead of which I was often wondering whether Polly had remembered
> to set the sponge for the bread, or to put water in the leach tub, or to turn the
> cloth in the dying vat, or whether the wool had been carded for Betsey to start
> her spinning wheel in the morning, or Billy had chopped lightwood enough for
> the kindling, or dry hard wood enough to heat a big oven, or whether some
> other thing had been forgotten of the thousand that must be done without fail.
> [Hechtlinger, p. 17]]

Household servants were rarely available in frontier settlements. If a family
kept slaves, they worked primarily in the fields. Occasionally an indentured girl
or boy lived with the family, bound over to serve the master for eight or ten years,
but most rural settlers relied on their children and extended family, as well as
their own skills and energy, to make a home in the wilderness. §

Pennsylvania towns. (above) Brownsville and Bridgeport from the National Road; *(middle)* Somerset; *(below)* Washington. *Engravings by Sherman Day, 1843.*

CENTRAL PART OF WASHINGTON.

Mansion House Hotel.   Court House.   National road to the West.

Moving to Town

Restless settlers in Western Pennsylvania, tired of trying to turn the wilderness into productive farmland, had three choices other than staying put. They could go back home to Philadelphia, Boston, or their place of origin in Europe, a choice most families found unattractive. They could continue to push westward into Ohio, Kentucky, and Illinois, and many did just that. Or they could move into town, where life was somewhat easier, there was money to be made, and like-minded people could be found closer than ten miles away.

Although Western Pennsylvania's population remained overwhelmingly rural well into the 19th century, the proportion of families living in towns was increasing. Urban populations in Pennsylvania's southwestern counties—Allegheny, Washington, Greene, Fayette, and Westmoreland—rose by four percent in 1800 and by seven percent in 1820. In 1790 there were 11 "towns" and by 1820 there were more than 60. Pittsburgh's greatest rivals for population and industrial growth were Washington, Uniontown, and Brownsville, all within reach of rich coal and ore deposits, all just off the National Road, all handy to river transportation to continue the westward migration on the Ohio. Washington County was the most populous of the western counties, and in 1810 had 36,289 inhabitants. In 1781 the village of Washington laid out a town plan, and although its population was not tabulated in the census of 1790, it boasted a greater variety of industries than Pittsburgh. In 1794 a soldier from Massachusetts wrote in his journal:

"The clear and beautiful Alleghany, the loveliest stream that ever glistened to the moon, gliding over its polished pebbles... was still the boundary of civilization."

—Henry M. Brackenridge

> Washington is a considerable town, consisting of framed buildings clapboarded and chiefly painted red, except the court house and two or three other buildings, which are of stone. The appearance of this place was very pleasing to me, as it resembled a *New England* town. [Harpster, p. 171]

Philadelphia businessman Joshua Gilpin, writing in 1809, was much taken with Southwestern Pennsylvania. He wrote with great enthusiasm about the Chestnut Ridge area, its beautiful farms, fertile soil and, wonder of wonders,

Uniontown from the East,
engraving by Sherman Day,
1843.

smooth roads. As to Uniontown, at that time boasting some 1,000 inhabitants, he noted:

> We found Uniontown very different from our expectation, it was founded about 30 years ago....[A]bout 17 years ago...it was made the County town—has a handsome Court house, Jail, and a more compact street of decent houses than in any place of the size I have seen in America—indeed there seems an unusual bustle & population about it—near the town are several mills on two branches of the Redstone. [Gilpin, pp. 42-43]

In 1816 Uria Brown, a surveyor from Baltimore, described Uniontown as having "some good building of brick" and "too many wooden houses for the Credit of the place." He noted that "its situation is handsome & the surrounding neighborhood is a handsome hill Country in a good State of Cultivation." [Harpster, p. 262]

Brownsville was another booming town because many immigrants who had planned to use it as a departure point for the Ohio River liked what they found and decided to settle there. Zadok Cramer in his 1802 handbook for river travelers, *The Navigator*, reported that "Brownsville (or Redstone)...is well known to migraters down the rivers. It is handsomely situated...a place of much business, and contains about 90 houses and 500 souls." When Joshua Gilpin visited in 1809, just seven years later, the town had more than tripled in size.

> The river forms a sweep or turn at Brownsville so that both above & below the town at the distance of a few miles it winds around the hills—Brownsville being at the bottom of the curve—has therefore a beautiful sheet of the river in view on each side....Brownsville united with Bridgeport contains ab 300 houses and 2000 inhabitants—the houses principally stores Taverns & tradesmen—there are many mills—for Corn—fuling—carding oil & ca. [Gilpin, pp. 47-48]

Gilpin noted "18 Stores at Brownsville," most designed to provide supplies to the boats departing for the Ohio. Mrs. Trollope relaxed her prejudices against all things American long enough to say a few kind words about Brownsville but couldn't let it get away without at least some criticism.

> Brownsville is a busy looking little town, built upon the banks of this river; it would be pretty, were it not stained by the hue of coal. I do not remember in England to have seen any spot, however near a coal mine, so died [*sic*] in black as Wheeling and Brownsville. [Trollope, p. 152]

View of Greensburg from Bunker Hill, *engraving by Sherman Day, 1843.*

John Heckewelder, visiting Greensburg in 1789, had found "30 handsome, trimmed log houses. The Courthouse is a wooden building & serves also as a church. The town lies on a pleasant hill where several springs gush out. East and west are streams and swamps. There is an English school there, and a German one nearby." Sally Hastings stopped in Greensburg in 1800 on a day of "Public Review," and found that "the Town was full of riotous People. There were parades and dancing…and they were very expert at this Exercise.…they were a Company of the most active and handsome Men I ever saw." However, as the bottles were passed around and the noise level rose, Hastings became increasingly irritable until one of the officers made a handsome apology for his men, "And for his own part, he carried his Politeness so far as to make Love to a Person of our Party; whom he entertained with a Song, which consisted of two elegant Lines and a—Hiccough…." She added that there were public races in Greensburg and "the Beaux are flocking into Town by the dozens."[Harpster, pp. 240-41]

By 1804 the town could claim 100 houses and a German Reform Church, according to a Swiss farmer, and a new brick courthouse as well as a jail. Margaret Dwight found Greensburg to be "a pretty little town, situated on a high hill." An unknown writer passing through Greensburg in 1822, found:

> [O]ne of the handsomest towns we have been in since we left home, the streets are laid out at right-angles, and the houses chiefly Brick well built, the Town is built on an elevated piece of ground commanding a handsome prospect of the surrounding country which is fertile and under a good state of cultivation, the public buildings are a Courthouse, jail, Three Meeting-houses one with a handsome cupilo…. ["A Diary of 1822," p. 71]

In 1809 Somerset had about 100 houses and 300 to 400 inhabitants, "a neat stone Court house and Jail—the houses are principally taverns, stores, & tradesmens houses." Gilpin commented on the price of land, an important consideration for farmers moving closer to town.

> [T]he land about here is very good for pasturage, oats and Indian corn but not so favorable for wheat—improved farms sell so high as $20 to $30 per acre, but other lands will not bring in more than $5 or $6 & if in stony ground & on the mountains degenerate to 25 cents per acre, all their value depending on the quality of the lands & the improvements made on it. [Gilpin, p. 31]

He found Bedford "a neat town of abt. 200 houses—many of them very good. It is the capital & and is rather an old town being founded in [1760] & was continued as a frontier against the Indians till the close of [the] last war...." However, he went on to comment that "it does not improve so much as other towns owing to its being surrounded by mountains and not having so large an extent of rich country as some other towns to support it."

Nevertheless, by 1811 Bedford had already established itself as a "notable watering place." The magnesia and sulphur-laden water attracted many visitors, "a vast concourse of people collected from different places, some of them very distant." For five or six dollars a week, visitors could stay at a large boarding house, complete with bath house, and enjoy a situation described as "very romantic and truly delightful."

Johann David Schoepf in 1783 put his finger on the key reason that women wanted to move to town. "Bedford is a little town," he wrote, "but a little town in a great wilderness may easily please without beauty."[Harpster, p. 132] A woman's first glimpse of Brownsville's 18 stores must have been a heady experience. Here was possibly her first opportunity in many years to pick out calico, have several kettles to choose from, and go to a proper church. Small wonder if she nagged her husband to settle there or go on to Pittsburgh.

View of Bedford Township and the Allegheny Mountains. HSWP Collection.

In 1754 George Washington noted Pittsburgh's strategic military location. After the Revolution the town became increasingly important as a transportation hub and manufacturing center, in large part because of the three rivers—the Monongahela, the Allegheny, and the Ohio. As settlers began to arrive from the East, there was praise for the available opportunities but criticism for the dirt and the slow development of cultural and educational activities. On one thing, however, almost everyone agreed. Pittsburgh's location was unsurpassed. In 1794 James Elliot wrote:

> It is almost surrounded by high hills, at the feet of which flow the large and beautiful rivers Allegany and Monongahela, and uniting their waters, form the celebrated Ohio, which flows to the northwest, changing its course after some miles to the southwest, and fully justifies the assertion of Mr. Morse, who, in the first editiion of his Geography, styles it, "The most beautiful river on earth." [Harpster, p. 172]

In 1827 the usually acerbic Mrs. Basil Hall, visiting from England, noted that "the situation of this town is altogether beautiful, surrounded by highly cultivated country and beautifully wooded hills which form an amphitheatre...." But it was left to Henry Marie Brackenridge, who, along with his father Hugh Henry Brackenridge, was among Pittsburgh's earliest and certainly most determined boosters, to wax rhapsodic over the location. "The clear and beautiful Alleghany, the loveliest stream that ever glistened to the moon, gliding over its polished pebbles, being the Ohio, or La Belle Riviere, under a different name, was still the boundary of civilization."

Despite its beautiful location, Pittsburgh in the late 18th century was still a frontier town, with all the pleasures and problems that phrase calls to mind. Visitors and prospective settlers arrived with high expectations, some of which were rudely shattered. "Disorder reigns in the streets," Heckewelder wrote, and Cuming reported that the streets were unpaved and consequently, "they are so extremely dirty, that it is impossible to walk them without wading over the ankle." Hogs and dogs ran unheeded through these streets, and residents became so used to them that they were astonished when visitors were critical. Most houses were wood or frame, but brick was beginning to take precedence as a building material. Cultural and educational amenities were scarce, and organized religion was slow to take hold. Growth was uneven, with no plan for the future but the promise of unlimited opportunity for all—which is why many had come in the first place. Visitors were bewildered and often distressed by what they found. In 1784 Unitarian minister Arthur Lee dolefully observed:

> Pittsburgh is inhabited almost entirely by Scots and Irish, who live in paltry log-houses, and are as dirty as in the north of Ireland, or even Scotland....There are in the town four attorneys, two doctors, and not a priest of any persuasion, nor church, nor chapel; so that they are likely to be damned, *without the benefit of clergy*. The place, *I believe*, will never be very considerable. [Harpster, p. 157]

When banker John Thaw arrived in 1804 from Philadelphia, he wrote to a friend that Pittsburgh was:

> [A] fine country town…[with] dear stores & bad society….It is a place by no means as so Enticing as Philadelphia & a person coming from thence should do it under the conviction of making Money and bettering his circumstances, but not of enjoying the pleasure either of a Country or City Life. [Thaw Papers, ALS, October, 16, 1804]

Perhaps the most negative aspect of Pittsburgh was the ubiquitous dirt and dust created by coal and increasing manufacturing activities. While the city's strategic location was enough to merit an 1822 traveler's designation of it as "the emporium of the world," the seemingly bottomless pits of coal provided an added stimulus to the development of manufacturing and commerce. Coal was in use in Pittsburgh as early as 1766, when the Reverend Charles Beatty wrote in his journal that he had ascended Coal Hill opposite the fort, where an underground fire had been burning "almost twelve months entirely under ground….the earth in some places is so warm, that we could hardly bear to stand upon it….the steam that came out was so strong of sulphur that we could scarcely bear it."[Craig, pp. 95-96] Coal mining did not become a major industry until the demand for coal rose during the War of 1812, but being cheap and plentiful, it was a popular household fuel, in use since Pittsburgh's earliest days. Fortescue Cuming, an observant traveler throughout Western Pennsylvania, wrote:

> A load of forty bushels, which costs only two dollars, will keep two fires in a house a month, and in consequence, there are few houses, even among the poorest of the inhabitants, where at least two fires are not used—one for cooking and one for the family to sit at. This great consumption of a coal abounding in sulphur, and its smoke condensing into a vast quantity of lamp black, gives the outside of the houses a dirty and disagreeable appearance. [Cuming, p. 62]

Pittsburgh from the Northwest, *engraving by Sherman Day, 1843.*

In 1816 David Thomas, visiting in Pittsburgh noted, "Dark dense smoke was rising from many parts, and a hovering cloud of this vapour, obscuring the prospect, rendered it singularly gloomy. Indeed, it reminded me of the smoking logs in a new field."[Harpster, p. 272] In 1821 John Pearson arrived from England with the intention of buying a farm and settling down. After one look at Western Pennsylvania, however, he immediately turned back and went home.

> We arrived at Pittsburgh, the Birmingham, the Manchester, the Sheffield of America, according to some, but in my words, a poor, gloomy, sickly receptacle, hardly fit for convicts of the worst description; no greater punishment, I am sure, upon our Bank note forgers, than to send them to Pittsburgh, yet this is the place where the hammers stunned your ears, and the manufactories struck you dumb with astonishment…. [Harpster, p. 280]

In 1828 Elizur Wright, Jr., serving as an agent for the American Tract Society, an evangelical missionary organization, wrote to his financée. "I hope at last to get clear of this noisy, smoky city," he told her, "…where the black mud on the pavements was over shoe—where the people are all either blacksmiths, or look like blacksmiths. Such is Pittsburgh. Ascend the hill around which the city lies and you may see hundreds of furnaces vomiting forth immense volumes of black smoke mingled with red flames."[Harpster, p. 272] Looking back on his arrival in Pittsburgh in 1829, newspaperman Russel Errett described his first reactions to the city.

> After traveling for two weeks through white, clean, cheerful-looking villages and towns, to come all at once upon dirty streets and dark, filthy looking houses stretched away in rows continually ahead and enveloped in an atmosphere of smoke and soot which blackened everything in sight, was not a pleasant transition. It did not make me homesick; but if there had been any place that I knew of that I should safely run off to, I should certainly have run away. [Harpster p. 288]

In 1841 William Reynolds noted in his diary:

> Pittsburgh looks as black as ever with the exception of the smoke of the manufactories. Many of which are at present closed….I went to a bath this afternoon and cleansed myself of part of the soot which two days residence in P. accumulated. The inhabitants do not mind, but it is exceedingly annoying to strangers. [Reynolds, p. 2]

The grime and soot may well have been unpleasant surprises for strangers, but to a woman who had traveled a long distance, her first view of the city must have been a welcome sight. A cluster of cabins, a few streets, some taverns, and a dozen or more shops spelled civilization. On July 18, 1788, the *Pittsburgh Gazette* ran an advertisement for Elliot, Williams and Company, a dry goods, hardware and cutlery establishment, which listed some of the new merchandise available from Europe and the West Indies. For sale were toothbrushes and combs, playing cards, and bottles of snuff. Dry goods included broadcloth in blue, green, scarlet, claret, brown, and bottle green. There were jeans and corduroys, chintzes, linens,

Beitler's Tavern *(located on the south side of Greensburg Pike), painting by Joseph Ryan Woodwell, 1857. HSWP Collection.*

silks, muslins, and calicos, hats for men and mantuas (loose robes) and fans for women. In the grocery department one could purchase tea, coffee, chocolate, spices from the Orient, molasses and sugar, as well as a fine stock of wines and rum. And for the householder lacking hard cash, merchandise could be exchanged for poultry, bacon, beef, cattle on foot, whiskey, flour, butter, cheese, tallow, candlewick, hard soap, and vinegar. In order to maintain a fair barter system, the prices for butter, eggs, rye, wheat, corn, and oats were regulated annually by town meeting.

Although luxury items were easily available, they could also be costly. Coffee and tea were in common use, but in 1807 coffee cost approximately 40 cents per pound and tea sold for $1.50 per pound. Chocolate cost 40 cents per pound and a bottle of mustard retailed for 25 cents. Everyday necessities were cheaper: in 1801 beef sold for 3 to 5 cents per pound, as did pork, mutton and venison; potatoes were 25 cents per bushel; flour $1.25 for 100 pounds. In 1817 a tailor charged 75 cents to make a pair of pants, $1.50 for a "small coat." In 1833 calico sold for 25 cents per yard; a man's pair of calf skin shoes for $1.37; a black silk dress for $6; and a pair of cotton hose for 50 cents.

Prices must be viewed in the context of wages. In 1800 a carpenter received 70 cents per day and by 1840 this had doubled to $1.40. Unskilled laborers earned 62 cents a day in 1800 and $1 by 1840. (In comparison, President James Madison's annual salary was $25,000, with Chief Justice John Marshall receiving $4,000.)

Before 1840 the work day was clocked from sunrise to sunset, but in that year President Van Buren mandated a ten-hour day for government shipyard workers and other industries followed.

In 1800 Pittsburgh had 1,500 inhabitants and 60 shops. There were 25 businesses on Market Street alone—general stores, shoe shops, medical stores, millinery shops, blacksmiths, bakeries, and taverns—a truly astonishing sight for the traveler whose long journey over the mountains had been dangerous, uncomfortable, and exhausting. But before the first shopping expedition, the family required temporary lodgings. The choices were narrow: friends or family for the lucky ones; a boarding house, or a tavern for the rest. To the modern American the word tavern brings to mind a noisy barroom, but many such establishments also offered accommodations and meals. The quality of the inns varied as much in the town as in the country, but by and large, the best-known taverns were clean, comfortable, but crowded, so that the traveler was lucky indeed who found first-class lodgings for himself and his family. John Ormsby kept a good house on Water Street, convenient to the ferry landing. Johann David Schoepf, visiting in 1783, commented on the Ormsby establishment. "We were directed to the best inn, a small wooden cabin set askew by the Monongahela, its exterior promising little; but seeing several well dressed men and ladies adorned we were not discouraged."[Buck, p. 254]

Henry M. Brackenridge wrote about both the inns and their landlords.

> The landlords or tavernkeepers are, in reality, the only lords we have in Pennsylvania; they possess a degree of intelligence and respectability of character which justly gives them an influence *dans la chose publique*, which very little corresponds with that of mine host in the country of John Bull....Before my time, BLACK CHARLES kept the first hotel in the place; when I can first remember, the sign of GENERAL BUTLER, kept by Patrick Murphy, was the *head tavern*; and afterwards the GREEN TREE, on the banks of the Monongahela, kept by William Morrow. The General Butler was continued by Molly Murphy for some years after the death of Paddy; she was the friend of my boyhood and youth, and, although as rough a Christian as I ever know, I verily believe that a better Christian heart, one more generous and benevolent, as well as sturdy and fearless, never beat in Christian bosom. Many an orphan, many a friendless one, many a wretched being has shed, in secret, the tear of gratitude over the memory of Molly Murphy! [Harpster, pp. 187-88]

Although Brackenridge's romantic description of Mrs. Murphy sounds as if it had been written by central casting, there were other female tavern keepers. General Washington actually slept at the Turtle Creek tavern owned by the Widow Myers. Margaret Allen kept an inn in Uniontown, and the area was later known as Granny Allen's Hill. Jean Hanna, whose uncle Robert Hanna founded Hanna's Town, was the host of a public house in Westmoreland County in 1773, and Mary Irwin's establishment was licensed in Pittsburgh in 1778. Names of other tavern owners—Letty Bean, Mrs. Woodrow, and Lydia Hoffman—have all been documented as doing business in or near Pittsburgh. In 1793 the *Pittsburgh Gazette* reported that a fine July 4th banquet had been enjoyed by patrons of Mrs. Ward's establishment.

> The company consisted of about 50 ladies and gentlemen, who, at 3 o'clock sat down to an entertainment prepared by Mrs. Ward which would have done honor to the first hotel in the United States—Mirth and good humour crowned the feast, and the evening closed with a splendid Ball. [Harpster, "Eighteenth Century Inns," pp. 14-16]

Taverns were clearly an important part of Pittsburgh's economy and social life. More like English pubs than American bars, the taverns served as meeting places for males who wanted to discuss politics or were eager to meet newcomers to the town. In 1770 Semple's Tavern advertised a billiard table and the Beaumont's Hotel and Ohio Coffeehouse promised that newspapers from Philadelphia and other Eastern cities would be available on the premises for patrons to read. Little or nothing is said about the social pursuits available for women in the taverns, and it is easy to envision a newly arrived wife sewing or reading in an upstairs bedroom while her husband is downstairs having all the fun.

There were a substantial number of Pittsburgh taverns in operation by 1795, inns with names instead of addresses on the unnumbered streets, among them the Black Bear Hotel, the Harp and Crown, the White Horse, the Sign of General Washington, and Andrew Watson's Tavern, where the first Court of Quarter Sessions of Allegheny was held. Several taverns had rooms set aside for dances. The Sign of the Green Tree advertised an Assembly Room, and the Sign of the Waggon and the Sign of the General Butler boasted ball rooms. A Masonic lodge met in a tavern, as did the Mechanical Society and even the Board of Trustees of the Pittsburgh Academy. The proprietor of the Sign of the White Horse advertised his establishment as a place "where all gentlemen travellers and others who please to favour him with their custom, may depend upon meeting with good entertainment and kind treatment, by the public's humble servant, Robert Erwin." James B. Oliver, who took over the Green Tree Inn at Fourth and Wood, renamed his establishment the Good Intent Inn and announced that the office for the stagecoach that traveled the Juniata route "is kept at this Inn."

Relations between the taverns and the clergy were surprisingly cordial. The Reverend Wilson Lee, a Methodist missionary, preached in John Ormsby's tavern in 1785, and John Reed, who owned the Sign of the Waggon as well as a race horse, "lined out the Hymns" and led the singing in the Presbyterian church where he served as precentor (choir director). William Eichbaum, who owned the Sign of the Indian Queen, was a staunch member of the German church. Indeed, generally speaking, tavern keepers were respected citizens of the community.

Nevertheless, because drinking was universal among both men and women, there were bound to be awkward incidents in the taverns and on the streets, and more than one innkeeper found himself before a magistrate on charges of keeping

Hannah Harwood Reed, 1745-1821

The first woman settler to live on Presque Isle, a peninsula on Lake Erie, was Hannah Harwood Reed. With her husband she built a log cabin on the island, which had previously served as a frontier military outpost, and operated a trading business there. As increasing numbers of travelers passed along the Lake Erie shore, Hannah suggested that the cabin be expanded to create an inn. The family agreed, and Hannah became the proprietor of the inn. By 1800 she had been widowed but continued to manage the family business, and also found time to teach the neighborhood children.

As Great Lakes trade and industry developed in the early decades of the 19th century, the population of the area continued to grow. By the time of Hannah Reed's death in 1821, several thousand people had made their homes on old Presque Isle, while the town of Erie had grown up all around the original settlement.

a disorderly house. In 1778 in Washington, prices were fixed by the court of Youghiogheny County so that the cost of a half pint of whiskey was set at two shillings and of a quart of beer at two shillings and six pence. A hot breakfast could not cost more than three shillings, while a cold one went for two and six. Dinner was four shillings, supper three. Lodging with clean sheets cost one shilling six pence, with no mention of the charge for a room with dirty sheets. At five shillings, stabling with hay and fodder for one's horse was substantially more expensive than accommodations for humans.

However, there were class distinctions among the taverns, both in Pittsburgh and on the road. Higher class and more affluent travelers could find adequate, if not luxurious accommodations, but even these did not please all of the guests. Mrs. Houston, an English visitor, was distressed by her unnamed Pittsburgh hotel.

> Such a hotel would not have been out of place in the oldest and dirtiest manufacturing city in the world (Birmingham). It was a great, wide-spreading, open-mouthed, building, lighted from top to bottom with most unpleasantly smelling gas and noisy with bustling waiters and flippant chambermaids. We were shown into large lofty gloomy rooms, with dingy red curtains and carpets, and looking as if the dust and dirt with which they were encrusted had been accumulating on them for a century at least. Take that hotel altogether, it was the oldest looking thing of any kind I had yet seen in America. [Houston, p. 266]

Lower on the social scale were the wagoners who needed large yards to park their wagons. John Masters's Eagle Hotel was a favorite stopover, where "at times fifty or sixty of these immense wagons would be corraled, and the sitting and bar rooms of the tavern filled with wagoners."

We know that Pittsburgh had boarding houses, but very little information exists about them. Hugh Brackenridge remembered the "pleasant and cultured" conversation he encountered at the table in Mrs. Earl's boarding house. In 1806 Thomas Ashe reported that there were boarding houses where one could arrange for lodging, boarding, and washing for $100 a year. He was surprised at how cheap accommodations were in Pittsburgh, commenting that the best taverns charged only half a dollar a day for three meals. During his sojourn in Pittsburgh, Fortescue Cuming tells us he:

> [B]ecame a weekly boarder at M'Cullough's, which though an inn frequented by travelers, I found to be as quiet, as regular, and as orderly, as any private lodging house; the beds equally cleanly, the table more plentiful, and the charge as moderate. As McCullough lays himself out to accommodate travellers, or regular lodgers, he applies himself solely to that, and discourages every thing which might subject his house to the noise, revelry, and confusion of a tavern. His wife an amiable and obliging woman, and three daughters, fine and good girls, just grown up, attend to the business of the house, and the accommodation of their guests, so well, that a man must be fastidious to a fault, who would not be perfectly satisfied with such quarters. [Cuming, pp. 62-63]

In 1816 Edward Carr advertised a boarding house on the bank of the Monongahela near the Steam Mill, with a "situation very pleasant, house airy and commodious." He invited gentlemen who "may think it proper" to call on him and noted that he also sold pickled oysters. Mrs. Boggs informed prospective guests that she had rented "that commodious Brick House corner of Front and Market Streets" and was ready to accommodate "a few genteel boarders." John May took lodgings in the "suburbs," just across the Monongahela from Pittsburgh, and found them to be far more reasonable than those in the city would have been.

> I have a room, with a bed to myself, a large store for the baggage, and for the people to lodge in, together with a kitchen to cook in: all for the very moderate price of 1s. 6d. per day....Had I taken lodging at Pittsburg, which is within call, it would have cost me seven times the money. [May, p. 37]

After 1790 the population grew at a phenomenal rate. In that year, the first U.S. Census reported 376 inhabitants. There were 1,565 in 1800 and 4,768 in 1810, a 204 percent increase in a 10-year period. By 1820 Pittsburgh boasted 7,248 citizens. In 1798 there were 74 wholesale and retail establishments in the town, 36 of them general stores. Others included cabinet makers, a bookstore, bakers, saddlers, tailors, blacksmiths, and four gold and silversmiths. By 1800 the general stores had decreased, replaced by "speciality shops," and there were larger numbers of mechanics and tradesmen, "giving an atmosphere of permanence and solidarity to the young town."

Despite its still muddy streets and unplanned look, Pittsburgh had some noteworthy public buildings by 1800. A market house had been erected in 1787 after much furor within the town over the need, location, and size of the building, and debate about the regulation of prices. Nonetheless, the semicircular structure with a wide projecting roof and a double row of brick pillar supports helped reinforce the notion that Pittsburgh was serious about business. Across the street was a new court house, the only high building in town. The square, two-story brick structure had a wooden spire, fluted wooden columns, and a court room paved with bricks. A few blocks away was the jail, a two-story stone building surrounded by a stone wall as well as a board fence. By 1815 there were three weekly newspapers and two "periodical literary works," three incorporated banks, a theater, a Masonic Hall, three market houses, and an academy in the town.

As early as 1786 the Presbyterians had erected a meeting house of squared timbers, but without a pastor the building fell into disrepair and the congregation apparently lost interest in regular services. By 1805 however, a brick church had been built around the old one, which was then torn down. In 1810 the Methodists built a brick church and another in 1818. Episcopalians erected a church in 1805 and the first Catholic church was built in 1808. By 1819 there were 11 houses of worship, "all destitute of every architectural pretention," but nonetheless, their presence, along with the public buildings and the increasing numbers of stores and shops, established Pittsburgh as a thriving, civilized town. §

Old Pittsburgh Market & Court House, *lithograph by Otto Krebs from a sketch by J. P. Robitzer. HSWP Collection.*

(left) Early Pittsburgh Scene, 1829-36, from platter attributed to Clews of Staffordshire, England. HSWP Collection.

(below) Engraving from Godey's The Lady's Book, *March 1837.*

Household in Town

Temporary lodgings may have been reasonable and comfortable, but for the family arriving from the East, with their funds virtually exhausted, it was best to get settled permanently as soon as possible. April 1 was Removal Day in Pittsburgh when everyone played musical chairs. Writing to a Philadelphia friend in 1804, John Thaw noted, "the population being equal to the dwelling houses, makes it very difficult to get one at this time, and also causes rents to be as high as with you." He finally found one in an "unfinished state" that rented for eight dollars a month, but he wanted to move to another which is "a very convenient two story Building, rents for 150$ (per year) & dont expect to get it for much less."[Thaw Papers, ALS, 1804] In 1818 rentals were still high and it was "difficult to procure a common room in an upper story under $100 per annum….a genteel private family can scarcely attain a good dwelling for under $300-400," while stores rented for between $300 and $500 for the year. One warehouse rented for $1,200.

Land speculation began early in Pittsburgh and vicinity. Before the Revolution the title of all newly discovered land had belonged to the king, who could allot it to one or more proprietors. William Penn was the beneficiary of Pennsylvania lands, but his "holy experiment" faltered with succeeding generations of land developers. Soon settlers were spreading out across the state, occupying land both legally and illegally. Possession or purchase of land required a patchwork of complicated negotiations with Native Americans, the authorities, and squatters who had set up housekeeping and started to farm without legal title.

When land was offered for sale in Pittsburgh in 1785, many residents quickly purchased the plots they were already occupying without benefit of title. Homes, commercial properties and land were advertised regularly in the *Pittsburgh Gazette*.

> *"Mrs. Preston dyed my leghorn….Cloches are quite the fashion while dresses are much trimmed with ruffles, puffs are said to be getting fashionable."*
>
> —Madelaine LeMoyne

> Any person wishing to purchase one or more excellent lots in Pittsburgh, will please to inquire of the subscriber, who will show the lots, and inform them of the price. [*Pittsburgh Gazette,* August 5, 1787]

In 1797 a 300-acre plantation on Sewickly Creek was offered, complete with grist and sawmills, plus a two-story house with a kitchen, barn, and still house, no price mentioned. In Elizabethtown, 60 x 120-foot plots were offered on condition that a one-and-a-half-story log, frame, or brick house measuring 18 x 22 feet be constructed within 18 months of purchase. The cost was £3 per lot, except for the corners, which went for £3.10. No buyer could purchase more than two lots "to prevent a monopoly," and the shrewd developer offered the first 20 purchasers an "out lot," absolutely free. Payment terms were easy; in 1825 the Holland Land Company advertised 150,000 acres in lots to suit the purchaser at $2 an acre, $10 down, and the balance in eight annual payments, with interest on and after the third year.

Land assessments were designated in English pounds and pence until 1796, and in that year Fayette County switched to dollar valuations. The conversion rate was approximately $2.50 to £1. In 1785 choice commercial lots with 58 to 160 feet of frontage on Market Street sold for £10 each, about $25. By 1790 similar parcels sold for $125, and in 1791 for about $300. By 1800 desirable commercial lots had been subdivided and prices had increased accordingly. A quarter interest in a lot of this size sold for $875 in 1804, three years later a sixth interest would bring $666. Many houses were built on leased land, which required ground rents to be paid to the owners and discouraged tenants from making improvements on property that was not their own.[Dahlinger, pp. 98-100]

Not unlike our own times, land was available, but the choicest areas required a diligent search. In 1805 a Swiss farmer turned down properties in Greensburg because they were "unsuitable" and he was not attracted to "this wild unfriendly region." He was finally directed to a property less than an hour from Pittsburgh which could have qualified for a "needs work" real estate ad, but he acquired it for $8 an acre. Despite the necessary repairs to both dwellings and soil, he still believed that "one of its acres is dearer to me than ten in Switzerland, because it is more earthy, and of far better quality, and the good climate hereabouts goes a long way to favor fruit trees."

Sophisticated travelers, primarily the British, found early Pittsburgh a motley combination of ugly log houses, dirty streets and unleashed livestock, but almost everyone noted that the city was growing. As early as 1786, Hugh Brackenridge boasted that the town had 100 houses and 1,500 inhabitants, which allotted 15 people to each house, a figure

FOR SALE,
A Tract of Valuable Land,

SITUATE in Unity township, within one and a half miles of the Loyalhanna, formerly the property of William Maxwell, deceased, containing upwasds of 400 *Acres of good LAND*, o which is a substantial

Log Dwelling House,

a Double Barn and other out buildings, a good Tan Yard and an excellent Orchard. There are upwards of one hundred acres cleared, a large portion of which is first rate meadow. The Farm is well calculated for raising stock, and has many other advantages which render it very desirable. Persons wishing to view the property and know the terms will please apply to
BENJAMIN ALSWORTH,
Near Hannahstown.

January 23 1819.

historian Neville Craig found "most extravagant." Later figures gave the town 200 houses in 1795; 300 in 1804; 767 in 1810; and 1,300 by 1815.

Travelers in Western Pennsylvania described Pittsburgh houses as not beautiful, but low and plain, scattered every which way across the town. Helping make the town liveable were the Lombardy poplars and weeping willows that lined the streets. In the earliest years the houses were the same simple log structures built by the wilderness settlers, rough-hewn rather than sawed. In 1795 it was reported that "The houses are generally well built for a new-settled place; though they have lately taken to building with brick, of which there are great quantities made near the town." Some of the homes utilized bricks made available by the dismantling of Fort Pitt and sold to the public. They could be readily identified by their soft (some said dirty) gray-whitish color.

Early brick houses usually had a central hall with rooms on both sides, heated by fireplaces with chimneys at each end. The front windows were frequently topped by plain lintels of sandstone, or sometimes with brick arches. Until 1797 window glass had to be imported from the East, and the cost of shipping and the frequency of breakage put the price out of the reach of most homeowners. Those who could afford it had to put up with tiny panes, usually 6 x 8 inches. Then General James O'Hara and his partners began manufacturing glass bottles and window glass, and by 1800 glass panes measuring 18 x 24 inches were available to Pittsburgh residents. But as late as 1829, at least one writer thought the town was "meanly built and gave no evidence of either wealth or refinement....There were no public buildings with any pretense to architecture, and every building in the city seemed to have been built to suit the then-present wants at the cheapest cost possible."

John Thaw might have taken issue with this assertion, since he built a Pittsburgh townhouse in 1808 with "party walls," eight three-story brick buildings, each divided from the other by separate fire walls. A porch was attached at the front, a kitchen, wash-house, and privy at the rear. The staircase in each house ran from the hall up three stories to the garret, "with hand rail and turned bannisters of Cherry," oakwood work on the first and second floors and an elegant "piazza." The owner planned to insure the house for $5,000 and it may well have been one of the residences about which another traveler said in 1807 that "it would be called elegant even in the city of New York."[Buck, p. 324]

When James O'Hara arrived in Pittsburgh with his bride Mary, daughter of a wealthy Philadelphian, she found that the house he had built for her was a simple one of logs, but she had brought as many luxuries as possible over the mountains. Apparently, "the carpets astonished the western country people. They expressed their astonishment that Mrs. O'Hara should spread coverlets on the floor, and hesitated to walk on them."[Darlington, p. 208]

The dictionary defines a town as larger than a village but smaller than a city, a flexible but somewhat ambiguous designation. To a woman, however, a town

BUSINESS DIRECTORY. 61

Smith Mrs. M., Dress maker and dry goods store, Fifth nr Market.
    Michael, Eagle Tavern, 113 Liberty st.
    Royer & Co., Iron and nail manufactury, c of Penn and Cecil's alley.
    Thomas, grocer and dry goods store, At.
    W. T., White smith, 67 Water st.
    Mrs., Midwife, 67 Water.
    Thomas, tailor, d h At.
Smither Nicholas, boot and shoe maker, N. L.
Smilie & Erseman, stone cutters, near Diamond, At.
Smyser H., Druggist, c. of Fifth and Market.
Snowden Samuel, d h c of Liberty and Irwin alley.
    Joseph, Druggist, c of Liberty and Irwin alley, b h c of 2d and Wood.
    John M. Esq., county Treasurer, office Ogden and Snowden's drug store, Liberty st. d h At.
Snyder Joseph, grocer, c of Factory and Liberty, N. L.
    John, Cashier Bank Pittsburgh, d h c of Pitt & Penn.
Soals Henry, merchant, M'Keesport.
Spang H. S. & Son, Iron and Nail manufacturers, warehouse, 55 Front.
Spaulding and Woodward, grocers, N. L.
Speer Dr. J. R., c of Penn and Irwin alley.
    & Ingrim, boat and house painter, 2d b Ferry and Short sts.
    James, Farmer's Hotel, Irwin st. Allegheny river.
    James A., House and boat painter, Front b Liberty and Redoubt alley.
Spence Mrs. E., dry goods store 102 Liberty.
Spencer Samuel, wholesale dry goods merchant, 78 Wood.
Splene George, Jackson Coffee House, Fifth b Wood and Market.
Spratt Joseph, grocery and dry goods store, Federal, at.
Sprattly James, boot and shoe maker, Fourth st.
Stackhouse and Tomlinson, Steam engine manufacturers and Founders, c Penn and Bell's alley.
    & Thompson,   do   c of Front and Short.
Stafford H., grocer and dealer, 18 Liberty.
Stark Ebenezer, dry goods and grocery, c of Smithfield and Front.
Stephens Wood, county surveyor, Ewings mill, Robinson tp

(left) Page from Harris' Pittsburgh Business Directory, 1837, *published by Isaac Harris. Few women's names are listed.*

(facing page) Pittsburgh's first post office, also the premises of the Pittsburgh Gazette.

was a place where goods could be easily purchased—all the items one had to make for oneself or buy from an itinerent peddler when living in the wilderness. When a family moved to town, life was somewhat easier for the women. Many of the tasks necessary to maintain a wilderness home could be given over to others, and even the less affluent found their household duties less arduous. In the town, one could avail oneself of the services of washerwomen, candlemakers, dressmakers, and shoemakers. Neighbors were just down the street, doctors were closer and more available, stores were becoming more numerous, as well as increasing the variety of goods they offered. Your neighbor, according to Riddle's *Pittsburgh Directory of 1815,* could have been one of 12 lawyers, 12 schoolteachers, 9 clergymen, 6 engineers, and 16 "gentlemen." The list of artisans and mechanics was a long one, including watchmakers, blacksmiths, saddlers, barbers, boat and barge builders, tinsmiths, and spinning wheel makers—men without whom Pittsburgh could not function. [Douds, p. 29; see also Lambing, p. 68] Most of these establishments were within the town, and many merchants and artisans lived over, or beside, their shops. Newcomers to Pittsburgh who possessed a skill could generally find work or open their own business.

Although the same 1815 *Directory* allegedly listed "all" residents of Pittsburgh, women were conspicuous by their absence. If a woman was married, it was sufficient to list only her husband, thereby denying her the privilege of being counted as an individual. Unattached females were designated as "Adams, Catherine, widow, laundress" or "Barn, Priscilla, widow, boarding house" or "Baird, Rosanna, widow, grocer." Men were listed as "Aitkin, Robert, laborer," or "Adam, James, gentleman," with no reference to spouses, if any. There was evidence of upward mobility, however; in 1815 Ebenezer Denny was listed as a merchant, but in 1819 he was designated as a "gentleman." [Riddle, p. 362]

Most towns were hardly an architect's dream, since houses were built with no thought to city planning. Their higgledy-piggledy sprawl and the increasing amount of coal smoke and dust were offensive to some, but the opportunities to make money made up for the lack of aesthetic qualities. Wrote the irascible Samuel Jones in 1816:

> Some who reside here, in apparent contentment, merely endure their oyster-like existence, in daily expectation of amassing fortune sufficient to enable them to retire to a more pleasant city, where they may spend in refined enjoyments, the wealth which they may have acquired, with much turmoil, amid the clang of iron bars, and the suffocating fumes which they were doomed to inhale. [Jones, p. 41]

Whether brick or frame, Pittsburgh houses were low and plain, some facing one another, others built sideways, still others facing the street. Many town houses had private fenced gardens, but since residences and businesses were mixed indiscriminately, some of the largest homes were located next to stores and warehouses.

After the War of 1812 the well-to-do began to move away from the center of town, building massive brick mansions on Penn Avenue. Life there was quieter, a pleasant oasis away from the noise and clamor of manufacturing and business. Inevitably, the rich moved further and further out of town, to the wooded acres of Point Breeze, Oakland, and Squirrel Hill.

If one's husband had a job, it was clearly possible to live very well indeed in the town. Zadok Cramer in his 1810 *Almanac* noted that Pittsburgh workmen went home loaded "with turkies, fowls, fat beef, fresh butter, &c. &c." It was no longer necessary to bake bread at home, since by 1807 there were six professional bakers, and even earlier, one who also outfited expeditions down the Ohio River, advertising in the December 2, 1786, *Pittsburgh Gazette*, "Biscuit ready baked and packed in barrels and keg, or loose for smaller demands."

Almost from its first issue in 1786, the *Gazette* advertised an abundance of products for the home. The housewife's kitchen could contain more and better utensils than she had ever dreamed possible. (At John Hamshaw's, kettles, pots, griddles, copperware were "as low for cash as it can be got in Philadelphia or

Lancaster.") Her table could be set with pewter and earthenware dishes. ("Adam French, Earthernware, reasonable terms for cash or fur. No credit.") Glassware became available locally when the first glass works west of the Alleghenies was established in 1797, and luxury tableware was sold at Craig and Bayard ("chream [*sic*] jugs, soup plates, mustard potts, pepper boxes and butter boats.") Ormsby's carried bone knives and forks as well as tablespoons of tin and pewter.

Table settings were more elaborate than the wilderness folk were accustomed to, and hostesses were not reluctant to use the best they had to impress visitors. Proudly displayed on the dining table or sideboard were treasured pieces brought from the East or ordered from local craftsmen.

Some women, reluctant to change, continued to use an open fire but others were happy to use stoves and ovens which allowed them to cook more comfortably and with less danger of serving themselves up as a burnt offering to the family. One company advertised a variety of stoves designed to meet the needs of everyone.

A native of a small Pennsylvania village, writer Agnes Sligh Turnbull spent her youth in what she called "the slow days of those calm and sunny years." In *The King's Orchard*, published in 1963 by Houghton Mifflin Co., Boston, she offers a fictional account of early Pittsburgh through the eyes of James O'Hara—Indian agent, Revolutionary officer, and highly successful businessman. Turnbull's descriptions of the expanding town and her interpretation of events are based on extensive research.

The dinner party described here, given by James and Mary O'Hara in honor of the Duke of Orleans in the late 1780s, skillfully evokes the way of life among the rising stars of an industrial society.

There were still chrysanthemums in the garden and Mary decided upon a large bouquet on the Irish table and an epergne for the dining room as soon as the date was fixed. Already on the buffet the decanters were filled with the best Monogahela rye and the finest Philadelphia sherry, Madeira and port....Mary arranged the flowers and set the great table. The food was planned, with O'Hara insisting upon something distinctively American....[T]hey settled on the main viands as roast turkey with baked apples stuffed with fresh sausage [and] Prudence's superlative cornbread and pumpkin pie for dessert....The doilies of Madeira lace, the tall silver candelabra, and the crystal glasses and epergne added elegance to elegance.

C. Postley's Patent Cooking Stoves or Portable Kitchens, the different sizes are calculated to do the cooking for small and large families, public houses, and Steam Boats, and are so extremely simple in their construction, as to be managed with ease by a child twelve or fourteen years of age. [Riddle, np.]

Although safer and more convenient than the open hearth, wood and coal-burning stoves nevertheless had their eccentricities to be mastered. It was still necessary to figure out how to obtain and maintain slow, medium, and hot temperatures for a variety of dishes. Caution had to be taken not to refuel the stove in the middle of baking cake or bread, since refueling drastically lowered the temperature and invited failure. As with the fireplace, different woods burned at different intensities, and quick-cooking dishes needed a different fuel from that required for a long-cooking stew or soup. A stove provided welcome heat in the winter and offered a useful spot to dry clothes, but there was little relief from the intense heat in the summer. Most stoves had a water reservoir which kept the cook supplied with hot water, and the somewhat complicated arrangements of dampers and drafts made possible a wide selection of temperatures—*after* one mastered it. Most cooks would have felt relieved to discover that the familiar Dutch oven was easily adaptable for use on the top of the wood stove.

By 1777 it was possible to give up spinning altogether if you lived in Pittsburgh and hired a spinning woman for 6 shillings a week. Shawls and aprons were available ready-made, and in 1786 fine boots and ladies' slippers of Morocco leather could be purchased at Thomas White, shoemaker, for 12 shillings and six pence. By 1807 Pittsburgh had weavers, dyers, cabinet makers, hatters, bakers, glassworks, breweries, book binders, mattress makers, bricklayers, plasterers, ship build-ers, spinning wheel makers, blacksmiths, carpenters, skin dressers, bookstores, saw mills, grist mills, watchmakers, straw bonnet makers, house painters, and one looking-glass maker. In 1818 in Greensburg, it cost "$2 per wife" to have a dress made and one could have a pair of pants made for 75 cents.

CHILDS & NESMITH,
WHOLESALE DEALERS IN
BOOTS & SHOES
PALM LEAF HATS,
AND
Leghorn, Straw and Fancy Bonnets,
No. 109 Wood Street,
BETWEEN FIFTH STREET AND DIAMOND ALLEY,
Pittsburgh.

Harris' Pittsburgh Business Directory, 1837.

The clothes worn in town were more stylish than those in the country. As textiles became more readily available and substantially cheaper, many city women bought yard goods and found a dressmaker to make up the latest fashions. Zadok Cramer's bookstore probably carried copies of Godey's *The Lady's Book* or other fashion magazines, and there were other ways to keep abreast of the latest fashions. Women travelers arriving by coach and later by trains from the East were closely scrutinized to note style changes in bonnets and coats.

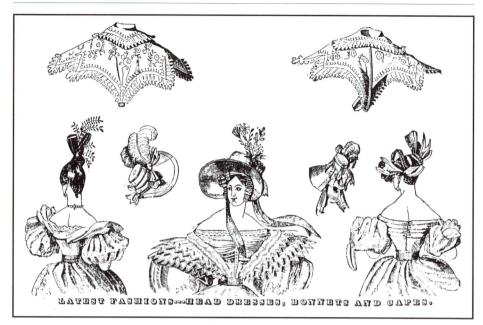

Latest Fashions...Head Dresses, Bonnets and Capes, *from Godey's* The Lady's Book, *1833.*

Family and friends back home sent pictures and brought the latest styles when they came to visit. "Sarah King brought all the Paris fashions from New York. Other ladies receive the fashions from Philadelphia every week," Nancy Swearingen reported to her Virginia family in the late 1820s. And later, "A great many dresses have been sent to the ladies here from Philadelphia ready made." [Dandridge Papers, ALS, February 19, 1827]

The Republican sentiments of the new country encouraged simpler fashions, and tight corsets gave way to loose chemise dresses of sheer and diaphanous materials, girdled just under the bosom in the Empire style, and dropping straight to the ground. Huge scoop bonnets, sometimes called "coal-scuttles," gloves reaching to the upper arm, and a cashmere shawl completed the outfit. Local merchants stocked a wide variety of materials, as well as readymade articles such as silk and cotton shawls, kid and Morocco leather shoes and slippers, wreaths and plumes, and a variety of gloves. By 1820 the fashion shifted back to bell skirts, filled out by stiff crinolines, large sleeves, and the whole decked with ribbons and laces.

In 1818 the *Pittsburgh Gazette* commented on the new cossack cut trousers for women.

> The wider they are the more fashionable the wearer. This appears to have put the other sex out of countenance for so very nearly have these cossack trowsers [*sic*] assimilated the sexes in their exterior appearance that the ladies have found it necessary to shorten their petticoats to prevent them from being mistaken for the beaux. [*Pittsburgh Gazette,* May 22, 1818]

Alice Morse Earle deplored the American custom of setting forth into the cold night so scantily clad and after looking at fashion magazines in the early 19th century, she declared "the chief emotion is that any of our grandmothers survived those years, so lightly were they dressed." The materials were usually sheer and light weight, even in January, and in general, "the neck and portions of the arms were left bare, even for outdoor wear." Mrs. Trollope was appalled at the American sense of fashion, or the lack of it, except in Philadelphia, where she felt there was a modicum of good taste. She too was astonished at the lack of proper clothing for the winter.

> I have often shivered at seeing a young beauty picking her way through the snow with a pale rose-coloured bonnet, set on the very top of her head: I knew one young lady whose pretty little ear was actually frostbitten from being thus exposed. They never wear muffs or boots, and appear extremely shocked at the sight of comfortable walking shoes and cotton stockings, even when they have to step to their sleighs over ice and snow. [Trollope, p. 238]

By 1804 Pittsburgh-made furniture of cherry and walnut was available at Philadelphia prices ("James Liggett cabinet maker—mahogany chairs and sofas"). Western Pennsylvania furniture styles followed those current in the East, notably in Philadelphia. If a family had sufficient wealth, fine pieces could be hauled over the Alleghenies, the freight sometimes costing as much as the furniture. Local cabinet makers, irritated at the thought of imported items, found a champion in Samuel Jones. Reporting that Pittsburgh boasted 6 chair makers employing 30 people with "products of the most elegant kind," and 14 cabinet makers with 65 employees, he admonished his readers that

(right) Slant-front Desk, 1808. This desk by John Huey, Washington County, is one of the best documented pieces of early Southwestern Pennsylvania furniture. (detail above) Signature in ink on a drawer. HSWP Collection.

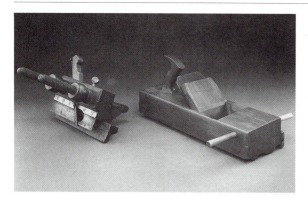

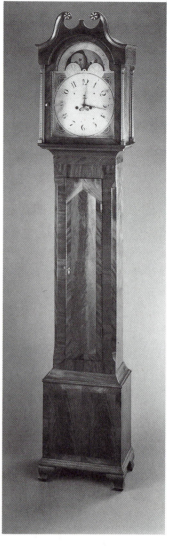

(above left) Plow plane used to cut grooves for joints, signed by its maker, carpenter J. M'Cully; (above right) Plane used to shape moldings, made by James Coates, who worked in Washington, Pennsylvania, between 1845 and 1860.
(right) Tall Case Clock, c. 1810. Its maker, Samuel Davis, was reported to have made at least 97 clocks at his business premises on Market Street. HSWP Collection.

"Sending to the east for cabinet furniture...is absurd as well as ungenerous towards our own workmen. The work that has been turned out of our own shops is equal to any made in Philadelphia or elsewhere."

Pittsburgh-made furniture was somewhat behind the times in fashion, but modern collectors believe that it had a structural integrity second to none in the United States. Solid, heavy, tightly joined, these pieces outlasted many of their Eastern counterparts, and the more imaginative cabinet makers improvised on the basic Chippendale, Hepplewhite, and Sheraton designs.

Families in town and on nearby farms had more servants than those living in the wilderness. Americans were reluctant to enter domestic service, however, since there were many better opportunities. Both men and women thought of domestic service as a temporary expedient before marriage. Why work in someone else's kitchen when one could have a kitchen of one's own?

Nancy Swearingen, who lived with her army captain husband at Fort Pitt, enlisted men for some tasks, but needed additional help with her household and children and turned to the army network to find it. "At last I have a good girl. [She] was with Mrs. Reed at Fort Mifflin. Her father belonged to James's old company that he left at Sackett's Harbor," she wrote to her family. Apparently it didn't work out, however, for a few months later she reported, "Have an excellent girl. Have nothing to do but sit in the parlor like a lady sewing or knitting." Three months later she complained, "I have to give a girl $1.25 a week, but what can I do? The children race all through the house, make so much dirt. I get out of all patience. I must endeavor to be resigned to my fate." A year later she reported that she had taken in two little orphan girls but did not detail whether they were hired, adopted or indentured—only that they were "very troublesome. Like all Methodists they think they must do nothing else but go to night meetings, class meetings, camp meetings, are constantly talking of such things. Such things give them idle habits."[Dandridge Papers, ALS, assorted letters, 1813-15]

Another means of getting help was through indenture contracts with immigrants. When the system worked well, the practice of indenture was useful to both parties. A young Irish girl, for example, would sign on as a ship's passenger bound for Baltimore, agreeing to be sold at the port to anyone willing to pay her passage. An agent met the boat and placed the girl with a family willing to pay his price, which included the passage and a profit for himself. In return, the girl would be bound to serve the family for a specified period, usually seven years, after which she would have her freedom, plus a small sum of money or some clothing. During those seven years she had the opportunity to learn how to keep house and cook, care for children, perhaps marry. She could advance her station by marrying into her master's family, a not unusual occurrence. One Quaker observer wrote, "I noticed many families, particularly in Pennsylvania, of great respectability both in our Society and amongst others, who had themselves come over to this country as redemptioners, or were the children of such."

Some men moved up easily in society by successfully completing their term of servitude. In addition, they had the opportunity to learn about their new country without taking the risk of buying land. They acquired new skills and utilized old ones, since many were experienced artisans. A Maryland preacher reported that a ship never arrived without a number of school teachers, tailors, and weavers aboard, although the school masters didn't bring as ready a sale or price as the others.

On the other hand, the indentured servants were legally only one step up from slavery. They were not free in a free country. Unscrupulous ships' captains and dishonest agents often conspired to gouge both passengers and purchasers, and even those who had prepaid their passage sometimes had such large charges added on that they were forced into servitude. Liwwät Böke wrote scornfully of her fellow countrymen's "unforgiveable and uncharitable trade...in humans.... No one is let off the ship except those had paid their travel costs or had good security.... No buyers bought the sick, the blind, or the elderly. Healthy persons were bought at once. The suffering and crippled often lay on the ship two or three weeks until they died." The English, Dutch, and Germans came to the ships to look over the stock of potential servants and "dispute[d] the whole time with those who are willing to serve for their travel costs....Families are broken up, children lost."

In 1774 the *Pennsylvania Messenger* advertised:

> GERMANS—we are now offering fifty Germans just arrived....to be seen at the Golden Swan, kept by the widow Kreider. The lot includes school masters, artisans, peasants, boys and girls of various ages, all to serve for payment of passage. [Cheesman, p. 263]

Often indentures were treated cruelly by their masters, but sometimes the master got a bad deal. Advertisements for runaways used phrases like he "cannot look you in the face,"..."blind in one eye." Nevertheless, each runaway represented a substantial investment, and the owner wanted the person back.

> Fifteen Dollars Reward.
> Ran away on the sixth instant from the subscriber an Irish servant, named Charles Jordan, 20 years of age, five feet six or eight inches high, short black hair, round-face, knock-kneed, large flat feet, has an old sore on the sole of his foot; took with him a straw hat, an old blue coat, linen hunting shirt, three coarse shirts, pair coarse trousers, a pair of coarse shoes; whoever secures said servant so that the owner near the forks of Cheat may get him, shall be paid the above reward and reasonable expenses, by
> John Wilson Fayette County, August 12 (1786)
> N.B. If taken out of the state Thirty Dollars reward.

John O'Hara, one of Pittsburgh's leading citizens, offered $100 for the return of John Buchanan, an indentured Irish servant who was "a notorious liar," who took two horses and a young woman he passed off as his wife. "As he had access to a large store in Pittsburgh [presumably O'Hara's thriving general store], it appears that he has carried off a considerable sum of money and other valuable property."

Like any property, indentures could be sold and the newspapers ran many notices offering good servants for sale.

Sterling Silver Tray, 1839. Tri-footed tray made by Grays, Dublin. This tray was given to Michael Allen, a commission and forwarding merchant in Pittsburgh, to commemorate his paying off his creditors in Ireland, although he had been forgiven the debt. An Irish immigrant, Allen was successful in many enterprises. HSWP Collection.

TO BE SOLD

For Ready Money Only

A German woman servant, she has near 3 years to serve, and is well qualified for all household work; would recommend her to her own country people, particularly since her present master has found great inconvenience from his not being acquainted with the manners, customs and language. For further particulars inquire at Mr. Ormsby's in Pittsburgh. [*Pittsburgh Gazette,* August 26, 1786]

It was generally agreed that conditions for most white indentures prior to 1818 were intolerable. In that year, a federal law was passed requiring passengers to be set ashore with their rightful goods. There would be no separation of husband and wife, nor could a redemptioner be sent out of state without his or her consent. Captains were required to provide proper food and drink on shipboard, and the sick had to be cared for.

Pennsylvania was never one of the larger slave-holding states. The census of 1790 reported that 97.6 percent of the population was white, while only 0.9 percent were slaves and 1.5 percent were free African Americans. In Allegheny County, 66 families held slaves in 1790, most having from 1 to 4. Only one

---

A LIST OF NEGRO AND MULATTO SLAVES

Registered in Westmoreland county pursuant to an act of Assembly of the State of Pennsylvania, entitled "An act for the gradual abolition of slavery," passed the 1st day of March, A.D. 1780, and to an Act of Assembly entitled "An act to redress certain grievances within the counties of Westmoreland and Washington," passed the 13th day of April A.D. 1782. The date of entry is first given, then the names of owners, followed by the sex, age and name of the slave.

Sept. 25, 1780.

James Gray. Female, 25, Beck.

Oct. 12, 1780.

Edward Cook. Male, 45, Jame; female, 35, Sail; male, 24, Davy; male, 22, Joshua; female, 17, Esther; female, 16, Nelly; female, 1, Sue. Providence Mountz. Male, 28, Sam; female, 22, Let; female, 2, Phillis.

Van Swearingen. Male, 25, Will; male, 30, Tony; male, 23, Winn; female, 13, Wester (or Hester); female, 9, Feby; male, 4, Harkless; male, 16, Jack; male, 18, Tom; male, 1, Will Jr. Joseph Jones. Female, 17, Cloe; female, 15, Bridget; male, 1, Dick.

Deverux Smith, Pittsburgh. Female, 43, Suck; female (mulatto), 7, Lucy.

Oct. 16, 1780.

Thomas Galbraith, Fairfield township. Male, 20, Ben; male, 13, George.

Oct. 18, 1780.

Joseph Dorsey. Male, 30, Charles; male, 32, Phil; male, 19, Aaron; male, 19, Tom; male, 25, Casse; female, 28, Jane; male, 12, Pompey; female, 6, Rachel; female, 4, Phillis; male, 2, George; male, 11/2, Frederick; male, 1/2, James; male, 5 months, Harmer.

John Hamal. Male, 40, Bigion; female, 30, Phillis; female, 8, Armice; female, 6, Dorrah; female, 4, Chisiah, female, 2, Hanna.

family posessed more than 10 enslaved people. Washington and Fayette counties, however, with their large farms and plantations had 123 and 100 families, respectively, retaining slaves. Figures for Bedford and Westmoreland counties were low, accounting for 53 and 24 slave-holding families.

The first petition against slavery in the United States was filed in 1688 in Germantown, Pennsylvania, by the Society of Friends. Not until 1780, however, did the state legislature pass a gradual emancipation law, mandating that all children born of slave mothers would be free at age 28. By 1788 any slaves brought into the state were immediately considered free.

Other than references to a school for young African-American children, there is little information about this population in early Pittsburgh. Charles Richards, known as "Black Charley," owned a tavern on the corner of Second and Ferry streets. McKnight reported that in Clearfield County, Fudge Van Camp, a very large African American "whose wool was a white as the wool of a sheep and whose face was as black as charcoal," worked in the local sawmill and was married to a white woman. He was described as fine-featured and thin-lipped. Born enslaved, he had purchased his freedom after serving as a teamster during the Revolution. It was reported that he had come to Port Barnett from Easton on foot in the winter of 1801, the last 33 miles in two feet of snow and without food. He liked the town and went back for his wife and four children. The only person of color in the area until 1810, he was a "fiddler and a great fighter and was the orchestra for all the early families." His son Richard also married a white woman, but left the county.

Though small in number in Western Pennsylvania, slaves were viewed as valuable property and were bought and sold like any other commodity.

> To Be Sold To any person residing in the County
> A NEGRO WENCH
> She is an excellent cook and can do any kind of work in or out doors. She has been registered in Westmoreland County. Produce will be taken, or cattle of any kind. Enquire of Col. John Gibson, Ft. Pitt. [*Pittsburgh Gazette,* June 16, 1787]

Rewards were offered for runaways, both in and out of state. A resident of Maryland advertised for "A negro man, WILL and a negro wench named SUE."

While the anti-slavery movement began to gather force in cities like Boston and Philadelphia in the early 19th century, it found little support in Pittsburgh, except among the Quakers. In this bustling town where business had begun to flourish, free men and women saw an unlimited horizon of opportunity. With energy, determination, and a little luck, there were fortunes to be made. Even though the unpaved streets were muddy and wet, the smoke from the booming manufactories unpleasant, the creature comforts of life which had been missing in the wilderness were abundant in Pittsburgh. §

From the Collections

The artifacts shown here are largely the finer things with which some early Western Pennsylvanians lived. It is not surprising that the beautiful, expensive, or rare things are the ones that most often survived. Fine things were so treasured by early inhabitants with means that they carted them from the East, bought them from merchants who imported them from all over the world, and paid local craftsmen to make them to order.

The early collections of the Historical Society of Western Pennsylvania do not reflect the rough and homemade possessions of the area's rural inhabitants, but they do include distinctive furniture, metalwork, glass, ceramics, and textiles that demonstrate the area's craftsmanship, the use of local materials, and creative adaptations of prevailing styles. The glass collection, ranging over two centuries, is one of America's finest.

Artifacts of the late 19th and early 20th centuries have stronger representation than earlier ones in the collections. Recent ethnic collecting initiatives have added materials that have normally not been collected by museums. A mosaic of ethnic, racial, economic, and religious groups live in Western Pennsylvania. The collections of the Historical Society now reflect the heritage of this diverse community.

Pittsburgh from the Salt Works on Saw Mill Run, *oil painting by William Thompson Russell Smith, 1843, produced for a geological survey of Pennsylvania.*

(left) **Dr. William Werneburg and children**, oil painting, c. 1850. A German immigrant, Werneburg practiced as an obstetrician in Pittsburgh. His daughters Ellenora and Mary were born in the city.

(below) **Earthenware Pitcher**, 1828. The decorations depict William Price's Round House, the Fort Pitt Glass Works he helped establish, and a dedication by his colleagues.

Cradle-settee, c. 1830. The removable front railing on this bench allowed a mother to rock her baby, leaving her hands free to perform other chores while sitting down.

Woven Wool Coverlet, *signed and dated, "John Mellinger, 1842." Mellinger was one of many professional weavers with Jacquard looms who worked mainly in Pennsylvania, Ohio, and Indiana from 1810 to 1840.*

Sampler/Mourning Art, *by C. Stotler, 1846. While mourning art in England usually honored patriots and historical figures, in America it also memorialized family and friends. Jacob Stotler, memorialized by this piece, probably died in 1840, but this kind of time-lapse before completion of a commemorative sampler was not uncommon.*

Silk Waistcoat with Silver Embroidery, *c. 1790, worn by Colonel George Morgan, father-in-law of Margaret Bunyan Morgan. As Indian Agent at Fort Pitt, he worked closely with regional Native Americans in the interests of peace but aroused the opposition of the settlers by his proposal that they exchange western lands for peace.*

Men's Shoes, *18th century. Shoes of this type were worn by immigrants from the northern part of the British Isles.*

Linen Shirt, *c. 1800, handwoven and hand-stitched. The fine decorative edging on the sleeve and at the bottom of the front opening indicates a highly skilled stitcher. The shirt was long, since often men wore only a shirt between their skin and their britches.*

Wedding Dress, c. 1855. This silk dress was worn by Annie Butterfield Link, an immigrant from Ireland in the 1840s. Her family owned a dairy farm on land that is now part of Sewickley near Pittsburgh. Not until the early 20th century did white become the favored color for wedding dresses. For many years after the ceremony, wedding dresses were worn for special occasions.

Silver Teapot, *by Andrew Osthoff, c. 1815. With its stylish lion finial and animal-form spout, this teapot stamped "Pittsburg," indicates that at this point the city already had both skilled artisans and well-to-do customers for their wares.*

Covered Dish, Platters, and Basket with Stand, *Chinese Export Porcelain, late 18th century. This handpainted ware is part of a set, bearing the monogram "M," made for Mary Carson O'Hara, wife of General James O'Hara.*

Flasks and Mineral Water Bottle, 1830-70. (left and right) Makers unknown, produced in Pittsburgh; (middle) **Flask** made by Bakewell Page and Bakewell, Pittsburgh. Much of the glass production of the Ohio River Valley was devoted to providing flasks, bottles, and other portable drinking vessels.

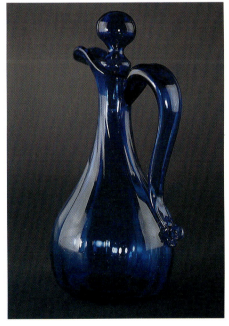

(left) **Molasses Can/Syrup Jug**, c. 1850. Molasses and syrup were inexpensive substitutes for sugar. This pitcher would have had its place on the table for use by the family. (right) **Cobalt Glass Cruet with Stopper**, c. 1830, probably made in Pittsburgh.

Handwritten Recipe and Remedy Books, *late 18th and early 19th centuries.*
(left) ***Margaret Bunyan Morgan's "Recipe Book,"*** *first entry 1790; (top)* ***"Receipts,***
Cures," *c. 1845; (right) Recipes and remedies in German and English, the cover*
shows the name "Müller," and the date 1826.

Copper Kettle, *mid- and late 19th century.*
This kettle was used by the Shaw family of
Glenshaw, Pennsylvania. Mrs. H.J. Heinz is
said to have cooked batches of relish in it.

Brass Andirons, *c. 1812. This pair of*
andirons was made in Joseph McClurg's
foundry, one of the earliest in Pittsburgh,
established in 1803.

Goods of All Sorts

If you dropped your last needle on the cabin floor and watched it disappear through the cracks right in the middle of a huge batch of mending, you had very few alternatives. You could dispatch a child to the nearest neighbor—possibly two or three miles away—to ask if she had a spare one for you to borrow. Or you could ask your husband to buy one on his next trip to the trading post, also several miles away, and if you were lucky, there would be some in stock. Or you could hope that a peddler would come trudging down the path out of the woods and save the day.

Trading posts were established in America in early colonial times to facilitate the exchange of goods and currency between the Native Americans and settlers. After the Revolutionary War, frontier posts were regulated by the government to prevent illegal trading, particularly in the sale of alcohol to Native Americans. The small stocks of household necessities found at these posts represented a lifeline to civilization to many frontier housewives. As traditional stores became more common in the East, the trading posts moved westward with the settlers and were still thriving in the 1840s throughout the Southwest and along the Pacific coast.

"Luxuries are cheaper now than necessaries were a few years since. …Yet it is a lamentable fact that it costs more to live now than it did formerly."

—Lydia Maria Child

The designation "Yankee" peddler that has come down to us over the years was absolutely accurate. In the early years of settlement, entrepreneurial merchants from the East who had a touch of wanderlust packed up some essential household items and took off to sell their wares. They started in New England and spread out across the country, to the South, the Midwest, and the West. Some traveled on foot, carrying a small tin trunk or backpack; later when the roads improved, they outfitted small wagons with everything from books to patent medicine to tinware.

In addition to goods, peddlers brought news, stories, jokes, and cheerful conversation to settlers in remote places. They were the quintessential salesmen—genial, gregarious, and sometimes charmingly unscrupulous. As early as 1720, Philadelphia merchants expressed concern about the character and dealings of peddlers and prevailed upon the Pennsylvania General Assembly to require evidence of good character before issuing licenses to them, since "they have greatly imposed upon many people, as well in the quality as in the price of their goods." Timothy Dwight, president of Yale, wrote "No course of life as the peddlers [*sic*] tends more rapidly to eradicate every moral feeling."

Moral or not, the peddlers performed a vital service for frontier families. Their packs contained essential items like needles, pins, thread, scissors, and thimbles, as well as articles meant purely for pleasure—ribbons, combs, lace, and perfumes. When peddlers progressed to using wagons, they expanded their stock to include more household goods, especially tinware, and added calicos, suspenders, steel pens, books, clocks, and coffee mills, as well as a vast array of other items. Tinware was a welcome advance in technology for the housewife, since it was lighter than both the heavy cast iron pots and kettles and the earthenware milk pans she had been using and, unlike the latter, was also unbreakable. Peddlers carried washboards, brooms, flatirons, and clothespins. Hanging dippers, pails, pots, and tea kettles banged against the sides of the wagon announcing the arrival of the merchant from a good distance down the road. Peddling was not confined to the roads, however. In Pittsburgh, itinerant merchants bought boats, loaded them with goods, and floated down the Ohio, stopping at ports along the way to sell whatever they could.

The mythology of the peddling trade is vast, and an aura of adventure and entrepreneurship surrounded these footloose merchants. Larkin tells us that at the age of 19, James Guild of Vermont "nerved himself to put on a peddler's face" and took off for the West, knocking on doors to sell small items—beads, button molds, sewing silk, and the like. When he met with little success, he took up tin repair, and in rapid succession played the tambourine in a traveling show, cut silhouettes, painted portraits, and ended up teaching penmanship, as he worked his way between Ohio and South Carolina.

Another Vermonter, Lon Newton, known as "king of the tin peddlers," was determined to make a trade with anyone he met.

> "Anything for the tin peddler this morning?" was Lon's usual approach. which enlarged to "Haven't you got any rags, iron, lead, copper, pewter, brass, zinc, any kind of old metal, hides, pelts, skins, furs or beeswax? H'ain't there anything you can trade with the tin peddler this morning?....I'll take....anything...excepting money and old maids." [Johnson, p. 46]

It was a good thing that he and his colleagues were not concerned about hard cash, as there was very little of it on the frontier. The barter system prevailed, and virtually anything could be traded for anything else, as long as both parties were satisfied. Women made butter and traded it for calico or tea; hides and skins were very welcome, as peddlers could sell those for cash. There was a demand for honey and beeswax, and on the East Coast, a market for ginseng, a herb used for "medicinal purposes," as polite society would have it, but more generally valued as an aphrodisiac.

 Conrad Richter, from *The Fields.*

Worth, father of the family living deep in the woods, brings news of a new trading post down the river and complains bitterly about the encroachment of civilization.

Wyitt had longed for a knife of his own, and he decides to take his small cache of pelts and trade them.

Out there in the clearing a brush cabin had been set up first. This was the store. He could tell by the squaws sitting on the logs outside while their near-necked young ones rolled and raced around....the squaws smiled broadly at him as he came up. Oh, they could tell the way he hung back he had never done anything like this before, hadn't ever seen the inside of a store up to now. But he was going to see this one....Wyitt wished [his sisters] could see him here. Not that they ever would. Women folks couldn't walk in a post like a boy and stand with all the riches of the settlement piled up in front of them: bars of bright new lead laid crosswise on the powder kegs; red and green blankets and black ones with broad white stripe...bolts of blue strouding and Turkey red goods... wooden buckets of beads, of bells for leggins, of rings for the nose and finger... and a half barrel that kept dripping from its tap in a wooden bowl, making the air sweet with whiskey.

Household Items, c. 1850. (top) Foot warmer in which coals radiated heat through the pierced sides; (middle) Bootjack; (bottom) Gambrel, used for processing slaughtered hogs. HSWP Collection.

Once or twice a year, families needed salt and other items they could not manufacture themselves. Liwwät Böke tells of the community joining together to send a pack train to Cincinnati loaded with pelts. "*The value was great!* Ten or a dozen men with guns and powder go, at times in snow. Three weeks later they bring back the things they were able to trade for, things which we cannot get or trade for here. With 30 horses we get sufficient salt, [plow] shares, iron, etc." Joseph Doddridge described how the pack saddles were filled with feed for the horses, and "on the journey a part of this feed was left at convenient stages on the way down to support the return of the caravan." The pack train would go to Baltimore, Frederick and Hagerstown, Maryland, each horse returning with two bushels of alum salt, 80 pounds to the bushel.

W. J. McKnight wrote of the difficulties of obtaining store-bought goods for his childhood home. "The nearest store was in Kittanning, thirty-five miles distant, and calico was fifty cents per yard, and the road but a pathway through the woods." The reward at the end of the path was a general store, where a splendid jumble of items spilled over the counters and floors. General stores remained in business for many years, but gradually specialty shops took over their function, as towns and cities acquired more sophisticated goods and the residents demanded a larger selection of merchandise.

Bakewell, Page and Bakewell, engraving. (inset) Tumblers, c. 1830. When Mrs. Anne Royall traveled through Pittsburgh in 1828, she visited the glassworks and saw tumblers being engraved with greyhounds. She wrote "The engraving is very neatly done, indeed, surpassing any I have seen in this country." The tumblers cost $5. HSWP Collection.

As early as the 1780s, residents of Brownsville, Greensburg, Bedford, Union-town, Washington, and Pittsburgh were able to purchase a great variety of goods, provided they had the wherewithal. Merchants imported items from Philadel-phia, New York, and New Orleans, as well as purchasing local products made by the growing number of skilled artisans. Despite the economic recessions that characterized the post-Revolutionary War period, Pittsburgh grew rapidly. Manu-facturing establishments like James O'Hara's glassworks, for example, produced window glass and inexpensive tableware at lower prices than were asked for equivalent items imported from the East. In 1798 the town boasted 74 wholesale and retail establishments. At the turn of the century the substantial number of merchants and tradesmen gave—as one historian put it—"an atmosphere of per-manence and solidarity to the young town." By 1810 there were iron works and rolling mills, foundries, and tanneries. In 1826 a total of 11 tinning businesses employed 65 people; 45 boot and shoe makers supported 225 workers; John M'Ilray owned a cotton manufactory employing 200 people, and 4 other textile factories together employed a total of 224 workers. In that year the amount realized by manufacturing enterprises added up to $2,553,549. The business of Pittsburgh was business, and opportunities for the industrious and ambitious seemed unlimited. [Jones, pp. 49-70]

Between 1785 and 1820, the range of goods advertised in the *Pittsburgh Gaz-ette* resembled that of the items advertised in newspapers published in Philadel-phia and New York. In 1794, for instance, William Christy advertised candlesticks and snuff boxes, violin strings "and a few good violins," Franklin stoves, essence of lavender, historical and novel books, "smoothing irons," assafoetida and "temple spectacles." Wilson and Wallace offered pewter dishes, powder and lead, salt, sealing wax, and ink powder, a wide selection of dry goods, along with "many articles too tedious to enummerate."

The eclectic general store with its crowded shelves and counters must have been a delight to the new female resident of Pittsburgh, who had only to step outside her town house, walk down the unpaved and frequently muddy street, dodge a few wagons, wild hogs, and noisy little boys and arrive at Ormsby's or Scott and Trotter's or William Herd's dry goods and grocery stores. Although the original log stuctures evolved into large, up-to-date frame buildings with increased space, products were also increasing in number and variety, so that the stereotype of the crowded, helter-skelter general store persisted in fact into the 19th century—and continues to exist in some sparsely populated areas of Vermont and the Midwest.

Specialized services also became available, so that a shopping trip might include a visit to Gregg and Barker, gold and silversmiths late of Wilmington, Delaware, who "mean to carry on their business in Front Street," and would also clean and repair watches. Or it might lead to a stop at Patterson and Lambdin to view the establishment's stock of "writing, letter, printing and wrapping papers. …all kinds of stationary and school books, the various kinds used in the schools of the Western Country." John Hamsher the tinsmith advertised that "his best known shop" sold wash kettles, stew kettles, pots, griddles, copperware "as low for cash as it can be got in Philadelphia or Lancaster."

The shopper could drop by Hugh Gardner's bakery for bread or cake; look in at James Liggett's, a cabinet maker, to order a new piece of furniture; or pop into Zadok Cramer's for the latest novel from Philadelphia or a look at his "hanging paper" for the parlor. There were opportunities to view the latest in stoves, Charles Postly's Patented Cooking Stove, which was touted as not only a stove for "extensive cooking" but was "a handsome piece of furniture for the sitting room." Potential buyers were advised they could take out the boilers and sit by the fire, and use the "multiple ovens for baking, wooden vessels for boiling water for washing, steamers attached to the boilers for cooking vegetables by the steam arising from the water while the meat is boiling."

Given a decent income, a Pittsburgh family could eat very well. Glasser and Company supplied shad and mackeral of "supreme quality" in one-half barrels, put up for family use. Bosler and Company offered coffee in bags and barrels, loaf and lump sugar, Young Hyson and Gunpowder teas in small boxes; chocolate, raisins, pepper, ginger, mustard, and figs in drums and boxes. Milles and Wilson stocked whiskey, gin, and cherry bounce, cheese, bacon, and venison hams.

When it came to fashion, the Pittsburgh stores appear to have been well stocked with both necessities and luxuries. Calico, chintz, dimity, muslin, gingham, and flannel shared the shelves with crepe, silk, velvet, and "Fine Irish linens." Also readily available were strange and exotic materials with names like kirsey, moreen, shalloon, and Tiffany, a thin gauze-like silk. Dress goods were offered in an array of colors, including scarlet, blue, salmon, yellow, brown, gray, olive, and snuff. Linens could be plain, striped, checkered, embossed, tamboured, or sprigged, while gloves were offered in black silk or superfine kid in white, pink, and green. Women could buy handkerchiefs and bandannas, and "Silk stockings from Paris in different colors." One could buy ostrich feathers, shawls and cravats, garters, shoestrings and suspenders in 1786, and sunshades, parasols and garden fans in 1800. No longer did wives have to make their own hats and dresses. Early city directories list dressmakers and milliners, including Julia Logan who advertised her "muffs, tippets, fancy turbans and umbrellas" along with her hats. Mrs. Teale "altered straw, chip and leghorn bonnets to any shape," and also made artifical flowers, dresses, and silk bonnets.

A man could buy all kinds of chewing and smoking tobacco—Scotch, Rappell and Maccauber snuff—at Rees Jones, tobacconist, or order footware from John Douthitt, boot and shoemaker ("fashionable work"). He could get a cast steel razor at J. Parsons, cutler, or order his house or his coach painted by M'Couch and Cresswell. A blacksmith would make his locks, keys, shovels, chafing dishes, ladles, and skimmers, and William and Robert Lesky could build or repair a coach, gig, or wagon "in the best manner or on the shortest notice." And if he wanted a shave, he could hardly do better than visit the barber shop of Edward F. Pratt, who took out a two-page ad in the *Pittsburgh Directory for 1815,* showing off not only his skill but his classical education as well. After a long introduction with many literary allusions, Pratt wrote that he would "for an instant abandon his usual occupation of embellishing the exterior for the task of enlightening the interior of that portion of the human figure, anciently denominated the Caput, but in more modern times, the Head." He continued:

> When the revolutionary struggle was over, Washington retired to his plough, and Hamilton became a barrister; after a similar event, in later times, Dearborn became a public writer, Rush an ambassador, and Pratt resumed his razor...henceforth all who wish to be shaved, either for the glorious and praiseworthy ambition of creating a beard, or for the comfortable purpose of getting rid of one, shall repair, at stated periods, to the antechamber of our "sanctum sanctorum"...[where they stand ready] to apply the mystic touch of the razor in such a manner that the chin will be instantly as smooth as the face of Belvidere, without the subject suspecting that he had been in the hands of an operator at all. Let all obey! [Riddle, n.p.]

Still, not everyone thought that Pittsburgh shops and services were as elegant as those of Philadelphia or other cities. Madelaine LeMoyne preferred to enhance her own bonnet.

> Mrs. Preston dyed my leghorn so when I arrived I had only to trim it, which did not take long, having all the necessary trimmings with me....Cloches are quite the fashion while dresses are much trimmed with ruffles, puffs are said to be getting fashionable. [LeMoyne Papers, ALS, 1824]

Nancy Swearingen prevailed on one of her husband's fellow officers to bring her back a winter bonnet from his trip to Virginia, but wrote her parents that she was a little nervous about the assignment since "he is a worthy goodhearted man, though not overburdened as you will soon discover." He apparently performed with credit, however, since she wrote her family that it was a Commodore Perry hat (commemorating a naval victory), "dark purple with black satin and black feathers, very handsome."[Dandridge Papers, ALS, January 9, 1814]

Mrs. Basil Hall, yet another acerbic visitor from England, was quite put out with Pittsburgh shops. "You cannot really form an idea of the trash that is to be found in the best shops," she wrote to a friend, "and the extreme difficulty and often impossibility of procuring what we consider the most common articles...." She also delivered a telling blow to Pittsburgh's pride and joy, the glassmaking industry:

> The glass is the best made in this country but it is very inferior indeed to good English glass, so dark in the color and the cutting is not nearly so good. I remember hearing some American ladies remarking one day that they thought the American glass quite as prettily cut as the English, which appeared to me a great stretch of national prejudice. [Hall, p. 289]

Pittsburgh's boat-building industry began in 1792 with the launching of a sloop destined for world trade. Some ten years later the international phase of the industry collapsed, primarily because of the difficulties of sailing large ships down treacherous river waters to the Gulf of Mexico. River commerce, on the other hand, continued to grow, with shipyards building boats not only to carry merchandise but also to transport families looking to settle in Ohio and Kentucky.

Boats of all sizes were built in Pittsburgh and Brownsville, and "a general assortment seems constantly on hand for the supply of Voyagers," wrote Joshua Gilpin in 1809. Once built, the boats needed to be stocked with provisions, and Pittsburgh merchants were more than ready to oblige. Since travelers were at the mercy of the river and the weather, the ability to gear up quickly for departure was important, and many merchants advertised, as did Florence Cotter, that he had on hand a complete assortment of groceries and liquors "of the best quality on the shortest notice." There was very little that John Stevens's establishment could not supply and deliver on board "with care and despatch on the most reasonable terms." Among the merchandise he advertised were cheese, butter, brandy, spirits, gin, bitters, old whiskey, and cider; ship bread, crackers, butter-biscuit and soft bread; sugar, tea, chocolate, coffee "burnt and ground"; coffee pots and cups, knives, forks, spoons, "segars," tobacco, snuff, pipes, beer, porter, paper, quills, ink, "and etc."

We know from announcements in the *Pittsburgh Gazette* that the barter system lasted well into the 19th century and was just as pervasive in the towns as in the wilderness areas. Almost all merchants accepted numerous items for trade—oats, eggs, butter, corn, cheese, vinegar, hard soap, flax, wheat, rye, pork, beef, bacon, "cattle-on-foot," tallow, potash or ashes, country linen, snake root, ginseng, whiskey, and furs. John and Daniel Craig opened a hat store in 1786 and agreed to take beaver, fox, racoon, and muskrat in lieu of cash. Zadok Cramer accepted clean linen and cotton rags to be used to make paper and wanted sheep and calf skins "clean tanned and well curried, without oil" for book binding. William Cecil, a saddle maker, offered all kinds of ladies' buckskin and plush saddles as well as "veleces [sic], travel canteens, fire buckets and mattresses," and announced that he would accept any kind of country produce as payment. Wilson and Wallace accepted "good merchantable flour, Beef Cattle, butter or cash." And even Monsieur Chovot of Paris would sell his fashionable gold jewelry "reasonably for cash, flour or whiskey."

In 1787 plans for a town market house were well under way, countered by vocal opposition determined to stop it. On March 10, 1787, the Gazette announced that there would be a public meeting when the "appointed committee will submit their resolves to the consideration of the people at large." On the same day a letter to the editor objected strenuously to the plan. "A market house with regular market days was certainly acceptable for those with cash," he complained, but most citizens "don't get as much cash in a week as would purchase a pound of beef, and we had better stay home and suck our fingers than go to market without it." He asked the "inhabitants" to consider the matter carefully, before the market was underway, "when it will be too late." As matters turned out, it was already too late, and the market house was built.

Merchants felt keenly the competition from eastern cities and tried to keep their prices low to encourage local purchases. "Western merchants will find their interest in purchasing at Pittsburgh," advertised Patterson and Lambdin, "as they will save, not only the expense of carriage, but also the exchanges between Eastern and Western funds." This was no small consideration, since after the Revolution, the money situation in Pennsylvania and other states was highly confusing. Federal money was not minted until 1792, but even then very little of it reached Pittsburgh. English money was the most common, but Isaac Craig's account book for 1791 shows that he had accepted dollars (from several states), half sous, English guineas, dubloons, French guineas, Spanish pistols, and banknotes. One pound of gold was worth 15 pounds of silver, but even that was confusing, since the gold and silver came from Britain, Portugal, France, and Spain, and each had a different value. The *Pittsburgh Directory for 1815* printed a formula for translating funds from various sources in the United States to clarify matters.

> To reduce currencies of New Hampshire, Maine, Rhode Island, Connecticut, Virginia into those of New York, North Carolina, to given sum add one third part thereof. Of Pennsylvania, New Jersey, Delaware, Maryland add one quarter of South Carolina and Georgia, subtract two-ninths.

> Directions to reduce currencies of the state to dollars: 6 shillings—add a cypher right hand of the pounds and divide by three. If there be shillings, add one dollar for every 6 shillings.

Small wonder that the barter system stayed in place for so long.

Every family in every generation has its share of financial discussions and warnings about extravagance, and some thoughtful Pittsburghers must have realized that the new abundance might incur more than economic costs. Lydia Maria Child in *The American Frugal Housewife* cautioned against the peril of shops now stocked with tempting goods. "Luxuries are cheaper now than necessaries were a few years since," she wrote. "Yet it is a lamentable fact that it costs more to live now than it did formerly....If the rich must have a new dress every fortnight, people of moderate fortune will have one every month. In this way, finery becomes the standard of respectabilty, and a man's cloth is of more consequence than his character." §

RECIPES

Sally Lunn

Sift a pound and a half of flour. Take 2 ounces of butter a pint of milk a salt spoonful of salt. Three well beaten eggs, and two Tablespoonfuls of fresh yeast.

Updated Version

1 package dry yeast
1/4 cup water
1 tablespoon sugar
2 large eggs, well beaten
2 cups milk, scalded
6 cups flour
4 tablespoons butter or margarine, melted
1/2 teaspoon salt

In a large bowl, sprinkle yeast over very warm water and sugar and let stand until dissolved. Beat in eggs. Cool milk to luke-warm and add. Beat in one-half the flour and butter cooled to lukewarm. Combine salt with remaining flour and add gradually, beating well until a soft dough is formed. Grease top of dough to prevent a crust from forming. Cover bowl and let rise in a warm place until doubled in bulk, about 1 hour. Punch down dough and spoon into well-greased loaf pan approximately 9 x 5 x 3 inches. Cover and let rise again until doubled in bulk, about 45 minutes. Bake in preheated 350° oven for 1 hour or until browned. Cool 10 min-utes on rack and remove from pan. It tastes best when served warm.

To Ragoo Cucumbers

Take two and two onyons—slice them and fry them—in butter—drain them—put them in a stewpan—add a littel wine and mace—lett them stew six minutes—then take a lump of butter as big as a wallnit rolled in flower stir all well—and when thick—dish them.

Updated Version

2 medium cucumbers, peeled & sliced
1 medium onion, peeled & sliced
1 clove garlic, minced
Butter or oil for frying
3 tablespoons dry white wine
(dry vermouth or sherry will do)
Pinch of mace
1 tablespoon butter or margarine
1 tablespoon flour

Fry onions and garlic briefly until soft but not brown. Add cucumbers and cook briefly. Add wine and mace, cover and cook 3–4 minutes. Cucumbers should still be crunchy. Work butter into flour with your fingers and add to pan. Serve when thickened.

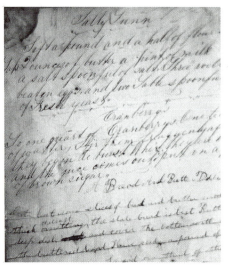

Page from Margaret Bunyan Morgan's cookbook. All but the recipe for "Pumpkin Pudding" in this chapter are from her book. HSWP Collection. The up-dated versions of the recipes are by Virginia K. Bartlett.

Food & Drink

Margaret Bunyan Morgan's handwritten cookbook contained a number of recipes for exotic fare with ingredients she was not likely to find in the little frontier town of Washington, including such dishes as grilled and stewed lobsters, clam soup, buttered crabs, and cocanut [*sic*] puffs and pudding. The recipes are an interesting mixture of basic foods (gingerbread, bread and butter pudding, stewed spinach); East Coast dishes calling for seafood and cranberries; and some somber remedies, learned perhaps after living on the frontier (strong paragoric, cure for a consumptive cough, how to deal with rattlesnake bite). Manuscript cookbooks like this one were clearly the work of well-to-do and literate women, a scarce commodity on the frontier. For the most part, frontier women cooked from memory or intuition, and since the diet was simple and very limited, written recipes were reserved for a more urban society.

Printed cookbooks were rare in America before the mid-19th century. Some settlers brought English books with them but in America women had to adjust to new foods. Corn, pumpkin, some fruits and berries, wild game, and new herbs—all strangers to the pages of British cookbook writers Susannah Carter or Maria Rundell—soon became old friends.

The first truly American cookbook was published by Amelia Simmons in 1796. A self-styled "American orphan," Amelia gave her book a subtitle that also served as a table of contents. "*American Cookery or the Art of Dressing Viands, Fish, Poultry & Vegetables and the best Modes of Making Pastes, Puffs, Pies, Tarts, Puddings, Custards & Preserves and All Kinds of Cakes from the Imperial Plumb to Plain Cake adapted to This Country & All Grades of Life.*" Simmons's book primarily dealt with standard English fare, but she also included several dishes using ingredients native to America, the first cookbook to utilize the products of the new country. A recipe for A Nice Indian Pudding used corn meal, for example, and the book also included recipes for Pumpkin Pudding made with stewed pumpkin, cream, eggs, and sugar, and baked in a crust; for cranberries, baked in a pie; for Indian

"It was a whole day's job to bake a handful of cookies and a few pumpkin pies, as only four cookies or one pie could be baked at one time."
—Sandra L. Myres

Slapjacks or pancakes; for Johny Cake or Hoe Cake; and for American Citron made of watermelon rind boiled with sugar and water.

Even though apples were not native to America, Simmons encouraged her readers to plant orchards and, as an aside, added some advice on dealing with young boys,

> There is not a single family but might set a tree in some otherwise useless spot, which might serve the two fold use of shade and fruit; on which 12 or14 kinds of fruit trees might be easily engrafted and essentially preserve the orchard from the intrusion of boys, &c. which is too common in America. If the boy who thus planted a tree, and guarded and protected it in a useless corner, and carefully engrafted different fruits, was to be indulged free access into orchards, whilst the neglectful boy was prohibited—how many millions of fruit trees would spring into growth— and what a saving to the union. The net saving would in time extinguish the public debt and enrich our cookery. [Simmons, p. 2]

We don't know whether *American Cookery* was for sale in the bookstores of Pittsburgh or Washington, but Margaret Bunyan Morgan's handwritten recipe for dressing a calf's head "Turtle Fashion" (turtles were a great English delicacy) is very similar to Simmons's recipe. In both instances, the cook is directed to boil the head, feet, and heart of the calf; boil again with spices; make forcemeat balls and fry them; add to the pot along with wine; and serve with eggs. Simmons's instructions are more detailed, but as in most handwritten recipes of the period, Morgan's version lists ingredients but is short on directions.

The Morgans had enough money to build a big house and settle into the upper ranks of Washington society. But when the average family arrived at its destination, survival was the first consideration. The men made a temporary shelter until the permanent house could be built. But the task of finding and preparing the food was primarily the women's. Men hunted, women cooked, and the food was very basic indeed.

If ever one food the settler found in America deserved paeans of praise, it was corn, as poet John Greenleaf Whittier proclaimed:

> Heap high the farmer's wintry hoard!
> Heap high the golden corn!
> No richer gift has autumn poured
> From out her lavish horn!

Without corn, the early settlers would have perished, and as others moved west, it was the first crop they planted. There was no need to plow. The farmer merely disturbed some earth with his axe or spade and dropped a few kernels in the ground. Corn was good eaten fresh from the ear (usually referred to as "green"), or dried for the winter. Made into hominy by soaking the kernels in wood ashes, then soaking it again, it was a staple to eat fried with pork or other meat. Corn was ground into soft or hard meal, coarse and fine, baked and boiled for puddings, fried for pancakes or johnny cake, cooked on the hearth for pone, made into mush, and sometimes served at every meal. Corn cobs could be boiled to make a kind of molasses or they could be burned to form the ashes that could be used as a substitute for baking soda, known as saleratus. A bag of corn meal lugged over the mountains provided sustenance until the first crop was in. Mush with milk constituted breakfast and usually supper as well. If milk was unavailable, mush could be made more palatable by the addition of bear grease, sweetened water, fried meat gravy, or corn cob molasses.

Perhaps the most ubiquitous food next to corn was pork. Many settlers brought their pigs along, thus ensuring a supply of bacon, salt pork, and ham, provided precious and expensive salt could be obtained. Hogs were an ideal pioneer beast, since they ate whatever meager scraps were left over and foraged in the woods for the rest of their food. A butchered hog yielded a remarkable number of products: tubs of lard and salt pork, hams, sides of bacon, scrapple and head-cheese, jowls, spareribs, and pickled pigs' feet; and the leftover fat and entrails went into the barrel for tallow to make candles. As a housewife in James Fenimore Cooper's novel *The Chainbearer* explains:

> As for bread, I count that for nothin'. We always have bread and potatoes enough; but I hold a family to be in a desperate way when the mother can see the bottom of the pork barrel. Give me the children that's raised on good sound pork afore all the game in the country. Game's good as a relish and so's bread; but pork is the staff of life. [Cooper, p. 82]

In the earliest days of settlement, game was available just outside the cabin door—squirrel, bear, deer, and fowl—a necessity until livestock was accumulated. Fat was obtained from bear and opossum and rendered into lard. Fruits and herbs were available for the picking, in itself a risky pastime. Wolves, panthers, rattlesnakes and Native Americans were all clear and present dangers; as a settler recalled, "Our time for gathering the…berries, as well as other fruits, was Sunday, and in large companies, under the protection of some of our warriors in arms."[Bryce, p. 26] Eighteenth-century writers, usually reminiscing rather than commenting at the time, were lavish in their descriptions of abundance.

> The wild meats were bear, elk, deer, rabbits, squirrels, woodchucks, and turkey and partridge in some areas…wild birds were plentiful—grouse, ducks, geese, pigeons, turkeys….wild fruits were abundant—crabapples, red and yellow plums, black-berries, huckleberries, elderberries, strawberries, choke cherries, raspberries, gooseberries. [McKnight, p. 82]

Daniel Drake remembered boyhood expeditions for paw-paws, grapes, honey locust pods, "and occasionally, the hard seeds of the coffee tree (guylandina Bonduc), of which…we made a substitute for coffee."

Early settlers in New England learned to use pumpkin in a wide variety of dishes, and that vegetable added not only flavor but nutritional value to the limited diet. Wrote Peter Kalm in *Travels in North America* in 1783:

> The Indians boil them whole, or roast them in the ashes and eat them, or sell them thus prepared in the town; and they have indeed a fine flavor when roasted....cut them through the middle, take out all the seeds, put the halves together again and roast them in an oven. When they are quite done, some butter is put in, which being imbibed into the pulp renders it very palatable. The settlers often boil pumpkins in water and afterwards eat them alone or with meat. Some make a thin pottage of them by boiling them in water and afterwards macerating the pulp. This is again boiled with a little of the water, and a good deal of milk and stirred about while it is boiling. Sometimes the pulp is kneaded into a dough with maize and other flour; of this they make pancakes. Some make puddings and tarts of pumpkins. [Phipps, p. 114]

Hickory, chestnuts, and butternuts were plentiful, as were fish. Settlers could hook, net, spear or shoot pike, bass, catfish, suckers, sunfish, horn-chubs, mountain trout, and eel. During John May's trip on the Monongahela, he noted the number of large and tasty fish caught almost daily, "two perch, weighing forty and one-fourth pounds together. They have been caught weighing twenty-four pounds. They are very handsome, good fish, something resembling a haddock; a little higher in the back, and much better eating." Little attention was paid to leafy vegetables, but settlers ate wild greens—dandelions, cowslip, pigweed, and ramps (wild leeks). But according to McKnight, the basic diet of most farmers in Western Pennsylvania, even after the first crops were in, was still limited to buckwheat cakes, corn mush and milk, rye mush and milk, bread, hominy, potatoes, turnips, wild onions or ramps, hog meats, wild meats, fish, and wild fruit.

Wheat bread was rare, since wheat, when grown, was a cash crop and few farmers wanted to sacrifice their limited resources merely to eat white bread. Prior to 1830, flour cost $3 a barrel, extremely expensive relative to the prices of other food items: beef cost 3 cents per pound, chickens 6 cents each, butter 6 cents and 8 cents per pound, and eggs 6 cents a dozen.[McKnight, p. 80] Benjamin Rush, a physician, statesman, and author, noted in 1790 that the profit to a farmer when he spread his gain from the sale of wheat over his lifetime was equal to the price of a farm for one of his children. Rye was more common than wheat and easily grown. Mixed with "Injun" meal, it could provide a very palatable yeast loaf and most households kept a crock of homemade yeast in the cellar. Buckwheat was a change from the staple corn dishes, either as pancakes or "souens," a kind of sourdough mix.

> Mix your buckwheat flour and water in the morning; add to this enough yeast to make the batter light; then let it stand until evening, or until the batter is real sour. Now stir the batter into water and boil until it is thoroughly cooked, like corn-mush. Eat hot or cold with milk or cream. [McKnight, pp. 81-82]

Although some staple dishes were common to the diets of all the early settlers, ethnic differences were pervasive and were observed as early as 1759 by Israel Acrelius, a Swedish settler who documented the habits of his countrymen. Early Swedish farmers, he reported, preferred cold milk and bread for breakfast, or perhaps rice, milk pudding, cheese, butter, and cold meat.

> For noon, in summer, soup, fresh meat, dried beef and bacon with cabbage, apples, potatoes, Turkish beans, large beans, all kinds of roots, mashed turnips, pumpkins, cashaws and squashes....Also boiled or baked pudding, dumplings, bacon and eggs, pies of apples, cherries, peaches, etc....In winter, hominy soup is cooked with salt beef and bacon. Then, also, pastries of lamb and chicken can be used and can be kept cold a whole week. [Fletcher, p. 408]

English settlers liked a common dish "filled high with boiled potatoes, cabbage and salt pork or corned beef. At every meal there was a large dish of fried salt pork swimming in its own fat....Indian pudding and pumpkin pies were also in great demand; and after butchering, sausages and mince pies were in daily use."

The German pioneers used less meat and more vegetables, especially turnips, cabbage (sauerkraut), onions, and salad greens. Milk and cheese were consumed in large quantities, as well as large amounts of pork, and some of the most famous Pennsylvania Dutch dishes like apple fritters, funnel cakes, *schmier-käse* (cottage cheese), liverwurst, *schnitz und knopf* (dried apple slices with pork), are still served in Central and Western Pennsylvania. The Scots-Irish, who settled Western Pennsylvania in large numbers, had to give up their oatmeal porridge for cornmeal mush but also ate substantial quantities of wild meat and game, as well as subscribing to the "hog and hominy" school of nutrition.

In order to provide the ubiquitous mush and pone, the corn had to be ground into meal, and this required either a long journey to the nearest mill or backbreaking effort on the part of somebody, usually the wife or the children. Most families owned a hominy block, a large hollowed-out stump. Corn was poured into the hollow and then crushed into meal with a pestle, a large stone often weighing as much as ten pounds. A sweep was a somewhat less labor-intensive device, consisting of a young sapling attached to the pestle and properly braced. The spring action of the "machine" considerably lessened the effort of grinding. Both of these methods worked well when the corn was hard, but soft corn had to be laboriously grated on a perforated half-cylinder made of tin and nailed to a wood block. Daniel Drake recalled rubbing the ear "up and down on this instrument over which, at the age of 7 or 8 and still later, I often tired my arm and sometimes lacerated my fingers."

The third alternative was the hand mill made of two circular stones placed in a hoop, with a spout for discharging meal. The upper stone was the "runner," the bottom called the "bed." Both stones were rigged to a pole and joist which allowed the mill to turn.

In Conrad Richter's novel, *The Fields,* young Guerdon was required to mill corn before he could go fishing.

Guerdon hated a sweep as bad as a grater. But what he held in the blackest abomination was their own sweat mill that stood in the chimney corner. It was the devil's own contraption and turned around hard as a four-horse wagon. A day's grinding seemed a month long, and no Sabbaths. The handle raised water blisters. The stones scraped and kept sticking. Those two millstones weren't more than a foot and a half across, but they could grind his body and soul between bed and runner. By the time he got through he felt like he had been bulled into samp, rough and lifeless as the meal that came through. That meal had to be hand-sifted in three sizes. The finest his mam could make bread out of. The coarsest she had to boil all day over the fire to soften for human guts.

Even when a mill was conveniently nearby, some of the poorer settlers felt they couldn't afford to have their meal ground professionally, since the miller took a substantial percentage of the product for his pay, sometimes as much as half.

This mill was erected by George Washington on Washington Run, adjoining the future property of the Washington Coal & Coke Co. HSWP Collection.

Even after grist mills became more common, there could still be problems getting the corn ground, especially during a summer drought, Doddridge reported.

> The mills were not expected to do any grinding after the latter end of May, excepting for a short time after a thundergust; our most prudent housekeepers, therefore, took care to have their summer stock of flour ground in the months of March and April. If this stock was expended too soon, there were no resources but those of the hominy block or hand mill. [Doddridge, p. 52]

The two staples that were difficult to do without and even more difficult to acquire were salt and sugar. Salt was necessary not only to season often unpalatable food but also to preserve meats for the winter. Hams and bacon were part of the daily diet and lifesavers for the cold winter months when inclement weather made hunting more difficult. Before 1800 salt had to be hauled over the Alleghenies in sacks on horseback and consequently was very expensive, selling for $8 a bushel in Pittsburgh. Then salt deposits were discovered in Western New York and salt from the new source began to flow, still laboriously, by ox-team, sailboat and flatboat into Pittsburgh. There is a newspaper report that in 1805, 11 flat-bottomed and 6 keelboats passed through Meadville, the keelboats carrying 170 barrels and the flatboats 60, which would sell for $13 a barrel. Between 1800 and 1819 salt was the major medium of exchange in Erie County. "Oxen, horses, negro slaves and land were sold, to be paid for so much in salt." A yoke of oxen could cost the trader eight barrels. In earlier days, Doddridge tells us, a bushel of salt could cost a "good cow and her calf." So valuable a commodity was it, he relates, that no one was permitted to walk across the floor while the measuring ritual took place for fear some might be spilled. Daniel Drake reported:

> When about six years old, I was sent to borrow a little salt of one of the neighbors. …It was a small quantity, tied up in paper, and when I had gotten about half way home, the paper tore, and most of the precious grains rolled out on the ground. As I write, the anguish I felt at the sight seems almost to be revived. [Drake, p. 31]

By 1813 salt was being produced in Western Pennsylvania and was more accessible to all.

Sugar was also a luxury and remained expensive and scarce until after 1840. Loaves or cones of sugar were sold in local stores and cut into usable size at home. But unlike salt, there were excellent substitutes. Honey was by far the most common sweetener, and although bees were not native to America, they had been brought by very early settlers and had quickly become wild. A good bee tree could yield as much as 75 pounds of honey and often more. The honey served not only as a sweetener for table use but as a preservative as well.

Since sugar maple trees were plentiful in Western Pennsylvania, farmers learned to tap them and make syrup as the Native Americans had done for generations. Fletcher tells us that the average farm family tapped 200 to 300 trees, which equaled between 500 and 1,000 pounds of sugar annually. Rebecca

Burland, the settler from Yorkshire, was intrigued by the process and described it for her son.

> A small cabin, or as it is termed here, camp, is built in the midst of trees; two or three large coppers, holding from five to ten gallons each, are set within it, to boil the liquor, which being drained from the trees into hewn wooden troughs, is carried into the camp. The incisions are made with an auger in the beginnings of March, when the sap is beginning to rise. Into each of these holes a tube is inserted, about an inch in diameter, so as just to fill the hole, through this the liquor flows as through a spout....After the liquor is thus collected, it is boiled down to the consistency of thin treacle. It is then strained through a coarse woolen cloth, and afterwards boiled again at a slower fire till it becomes hard and firm like raw sugar. [Burland, pp. 55-56]

Once food was obtained, it had to be cooked and served. Women had a minimum of utensils to work with and always cooked over an open fire, either in the cabin or outside. Chances are they brought a kettle and a skillet with them over the mountains, the pot and the pan that would cook almost anything. Liwwät Böke, a methodical and well-organized young girl, made up packing lists for herself and her future husband before they left Germany. Bed linen, clothing, farm implements, medicine and chewing tobacco were some of the necessities of life for the New World, but prominent on the lists were her cooking utensils including a kettle and bucket; silver, dishes, spoon, knife, forks; drinking cup and plates; plus a trunkful of seeds, both for vegetables and flowers, and the couple's baptismal certificates, a rosary, and a bottle of holy water.

Perhaps the most important utensil was the stewing pot or kettle, sometimes made of copper, more often of cast iron, but always heavy, weighing as much as 20 pounds or more when empty. Meat and game could be stewed in the kettle, soup simmered, and large quantities of mush boiled up. Bread was made in a smaller kettle with legs, the original Dutch oven, designed to be set directly over the coals. The bread was placed inside, a lid set in place, and coals heaped on top. A long-handled frying pan was a must and a spider (a frying pan with legs which could be set directly on the hearth) was useful. Sometimes a griddle for pancakes, as well as a gridiron, a footed wrought iron trivet for broiling meats, were part of the *batterie de cuisine.* Long-handled utensils, such as a skimmer, a ladle, a spoon and fork, were also common and necessary to keep the housewife from catching fire as she reached over the hearth. Such implements appeared to be a part of every household, yet there is rarely a reference to their being purchased. If these items were too bulky to bring from the East, where did they come from? Perhaps like the ladies of Dedham when asked where their hats came from, the owners of these housewares would have responded, "We don't *buy* them, we *have* them!"

An iron crane attached to the wall of the fireplace swung out to allow the housewife to attach pots to a series of hooks, regulating their distance from the fire. A trammel, a notched hook which made it easier to adjust the heights of the

Baking Scene *by Lewis Miller, carpenter and folk artist from York, Pennsylvania.*

pots, was often used. Rather than a roaring fire, small fires of various intensities were placed in different areas of the fireplace to accommodate different cooking techniques. The Dutch oven bread, for instance, was baked near the front on a bed of coals. In the center, a more briskly burning fire roasted meat on a spit, while a stew simmered on a trammel hook near the back of the fireplace on medium heat.

Ovens, no doubt designed by a man, were originally built into the backs of the fireplace, where a woman had to literally reach over the fire to gain access. Presumably, the advantage of this arrangement was that only one flue was necessary. The folly of this placement, however, was soon recognized and small dome-shaped or beehive ovens with their own flues were situated at the side of the hearth. The oven was usually about 26 inches in diameter with a much smaller opening to minimize heat loss. The oven door was first a wooden slab, then cast iron.

Lydia Maria Child, writing in *The American Frugal Housewife* in 1832, assumed even then that hearth ovens were universal. "Heating ovens must be regulated by experience and observation," she told her readers. A fire was built directly in the oven to heat the bricks, and when the interior was judged hot enough, the ashes were raked out and the food placed inside. A woman needed a substantial amount of that experience and judgment to know when the oven was the right temperature for that day's baking. A common method of determining this was to place one's hand inside and count to a certain number, which presumably varied with the intestinal fortitude of the baker. If your hand had to be withdrawn before that number was reached, the oven was too hot. Likewise, keeping your hand there beyond the magic number indicated that the oven was not yet hot enough. Joyce Carlo tells the story of one pious woman who sang the Doxology through a specified number of times rather than counting. Mrs. Child preferred a less tortuous method. "If you are afraid your oven is too hot," she counseled, "throw in a little flour, and shut it up for a minute. If it scorches black immediately, the heat is too furious; if it merely browns, it is right."

The development of a small oven made of tin represented a major step forward. The oven was built to resemble half of a small barrel with the side away from the fire closed to allow the heat to be reflected back into the oven. A built-in spit with a handle allowed the meat to be turned as needed and basted through a small door in the back, offering the baster some protection from the fire. Children were frequently allotted the tedious job of turning the spit, and there were even reports that small dogs had been hooked to treadmills and made to perform the task.

Despite the gradual appearance of "labor-saving" devices such as cranes and hooks, cooking over an open hearth remained both dangerous and exhausting. Pioneer women were prone to suffer from singed hair and clothes, smoke in their eyes, and strained backs and blistered hands, to say nothing of having the critical responsibility of keeping small children away from the fire.

> It was a whole day's job to bake a handful of cookies and a few pumpkin pies, as only four cookies or one pie could be baked [in the bake kettle] at one time. The lid had to be lifted and the hot coals removed often. If your hand would suddenly lose its grip, or someone jostled your elbow, down the lid would come and the coals more often land in the kettle. The fronts of my dresses would be scorched, the toes of my shoes, burned and my face blistered in the process. [Myres, p. 147]

An early account of a bad accident illustrates one of the serious hazards, and although this was written in 1722, little had changed for the housewife by the end of the 18th century. A husband recorded in his journal:

> April 1 sund fair. Molly is scalded in ye back and neck. a dis of hot milk Spilt on her by Nathanll. wed 4 cloudy. I was at home all day making a plow and looking after Molly who is bad with her Scald. Ye ague hath been in itt & she hath ye fever. [Phipps, p. 98]

Travelers spoke in glowing terms of the abundance of America, and indeed there seemed enough for all. But American life was defined by the seasons, and the lush days of summer and autumn were spent preparing for the harsh winter to come. Most, if not all, of this burden fell to the women. It is hard to know where to begin the chronicle of food-related tasks, other than the actual preparation of meals, not only because there were so many of them but because they overlapped in a kind of domino effect and literally never ended. Women's cooking chores were bound by the weather and the fact that certain tasks had to be accomplished when the food was there and ready to be dealt with. Herbs had to be picked on a dry day before they went to seed. Butter was best made, so went the conventional wisdom, in June and September, because cow's milk was sweeter then. Churned butter had to be packed into tubs and stored as long as possible in salt brine (which also had to be prepared ahead of time), or in the spring house, a small stone structure built over a spring, where the cool running water prevented spoilage. New corn was ready in midsummer and had to be cooked or dried or ground into meal: corn meal had to be baked or boiled into something palatable like mush, johnny cake, or pudding.

A newly killed bear yielded fresh meat to be cooked without delay plus some to be dried, grease to be rendered for cooking and preserving, and a skin to cure for a blanket or rug. Deer and other game had to be cleaned, and prepared and preserved, if possible, by drying. Summer and autumn berries had to be picked, cleaned, cooked, and preserved for the winter. Vegetables had to be picked when they were ready and pickled for the winter, with the brine skimmed and changed at the right time to avoid spoilage. Drying foods could be a tricky process, requiring good air circulation and frequent turning. Bird droppings, insects, and blowing dust were all hazards, but the resulting bounty of preserved apples, peaches, and pears, as well as venison and other meats and fish, saw the family through the long winter. *Food of Our Fathers*, a report from a group of food technologists, describes an early method of making bouillon cubes:

> They would boil calves' feet and other bones in water to extract the jelly, cool the solution, remove the fat and sediment, and then boil again to concentrate the solution. When sufficiently condensed, this would be cooled in a shallow pan, where it would solidify to be cut into strips. Dubbed "portable soup," these strips could be carried on long trips, and redissolved in hot water to yield a tasty broth. [*Food of Our Fathers*, p. 13]

Unfortunately, adds the report, the soup had very little nutritional value. For a more nutritious cold weather lunch, the wife could make a bean porridge and freeze it with a string attached so that her husband could hang it from his sled. When he was hungry, he could break off a piece and eat it.

Butchering had to be carried out on a cold autumn day so that the animal carcass would cool quickly. The occasion called for extra food to be prepared for the neighbors who helped. Meanwhile, the housewife fell behind in other important tasks. Butchering has been called a frolic by some writers, a sport by others, an opportunity for sociability by many, and a great deal of work by most. When the word went out that butchering day was imminent, as many neighbors as possible turned out to help. Huge fires were built at dawn and breakfast cooked and served to the dozens of helpers by the women. Large barrels, or hogsheads, of scalding water were readied. The hogs were driven from their pens, shot and stuck, popped in the boiling water, denuded of their bristles, and then gutted and dressed. This was men's work, and one of the goals was to finish with the six or eight hogs before 9 in the morning so that the rest of the day could be devoted to shooting matches and other sporting events. In the meantime, the women were preparing a large dinner, "one of the biggest and best dinners of all the year."

RECIPES

A Bread and Butter Pudding

Cut some slices of bread and butter moderately thick omitting the crust, the stale bread is best. Butter a deep dish and cover the bottom with slices of the buttered bread. Have ready a pound of currants or raisins. Spread one third of them thickly over the bread and butter and strew some brown sugar. Then put another layer of bread and butter and cover it also with currants and sugar. Finish with a third layer of each and pour over the whole four eggs beatten very light and mixed.

Updated Version

1 loaf French or Italian-style bread, cut into 1/2" slices, crusts removed
Butter for spreading on bread
1/2 cup raisins or currants
2 tablespoons brown sugar
4 eggs, well-beaten
2 cups milk, scalded
1 teaspoon vanilla
2 teaspoons granulated sugar

Butter a deep 2- or 3-quart casserole. Butter bread slices and cover the bottom of the dish, buttered side up. Spread 1/3 of the raisins or currents over bread and 1/3 of the brown sugar as well. Add 2 more layers of bread, raisins and sugar. Cool milk and add slowly to beaten eggs with granulated sugar and vanilla. Pour egg mixture over bread slices and press down gently with spatula to make sure all bread slices are moistened. Bake in preheated 350° oven for 40–45 minutes or until a knife inserted in middle comes out clean. Pudding can be served warm or cold and can be reheated in the microwave oven. Serve with a little cream if desired.

Pumpkin Pudding

Stew a fine sweet pumpkin till soft and dry. rub it through a sieve mix with the pulp six eggs quite light a quarter of a pound of butter half a pint of new milk some pounded ginger and nutmeg a wine glass of brandy.

Updated Version

5 large eggs
1 can plain pumpkin
1/2 cup sugar
1/4 lb. butter or margarine, melted
1 cup half and half
1/2 teaspoon nutmeg
1/2 teaspoon cinnamon
1/4 teaspoon ginger
1/4 cup brandy (optional)

Beat eggs until light and mix with pumpkin, sugar, melted butter, half and half, spices, and brandy if desired. Pour mixture into a shallow buttered 3-quart casserole. Bake in preheated 350° oven for about 55 minutes, or until a knife inserted in the center comes out clean.

Handwritten Recipe and Remedy Book. F. Key's "Receipts to make some of the good Things of Life, 1800." HSWP Collection.

The ladies devoted the rest of their afternoon to hard work, and "rending the lard, making sausage, liver wort, scrapple, puddings, mince-meat, etc., would keep all hands busy for the afternoon and evening."

Making mincemeat was labor intensive: the meat was chopped up on a large plank by a person wielding two large cleavers, one in each hand, and working them up and down until the meat was fine enough for its intended purpose.Then the remaining ingredients were mixed in—apples, raisins, cider, and a long list of spices. To make sausage, a knowledgeable person who understood the proper proportions of fat and lean meat and spices mixed the ground meat with the other ingredients. The mixture was then stuffed into cleaned hog gut casings through a funnel held tightly by hardy folk. Endless lengths of sausage were thus prepared and hung in the smokehouse for curing. The meat itself—hams, shoulders, and sides—was packed in brine barrels for several months, then subjected to the same smoking process as the sausage.

Even if the householder didn't do his own butchering, meat still had to be cut and processed, and even if the settler was adept at this, cutting up half a cow could still be difficult. But Christiana Tillson's husband knew nothing about it, and the task fell to her.

> We usually had a quarter of beef—nothing less—brought at a time; sometimes a whole animal. Your father knew nothing about cutting and dividing meat, so by the help of directions laid down in a cookery book and a little saw I attempted this art....A part would be salted down to be used for corn beef when the fresh had been eaten; the pieces for roast and steak set apart; the fat about the kidneys carefully picked out and put to dry for suet, and the remained of the fat melted, strained and put away for candles; a part made into "collared" or "pressed beef;" the round made into "hunter's beef," and the shins hung up in a cool place for soup. [Tillson, p. 149]

Another activity that combined hard work and sociability was making apple butter, although this was done in stages. The first stage was making cider, either on the farm, if a press were available, or at a communal press in the vicinity. Some fresh cider was saved for drinking, some was allowed to get "hard," and some was made into vinegar. Two or three barrels of fresh juice were boiled down in large kettles until a few gallons of syrupy liquid remained. These could be stored indefinitely until it was time to make apple butter.

"Apple bees" combined the chores of peeling apples to be dried—cut in rounds and strung on long threads—with preparing the butter apples—pared, cored and put in a barrel until the following day for boiling. The rest of the time was devoted to "playparties" with dancing, games, and eating, for the hostess was expected to provide substantial refreshments for the working group. The next day cider and apples were put in a huge kettle over a fire, either indoors or out-side, brought to a boil, and cooked for hours until the dark red mass "tested" done. Someone—or several someones—had to stir the pot continuously so the apple butter would not burn, and as it thickened, it became more difficult to stir.

RECIPES

Apple Pudding

Take 3 or 4 apples peel them and cut them in slices and lay them a covering of apples and one of sugar till your dish is almost full then take a custard and throw on the top of it put a paste in your dish.

Updated Version

This "pudding" is more successful when the custard is made separately and served as a sauce.

> 3 or 4 Granny Smith (or other
> tart apples), thinly sliced
>
> 1/3 cup brown sugar, firmly packed
>
> 1/4 teaspoon nutmeg
>
> 1/2 teaspoon cinnamon
>
> 1 tablespoon butter

This recipe works best in a deep pie dish or a shallow casserole. Arrange a pie crust in the dish, leaving enough overhang to crimp the edges. Place a layer of apples in crust and spread brown sugar and 1/3 of spices over them. Repeat until there are 3 or 4 layers. Dot with butter. Bake in a preheated 350° oven for 45–50 minutes. Serve with custard sauce, either warm or very cold.

Custard Sauce

> 6 egg yolks
>
> 1/2 cup sugar
>
> 3 cups milk (or 1 cup cream
> and 2 cups milk), scalded
>
> 2 teaspoons vanilla

In the top of a double boiler, mix eggs and sugar and slowly stir in milk. Cook over simmering hot water, stirring constantly, until mixture will coat a metal spoon or reaches 180° on a candy thermometer (about 10 minutes). Wipe down sides of pan with a heat-resistant rubber spatula while stirring. Remove from heat and add vanilla. Chill well, stirring occasionally to prevent crust from forming. May be served warm or cold.

To Make a Paste for Tarts

Put an ounce of loaf sugar, beat and sifted, to one pound of fine flour. Make it into a stiff paste with a gill of boiling cream and 3 ounces of butter. Work it well, and roll it very thin.

Updated Version

The original recipe makes a great deal of VERY tough pie crust. You might wish to use your favorite pastry recipe for the apple tart, or try this modified version.

> 1 tablespoon sugar
>
> 2 cups flour
>
> Dash of salt
>
> 2/3 cup butter or vegetable shortening
>
> 1/3 (approximate) cup cold milk

Mix sugar, flour and salt together. Cut in the shortening with a pastry blender or two knives until it resembles coarse corn meal. Add the milk a little at a time and mix in with a fork until the mixture holds together. Take care not to overmix, or crust will toughen. Form into a ball with your hands and roll out very thinly on a floured pastry cloth or board. This is a crumbly pastry, so you will probably have to roll it more than once. Lift the crust into the dish, leaving an overhang. Add the filling and crimp the crust with a fork or your thumb and forefinger.

When it was finally done, with as many as 30 gallons made at one time, it was poured into crocks covered with paper, tied, and stored for the winter.

The tableware of the early settlers was as basic and primitive as their diet. Wooden bowls, plates or trenchers, and cups or mugs were the rule of the day; rarely was glass or china seen, and pewter only occasionally. Whatever precious pieces existed had probably been brought carefully over the mountains from Philadelphia, Boston, or even Europe. Pewter, as late as 1807, cost $2 for six plates, more than the cost of four bushels of oats.

The trencher was the all-purpose dish, a square or oblong piece of wood, usually maple, hollowed out to receive the food, which was served from a common dish. Forks were slow to arrive in America and food was delivered to the mouth by knives. Since much of the food was partially liquid—gravy, mush, milk, and stews—spoons were the most useful utensil, carved from wood or horn.

Water was generally pure and plentiful in the late 18th and early 19th centuries, but one needed a herd of small boys and girls to lug it from the springs and rivers. In the 1770s, "real" tea was popular but expensive, selling for 50 cents to $1.50 a pound when butter cost 12 1/2 cents a pound and eggs were 6 cents a dozen, but there was a variety of options available. A palatable tea could be made from fern or sassafras, sage, mint, dittany, and many other herbs. Coffee was virtually unknown for many years and also expensive. Substitutes for coffee were less successful than herb teas, utilizing roasted wheat, rye and barley, and even roasted chestnuts or potatoes. The author of a work on the settlement of Virginia and Pennsylvania in the 1760s to 1805, Doddridge tells us that in his first experience with that beverage as a young lad he found "the taste of coffee nauseous beyond anything I had ever tasted in my life." Buttermilk was always available after butter churning, homemade beer was usually present in quantity, but the outstanding beverages of choice were cider and whiskey.

The ingredients for hard liquor were as close at hand as the game and fish that settlers used for food. Apple orchards proliferated and by mid-century, farmers were putting up as many as 40 barrels of cider a year. "Prime" cider was over a year old, and very hard. Mixed with honey, it became metheglin, a powerful sweet drink. Diluted with water, it flavored the obligatory mush. And everyone drank it—men, women, and children—in prodigious quantities.

Whiskey was a natural product for Pennsylvania. Rye and corn were the chief crops and each farm seemed to have its own small still. It was the basis for much of the settlers' legendary hospitality, and the "green glass, long-necked bottle was a kind of household god. It was present on nearly every occasion—at weddings, corn-huskings, log-rollings, flax-pullings, sheep-washings, fish-swabbings, house and barn-raisings." Families regarded it as their duty to supply guests and keep the bottle always available. If a friend should call and find it empty, the host was embarrassed and the guest disappointed. Farmhands expected strong drink and plenty of it as part of their board. Children's bread was sometimes soaked in whiskey. Clergymen drank as freely as their parishioners, and lawyers and businessmen in the towns were often observed drunk and disorderly. Liquor was seen as "the indispensable emblem of hospitality and the accompaniment of labor in every pursuit, the stimulant in joy and the solace of grief." In 1810 traveler Fortescue Cuming observed:

> So far do they carry this mania for whiskey, that to procure it, they in the most niggardly manner deny themselves even the necessaries of life; and, as I was informed by my landlord Fleming, an observing and rational man, countrymen while attending the courts (for they are generally involved in litigation, of which they are all very fond) occupy the bar rooms of the taverns in the country towns, for several days together, making one meal serve them each day, and sometimes two, and even three days—but drinking whiskey without bounds during the same time. [Cuming, p. 47]

Drinking in the taverns may have been more visible, but accounted for only about one quarter of the total consumption. It was estimated that during the Revolutionary years, Americans drank the equivalent of three and a half gallons of 200-proof pure alcohol per person each year. Drinking increased, until by 1820 the total had risen to four gallons per person annually. Largely because of the determined efforts of temperance activists, drinking began to decline, and by the mid-1800s the estimates had dropped to less than two gallons per person.

This heavy drinking was fertile ground for the reformers of the 19th century, who rightly saw American women and children as the chief victims of alcoholism. Although women drank, they usually consumed less than their men. Estimates in the 1820s suggest that men drank some 15 times the amount that women did. And the standards of the day found drunkenness in women more objectionable than in men. One observer in Ohio reported that he rarely paid much heed to men in their cups, but one stormy night he found a shocking sight, "nothing less than a *woman beastly drunk*....with a flask of whiskey by her side." As Larkin points out, "Americans traditionally found drunkenness tolerable and forgivable in men but deeply shameful in women." Excessive drinking was clearly a problem that affected families adversely—their incomes, health, emotional stability, employability, social acceptance. As Scott and Wishy note, intemperance became a metaphor for everything that was wrong with the family and with society. Popular magazines published stories about the sufferings of women who were married to drunkards, and songs and poems reinforced the evils of drink. By 1826 temperance societies were proliferating across the state, and drinking began to decline.

Although hard drinking was an important part of early American culture, whiskey was also a cash crop. Corn and rye could be easily converted to whiskey, and most farmers with stills—which meant almost all of them—could produce a surplus that not even the hardest drinking family could consume. By 1800 there were more stills than grist mills in the state.

Whiskey was a valuable item of barter, and some farmers alleged it was a better asset than a cow. But it was also a cheap and convenient way of sending

Temperance Song: *Father, Dear Father, Come Home with Me Now*

Father, dear father, come home with me now!
The clock in the steeple strikes one;
You said you were coming right home from the shop,
As soon as your day's work was done.
Our fire has gone out, our house is all dark,
And mother's been watching for you;
With poor brother Benny so sick in her arms,
Without you, oh, what can she do?
Come home! Come home! Come home!
Please, father, dear father, come home.

Father, dear father, come home with me now!
The clock in the steeple strikes two;
The night has grown colder and Benny is worse,
But he has been calling for you.
Indeed, he is worse, Ma says he will die,
Perhaps before morning shall dawn;
And this is the message she sent me to bring,
"Come quickly, or he will be gone."
Come home! Come home! Come home!
Please, father, dear father, come home.

Father, dear father, come home with me now,
The clock in the steeple strikes three;
The house is so lonely, the hours are long,
For poor weeping mother and me.
Yes, we are alone, poor Benny is dead,
And gone with the Angels of light;
And these were the very last words that he said,
"I want to kiss Papa good night."
Come home! Come home! Come home!
Please, father, dear father, come home.

"Don't marry a man to reform him,
To God and your own self be true;
Don't link his vice to your virtue;
You'll rue it, dear girl, if you do."

—From a temperance poem.

    Chorus
Hear the sweet voice of your own little child,
As she tearfully begs you to come!
Oh, who could resist this most pitiful pray'r,
"Please father, dear father, come home!"

       —Music and lyrics by Henry C. Work, 1864.

grain to the East. A pack horse could carry 4 bushels of grain in its original state; but in the form of whiskey, the horse could carry the equivalent of 24 bushels of grain. In 1791, when the government slapped an excise tax of four pence a gallon on all distilled spirits, the farmers of Western Pennsylvania were understandably irritated. The ensuing Whiskey Rebellion cost lives and property before being quelled by military force sent from the East. Ironically, once the rebellion was put down, the tax was repealed.

Over and over again travelers' accounts expressed amazement at the abundance of food in America, particularly meat. Venison, bear, squirrel, and a variety of fowl and fish were available with very little effort on the part of the householder. How well the food was cooked was another matter, since the settlers in the wilderness above all wanted full stomachs. The available cooking paraphernalia and the methods cooks had to resort to did not lend themselves to sophisticated meals, but except in times of extreme hardship—drought, standoffs by Native Americans, floods, and difficult winters—starvation was only a memory of the old country. Travelers also commented on the large amount of protein consumed in America. Some writers have suggested that our country's energy and inventiveness in its earliest years was due to the effect of plentiful protein on growing children, as well as on their parents.

It is interesting to trace the movement of settlers westward and note how they carried their customs and patterns of daily chores with them. The experiences of women in Western Pennsylvania were replicated by those of women in Illinois, Ohio, Kansas, and beyond. If one examines the kitchens of the early 17th century and compares them to those common at the beginning of the 19th century, one sees very little change. In 1832, despite the fact that many women were purchasing new stoves, Lydia Maria Child's *The American Frugal Housewife* gave detailed instructions for cleaning kitchen hearths. "Wash them with soap, and wipe them with a wet cloth; some people rub in lamp oil, once in a while, and wash the hearth faithfully afterwards. This does very well in a large, dirty family; for the hearth looks very clean and is not liable to show grease spots." In 1847 Sarah Josepha Hale's cookbook *The Way to Live Well and to be Well While We Live* advised housewives to sweep the chimney often so that soot would not fall down on the dishes at the fire. The hearth, she declared, must be as neat as a pin. In 1837 "A Lady" published *The Housekeeper's Book* and deplored the onset of stoves.

> I have not, it is certain, been so circumstanced as to witness the operations of *many* of the newly invented steam kitchens and cooking apparatuses which the last twenty years have produced. but those which I have seen, have failed to give me satisfaction. To say the truth, the inventors of cast-iron kitchens seem to me to have had every other object in view, but that of promoting good cooking. It is certainly desirable and proper that every *possible* saving should be made in the consumption of fuel; but I am sure it is *not possible* to have cooking in perfection, without a proper degree of heat, and, as far as my observation has gone, meat cannot be well roasted unless it is before a good fire. [*A Lady*, pp. 31-32]

Frances Phipps tells us that the kitchen was the first room built in early American homes but the last one to change. The hearth, the basic utensils and even the recipes were essentially the same from the time the earliest Americans settled Plymouth until the mid-19th century. "It was not until industry followed the settlers' trails, until mills were constructed with furnaces to fire new and more powerful forges, that the iron cooking range with its built-in oven supplanted the colonial hearth."

When families moved to the towns and cities of Western Pennsylvania, stoves and many other items relating to food and its preparation were available—for a price. Meals became more sophisticated, entertainments more lavish. The local merchants carried luxuries undreamed of in earlier days—almonds and China tea, mustard, French brandy, coffee mills, and pewter plates. But the basic necessities for daily meals were still essentially the same—bread, meat, and vegetables. Women in the towns still cultivated gardens, preserved their vegetables, and dried their herbs. Just a mile or so out of town, they kept poultry, cows, and pigs, and made butter. It is true that not only were more resources available, but also more artisans to do work formerly done by both men and women. However, unless a family had substantial funds, they were forced to rely on their own energy and talent.

Baking bread was a never-ending task for the housewife, but in the towns, she had her choice of bakers if she preferred to purchase baked goods. Some experts, like Lydia Maria Child, cautioned against using professionals:

> Make your own bread and cake. Some people think it is just as cheap to buy of the baker and confectioner; but it is not half as cheap. True, it is more convenient; and therefore the rich are justifiable in employing them; but those who are under the necessity of being economical, should make convenience a secondary object. [Child, p. 9]

John May took an interest in bread making, and wrote down the recipe he obtained from his landlady, whose bread, he declared "is as good as any that I ever tasted." The instructions sound very vague to the modern bread baker; they called for taking "a piece of leaven of the bigness of her fist," pounding it and mixing it with three quarts of cold water; letting it stand until time to mix it; then draining the water to use the yeast. Next the "dough [is] mixed with tolerable warm water, and left to stand while the oven is heating. By this time the batch will have risen sufficiently." The landlady then put the dough in baskets and let them stand "a little time before they are put into the oven. If the right temperature is secured in the oven you are sure of a good batch of bread."

In 1810 a carpenter in Western Pennsylvania received $1.09 a day, a common laborer 82 cents. At the time beef cost 3 cents per pound, a flitch of venison, $1. Butter cost 14 cents a pound, eggs 5 cents a dozen.[McKnight, p. 84] These prices may have seemed reasonable to a "gentleman" with a private income, or to a professional man, a doctor or lawyer, but on a weekly salary of $6.54 or $4.92 and a family of five to feed, house, and clothe, there was little room for almonds and Madeira. A man's work day was sunrise to sunset, which left him virtually no time to work on his own home or small farm. Not until 1840 did the work day settle in at ten hours, after President Van Buren made that accommodation for the workmen at the Washington Navy Yard. The long work day required women to bear most of the household burden as in the past, and perhaps even to add some of the tasks her hard-working husband was unable to carry out, like caring for livestock or growing foodstuffs.

In 1810 families with average means—small merchants and skilled artisans —could afford to buy sugar (35 cents a pound) and salt ($1.35 a bushel). Pepper cost 30 cents a quarter pound, coffee, 58 cents a pound. Living on the elegant "Morganza" estate just outside of Washington, Pennsylvania, Margaret Bunyan Morgan undoubtedly supervised her cook and servant girls in the preparation of some of the more elegant recipes she recorded in her cookbook. Brandy peaches call for fruit, sugar syrup, and two pints of brandy. Plumb [*sic*] pudding requires raisins, citron, currants, brandy, spices, and 14 eggs. Honey cakes call for 7 pounds of "flower" and 4 pounds of honey. Roasting a 12-pound haunch of venison required three hours, and she suggests serving it with a gravy "with a deal of clarett and your Sweet Saus current Jelly or Cranberry."

Roasting a pig was a major undertaking, requiring cleaning the beast, stuffing the belly with bread crusts and herbs, and basting it first with water and then butter until it was half roasted. "When the eyes drop out it is done." In addition to the more complicated recipes, Margaret Bunyan Morgan wrote out instructions for pickling ham, using salt, beer, or an egg, and an eight-day recipe for cured beef.

Americans developed their own taste and cooking style based on what was available to them, and although their meals were essentially simple, they ate and drank well. Visitors from abroad found some of their eating habits difficult to understand in some instances and downright appalling in others. Mrs. Trollope reported her own prejudices with her usual lack of restraint, administering the *coup de grâce* to our national crop.

> They consume an extraordinary amount of bacon. Ham and beefsteaks appear morning, noon, and night. In eating, they mix things together with the strangest incongruity imaginable. I have seen eggs and oysters eaten together; the sepiternal ham with applesauce; beefsteak with stewed peaches; and salt fish with onions....They eat the Indian corn in a great variety of forms; sometimes it is dressed green, and eaten like peas; sometimes it is broken to pieces when dry, boiled plain and brought to the table like rice; this dish is called hominy. The flour of it is made into at least a dozen different sort of cakes; but in my opinion all bad. [Trollope, pp. 235-36]

Liquor flowed freely in Pittsburgh, sold in both licensed and unlicensed establishments, but despite sporadic attempts to form temperance societies, little impression was made on Pittsburgh's heavy drinkers—both men and women. An increasing number of brawls and street fights, as well as the rising number of dysfunctional families, encouraged the small groups of temperance workers to join together to form a substantial union, and in 1830 they began a major campaign to educate citizens on the evils of excessive drinking. Local clergymen joined the crusade as did many notable city leaders. Nationally known reformers came to Pittsburgh to speak—Wendell Phillips, Lucy Stone, and Abby Kelly, among others. The George Washington Hotel was a temperance hotel and another hotel owner who was converted to the cause replaced his stock of liquor with ice cream and lemonade. In 1841 nearly 6,000 men signed a pledge of abstinence. Temperance societies like the Washingtonians, the Marthas, and the Sons of Temperance organized parades and enlisted children into the Cadets of Temperance. Similar crusades were taking place throughout America, but with little effect on public policy. By 1850 few states had passed regulatory legislation. The Pennsylvania law was far weaker than the reformers would have liked, and little effort was made to enforce it.

The most remarkable development in the diet of Western Pennsylvanians was the rapidity with which a large variety of foods became increasingly available. The basic diet of bread, meat, and whiskey prevailed among the poorly paid laboring classes, but affluent professional men and merchants, as well as artisans with some disposable income had access to a seemingly endless stream of luxuries never before seen on their pantry shelves. In Pittsburgh in the 1790s housewives could purchase Hyson and Souchong tea; pepper, allspice, nutmegs, cinnamon, mace, cloves, and ginger; rice, chocolate, raisins, prunes, figs and juniper berries; Madeira, table wines from Portugal and France, Jamaica spirits, Holland gin, lime juice, and cherry bounce. A wife's marketing basket could be filled with a wide variety of vegetable seeds, including yellow, green, and "valentine" beans; peas, beets, parsnips, celery, cress, cucumbers, "spinage," sweet basil and summer savory. In 1800 Ormsby's stocked olives, anchovies, salmon, vanilla pods, and French and Spanish brandies. In December 1817 Mrs. Mercer advertised in the *Pittsburgh Gazette* that fresh oysters could be shipped from Philadelphia and New York throughout the winter. "Parties can be supplied, served up, either stewed, fresh, or in every other manner." The abundance of food was very much in keeping with the optimism of this frontier city, where the enterprising could make money and the future looked rosy indeed. §

HERBS—Aromatic, Culinary, and Medicinal, 1776-1850

Many of the common names for plants listed appear the way they were spelled in this period of time.

Sweet Yarrow
Marsh Mallow
Pimpernel, Poor Man's
    Weatherglass
Smallage
Virginia Snake-root
Wormwood
Common Mugwort
Celandine
Wormseed, Goosefoot,
    Mexican Tea
Carduus Benedictus,
    Blessed Thistle
Scurvy-grass
Ague-weed, Thoroughwort,
    Common Boneset
Gromwell
Pot Marjoram
Mandrake
Horehound
Opium Poppy
Rhubarb, True Turkey
Castor-oil Nut, Palma Christi,
    Castor Bean
Summer Savory
Winter Savory
Carolina Pink-root
Wood Betony, Woundwort
Common Thyme
Fenugreek
Stinging Nettle
Corn-sallad

A mid-19th-century engraving showing a sprayer being used to treat the soil against troublesome worms.

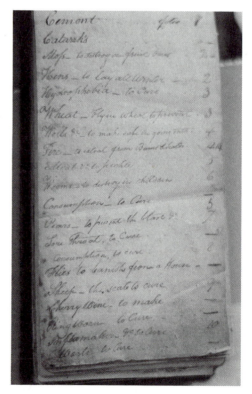

Contents page from "Receipts, Cures," c. 1845. HSWP Collection.

MATTERS OF HEALTH

Handwritten household books like Margaret Bunyan Morgan's usually devoted equal time to food recipes and medical remedies. Directions for gingerbread were apt to be placed cheek-by-jowl with instructions for making cough syrup. This made sense at a time when doctors were ill-trained and scarce, even in the towns, and wives and mothers had to make do with home remedies and the advice of neighborhood "grannies" wise in the uses of herbs and medicines.

If the trip across the Alleghenies was difficult, imagine what it must have been like to make that journey if you were ill. Elizabeth Van Horne and her family transported her seriously ill father across the mountains to Pittsburgh. Just east of Harrisburg she wrote, "through fatigue with travelling and his disordered state of body my Father was taken with faintness and talked unintelligibly which alarmed us very much." Once in the town they sent for a barber, whose profession of cutting hair was supplemented by his knowledge of bleeding and other surgical procedures. Her father was cupped, a bloodletting method requiring that an incision be made and the blood drawn out by means of a vacuum. She wrote, "We are since astonished at the change in him he seemed to enjoy his days ride in observing the buildings, the Soil, the timber &c." Later she marveled at his fortitude:

> *"...a mixed decoction of about all of our roots and herbs, to be administered, as he said, with the hope that some of the ingredients would hit the disease."*
>
> *—a frontier doctor*

Oh! my friends, you can have no conception of what we suffer in mind to see him so fatigued, so weak, and to lay on the floor, so restless getting up and down without a murmur or complaint....This morning he is confined to his bed....We are detained at an indifferent house—far from a home or any friends—not a Dr in 8 miles nor a Town near that we can obtain any thing necessary that should be needed....[Finally reaching Pittsburgh] his soul took its flight (we trust) to happier regions. [Van Horne, pp. 14-15,17]

Three days after the burial, the grieving family continued their journey to Ohio, having been shown "friendship, kindness, and simpathy" in Pittsburgh.

When it came to health and well-being, living on the frontier was a mixed blessing. The simple, outdoor life with plenty of exercise, plain food, fresh air, and lack of urban stress was a plus. On the minus side was even less knowledge than in cities of rudimentary sanitary procedures, or the manner in which disease was spread. Bishop Asbury wrote that he visited a cabin where the inhabitants "were but one remove from savages," and missionary David McClure noted that while lodging at a Dutchman's home, he couldn't sleep because "such swarms of fleas from the blankets attacked us on all quarters."

The monotonous diet was high in red meat and bread, low or totally lacking in vegetables and fruits. Malnutrition was common, lack of access to medication, fear of Indians, crop failures, and isolation took their toll. Infant mortality was high, and although an adult who reached age 21 could expect to live into his or her mid-60s, one out of every five white children would not survive from birth to maturity. The cemeteries were filled with small graves, and a family counted itself lucky if a child lived beyond the age of two.

Small wonder, then, that a housewife's recipe book was filled with home-made nostrums and concoctions designed to cure everything from worms to cancer. Prominent as one reads through the pages is the assurance that everything is going to be all right. "A sure cure" is a common notation. "Absolutely guaranteed to work" is another, as is "never known to fail." If the medicine did not do the job, perhaps positive thinking would.

Housewives relied heavily on herbs and other local plants to stock their medicine cabinet, some of their knowledge doubtless gleaned from Native Americans. "Take a large handful of camimile [*sic*] flowers," Margaret Bunyan Morgan noted in "A Receit for a Cough," and "an equil quantity of white balsam. Boil them in a quart of water until it is wasted to a pint. Strain it and put to it a pint of brown sugar lett it boil to a Syrup." This was undoubtedly preferable to another "cure for a Sore-Throat, never known to fail."

> Take a small piece of allum [*sic*] in your mouth and let it dissolve, spitting out your spittle untlll it has all dissolved a little before you go to bed, without rinsing your mouth. There is some quality in the allum that draws the humour from the throat and the patient will find himself much better next morning—repeat if necessary.

Settlers suffered from a variety of diseases with the generic designation "fevers." The ague or "shakes" induced alternate chills and fever, severe headaches, and muscle pains, sometimes lasting for weeks and leaving the patient weak and listless. Mothers forced to tend to their children or husband added these exhausting nursing tasks to their regular work and often became ill themselves. Modern medical experts believe that these fevers were probably typhoid or malaria. Water supplies were suspect, drainage and disinfection unknown. Some fevers were thought to come from "noxious vapors" rising from the swamps, and although the mosquito was not identified as the culprit until much later, settlers were getting close to the truth when they avoided the wet marshlands, especially at night. Other causes believed to be responsible were decaying refuse, grief, worry, lack of sleep, too much thinking, and unripe fruit.

Most families had their own cures for the ague which were passed along to neighbors and friends. The remedy suggested in one cookbook was:

> A Frankencense plaster, in the form of a heart, to be placed before the fire and an entire nutmeg to be grated over it. This done, the plaster to be applied to the pit of the stomach, with the point of the plaster upward.

Dr. Jonas Rishel writing in *The Indian Physician* believed all fevers originated either from external cold or "inhaling a miasma or contagious vapour." He advised opening the pores and inducing perspiration by administering vast quantities of tea, emetics, and draughts of alkali. He noted that sometimes "the bile is carried in the mass of blood, to the extremities, and gives the skin a yellow tinge. From this appearance, the yellow fever has derived its name." In other fevers, he explained, when the blood flows incorrectly, it remains in spots which turn dark, hence the spotted fever.

In Pittsburgh, city boosters were quick to point out the small incidence of fevers compared with those in rural areas. Historian Neville Craig declared, "As to miasma, there is not and never has been any thing of the kind; probably no city in the country is more healthy than Pittsburgh and Allegheny." He also defended the dark clouds over the industrial city and wrote that the gases and smoke emanating from the factory stacks had a salutory effect on the citizens' health.

> The combustion annually of ten millions of bushels of bituminous coal fills the atmosphere with carburetted hydrogen, sulphurous gas, and the all-pervading impalpable dust of carbon. The smoke is thickest in the calm, cool and foggy morning of autumn. It is anti-miasmatic; and hence it is, that formerly the natural ponds, and latterly the foul and stagnant artificial basins, have never generated remittent or intermittent fever....Strangers with weak lungs, for a while, find their coughs aggravated by the smoke, but nevertheless asthmatic patients have found relief in breathing it. [Craig, pp. 307-9]

Title page from The Indian Physician.

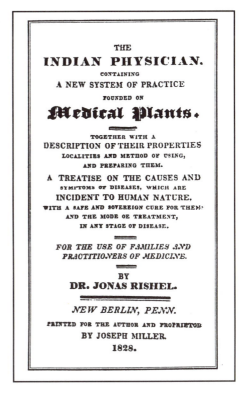

THE
INDIAN PHYSICIAN.
CONTAINING
A NEW SYSTEM OF PRACTICE
FOUNDED ON
Medical Plants.

TOGETHER WITH A
DESCRIPTION OF THEIR PROPERTIES
LOCALITIES AND METHOD OF USING,
AND PREPARING THEM.
A TREATISE ON THE CAUSES AND
SYMPTOMS OF DISEASES, WHICH ARE
INCIDENT TO HUMAN NATURE.
WITH A SAFE AND SOVEREIGN CURE FOR THEM;
AND THE MODE OE TREATMENT,
IN ANY STAGE OF DISEASE.

*FOR THE USE OF FAMILIES AND
PRACTITIONERS OF MEDICINE.*

BY
DR. JONAS RISHEL.

NEW BERLIN, PENN.
PRINTED FOR THE AUTHOR AND PROPRIETOR
BY JOSEPH MILLER.
1828.

It is hardly surprising that rheumatism and lumbago were common complaints. Settlers were frequently exposed to the wet and cold, and because deerskin clothing absorbed water so easily and stayed damp a long time, it was not the best protection against inclement weather. Handwritten household books abound in solutions for these painful afflictions.

Dr. Wainman's Recipe for a Lumbago or pain in the back.

> The best sweet oil   4 oz.
> Spirits or Sal Animonac   3/4 oz.
> Tinchure of Opium   1/4 oz.
> Mix'd well together.
> Rubb'd well in with a softhand.

A Mrs. Zorke, recommended three parts of Sal Volatile and one part volatile Tincture of Quiacum, with a teaspoonful to be taken every night in a little cold water. Seneca Oil, that great nostrum touted by peddlers and traveling medicine men, was pure petroleum, free for the asking as it oozed out of the ground. Thaddeus Harris observed it could also be found floating on spring water, skimmed off and used "as an infallible cure" for chilblains and rheumatism.

When rheumatism was accompanied by fever, bloodletting was the appropriate remedy. As bizarre and brutal as this practice sounds today, it was a common and well-respected treatment among many practitioners until well into the 19th century. While physicians advised this cure, others, including midwives, barbers, and farriers, were also called upon to perform the operation, using a lancet and sometimes a suction pump to draw the blood out, or by applying leeches (worms that live in water and suck blood).

Bleeding was the remedy for a long list of ailments, from fever to epilepsy, from sunstroke to pneumonia. When in doubt, the doctor might well draw a pint of blood. Some medical experts decried this treatment, however, and Dr. Rishel declared that "the fatal and disastrous consequences arising from it daily, ought to convince those who use such unnatural means that they are not only squandering the most precious fluid, but life itself." He was especially distressed at the practice of periodic bleeding as a preventive measure:

Those persons, who from a notion of preventing diseases, suffer themselves to be bled regularly, once, twice or oftener in a year, whether they are indisposed or not, ought to be informed that they are using means which, if persisted in, are likely prematurely to bring upon them those very diseases which they profess so much to dread. [Rishel, p. 68]

Children were especially vulnerable to wounds, burns, and insect bites, and most mothers had a sure-fire remedy for whatever ailed their children. One recommended cure for a rusty nail wound involved the use of raw beets, while another for insect and rattlesnake bites required salt and eggs. An unusual remedy for the bite of a rattlesnake or copperhead called for the belly of a live toad to be applied to the wounded part. The frog would soon expire and be covered all over with livid spots, another "certain cure." Or the wound could be "emerged" in mud or covered with a mud plaster to be repeated every ten minutes. "Never known to fail."

Colic could be relieved with a decoction of cardamon seeds, sliced rhubarb, strong brandy, and essence of peppermint. And according to many frontier accounts, worms were thought to be ever-present in children, so that remedies for this ailment abounded. The most common cure was a solution of salt, sometimes mixed with the scrapings from a pewter spoon. Sulphate of iron, or copperas, was another possibility, and once again, mothers devised their own variations.

To destroy Worms in Children

Take the tops of Fern when at full growth: burn them to ashes, make those ashes into balls about the size of a hen's egg & lay them by for use.
When you have occasion to administer it, put one of those balls into the fire, let it remain there until it is red hot—Take one teaspoon from the middle of the inside of the ball when cold, mix this with as much molasses or any other sweetening and give it to the patient—has never been known to fail.

John May collected odd bits of information on his travels, including his landlady's "sovereign cure" for worms.

Take a half-pint of live angle-worms, put them in a thin linen bag, and sew them up. Then put them, while yet alive, on the child's stomach. There let them remain six hours; then remove them to the navel; there let them remain for the same time; then remove them to the bottom of the belly, for six hours; then take them away, and the child will never be troubled with worms again. [May, p. 41]

(facing page) Illustration from Dilworth's
A New Guide to the English Tongue.
(right) From "Receipts, Cures," c. 1845.
HSWP Collection.

With open fires a severe hazard, children frequently suffered burns on many parts of their body. Joseph Doddridge recalled that common remedies in his childhood were poultices of Indian meal or scraped potatoes, while roasted turnips were also used, as was slippery elm bark.

Frostbite was treated with chicken fat, applied with a woolen cloth; cut radishes were applied to warts, raw turnips or rotten apples to running sores. Mullen leaves relieved hives; the "itch" was treated with a salve of lard, sulphur, and brimstone. A "universal and infallible Salve" was made with "one pound of good sound Tobacco" boiled with a quart of good "Cyder" until reduced, then filtered through a "fine piece of linnen" and beeswax added.

Herbs were grown in every frontier garden and utilized more as medicines than as enhancers of flavor. Each herb had its own special properties, and frontier housewives knew them all. Burdock leaves reduced fever, as did Virginia snakeroot, by causing the patient to perspire. Foxglove (still useful as a source of digitalis) was used for heart problems, while sweet fern and goldenrod tea cured bowel trouble. Cedar berries strengthened a weak spine, jimson weed was good for asthma, catnip tea for colic, boneset tea cured the ague, and grapevine sap judiciously applied caused hair to grow on bald heads. Lobelia tea was an excellent cathartic. Angelica helped digestion, elecampane was "an antidote to all humors," and winter clover tea "gives much relief to women in travail." Red henbane was useful in treating the bite of a mad dog, while green wheat or motherwort tea usually afforded relief from "hysterick passions," a disease "most common to females of delicate minds, and irritable nerves."

Liwwät Böke had her own list of uses for herbs. "Roots of Chinese briar and sassafras we use frequently for cleansing the blood," she wrote. "We use the caustic and cleansing ability...of the roots of the white nettle...to clean old sores and boils and festering proudflesh." May apples and ginseng had purifying qualities, while white carrots were good for stomach and diarrhea disorders.

Sampler, signed and dated by Elizabeth Keneby, 1805. HSWP Collection.

Many home remedies were a mixed bag of common sense, experience, superstition, and rumored witchcraft. Unexplained illness or death and odd behavior of any kind would raise eyebrows and start the whispers about witches. The latter, or "some supernatural agency of a malignant kind," were often thought to be responsible for diseases of childrens' internal organs, such as dropsy of the brain and rickets, about which little or nothing was known.

To prevent witches from entering their homes, some Germans laid brooms across their thresholds or nailed horseshoes to the front door in a particular pattern. Special potions were given to those suspected of having been bewitched, and such bizarre items as children's urine and silver bullets were employed in attempts to rid the home of witches.

Even when witchcraft was not suspected, superstition played a large part in the prevention and cure of disease. Doddridge tells us that erysipelas, an acute inflammation of the skin, was thought to be cured by the blood of a black cat, with the result that it was hard to find one whose ears and tail had not been clipped in the service of its owner. Some children wore a chicken breast bone tied around their neck to prevent whooping cough, and until well after 1800, youngsters were sent off to school wearing amulets filled with foul-smelling herbs to ward off a variety of diseases. If a child could procure the middle toe of an owl with which to pick his teeth, he would never have a toothache. Rubbing a sprain on the first Friday after the full moon was a certain cure, and a goiter would disappear if the neck were rubbed three times with the hand of a corpse. If a boy had a pain anywhere, he could be cured by putting a buckwheat cake on his head, and if he were homesick, salt was put in the hems of his trousers and he was made to look up a chimney.

Nanny tea, a concoction made with sheep dung, allegedly brought out the rash of measles. A whooping cough remedy was to take the child to a flour mill and "give it a good shaking up in the hopper." Rubbing a child's jaws against the side of a hog trough was a sure cure for the mumps. One old lady reminisced that as a girl, she was told to cure asthma by cutting off a lock of her hair, boring a hole in a sweet apple tree, inserting her lock, and plugging up the hole.

> In some reminisences…it is told just how high to bore the hole and when to expect results.…Judging from the number of persons who tried this treatment, we must conclude that phthisic [asthma] was formerly a very prevalant complaint, especially among girls. This conclusion is also strengthened by the statement of a lumberman who had been cutting timber all through this region for the past thirty or forty years, and who says he has found many a tree with the tell-tale hole and plug in it. [Galley, pp. 380-81]

Consumption (the term used for tuberculosis) and cancer were common, and the recommended cures varied. One of the household books noted that a consumptive cough could be cured by stewing together a pint of molasses, six pennyworth of flower brimstone, and the same amount of flower "Liquerish," together with a lump of fresh butter. The patient was to take a spoonful before meals and whenever he or she coughed. Another remedy, guaranteeing the restoration of perfect health, recommended collecting the dew from camomile and letting the patient drink a small quantity every morning.

To cure cancer, a strong decoction of the herb pipsissiway must be made and the patient must drink freely of the tea as well as allowing external applications with a soft cloth which "can't be too often applied. A certain cure." An appended note indicated that the household book owner didn't know what pipsissiway was, but thought it "worth an inquiry."

Many of these remedies seem amusing and quaint, but it is well to remember that settlers were above all pragmatists. In the absence of doctors, mothers clung to remedies that had been known to work on somebody, somewhere. Perhaps the patient had recovered of his own accord, but perhaps it was the prescription she had administered that effected a cure. A frontier doctor wrote of his early experience, "My partner made what he called 'Devil's Broth' —a mixed decoction of about all of our roots and herbs, to be administered, as he said, with the hope that some of the ingredients would hit the disease."

Frontier mothers must have lived in a state of apprehension bordering on terror as they watched their children become ill, knowing there was so little to be done. Ordinary contagious diseases like measles and mumps were generally allowed to run their course, but an epidemic of a serious disease such as smallpox would carry off thousands of children and adults and disfigure many others. Although vaccination against this disease was available as early as 1731, many religious figures opposed it as "a distrust of God's ever-ruling care," and most people failed to take advantage of this preventive measure.

Smallpox and tuberculosis were essentially city problems, often contracted through close contact in confined quarters, as was cholera, a fierce, rapidly spreading disease that could carry people off in a matter of hours. Marked by violent dysentery and dehydration, cholera was much to be feared, and the epidemics in New York and Philadephia in 1832 greatly alarmed

Page from Müller's recipes and remedies in German and English, 1826. HSWP Collection.

the citizens of Pittsburgh. A group of ministers assembled and recommended "a day of fasting, humiliation and prayer that God avert the danger threatening the country from Asiatic cholera." Ordinances were passed requiring strict sanitary measures, but on October 22, 1832, a man from Cincinnati died in Pittsburgh and the disease spread rapidly, despite all the precautions. Four days later there were 5 cases and 3 deaths. Although the disease was checked, some 35 people died within the next two months. In 1833 cholera reappeared, with 17 cases and 8 deaths reported in two months. The Board of Health and the doctors were at odds both over methods of treatment and ways of reporting cases, and the seriousness of the situation was played down. Hydrants were turned on all over the city to clean the streets, and a temporary hospital was set up. Although 75 deaths were reported, physicians believed that the newspapers had supressed the actual numbers and given inaccurate figures.

For the next few years, cholera returned to Pittsburgh. In 1848 there were 10 deaths in one day; business was suspended, streets were empty, and many people left town. In 1849 between 150 and 200 died, and in 1854, the worst year, it was estimated that 1,000 died of this dread disease.[Diller, pp. 178-83]

Some notion of the anxiety which gripped many families during the epidemics is gleaned from one of the manuscript household books. In addition to a compilation of many cholera cures, it includes newspaper clippings, one with a listing of cholera deaths in cities other than Pittsburgh. Some are in German, some in English, including this one from the *National Gazette* of June 1833.

> The most severe fasting—much drinking of cold water—much washing with cold water. In short, a complete inundation of the whole human body with cold water, both inwardly and outwardly.

When doctors were scarce, midwives were called upon to do more than just deliver children. "Because people know that I am a midwife," Liwwät Böke wrote, "I get many questions. The usual cause of the sicknesses and of the unsound outlook is that the people here do not use enough soap." Many of her neighbors scoffed at her, calling the advice "Dumb stuff! …until they are dead," she said. "Unlearned, filthy people, ever such simpletons." She preached the doctrine of hand washing before meals, before holding the children, after feeding the stock and after going to the outhouse. She warned against going barefoot and cautioned wives to cook meat thoroughly. Rid the house of flies, ants, and lice, she said, and when the throat is sore, gargle with hot water every two hours. Above all, drink only fresh spring water, never stagnant or dirty water, and "every few days, wash our bodies with soap, back and front, man and woman, every child."

An unusual story of one woman's achievement in medical matters was that of Mrs. Eunice Sprague, who died in 1814 at the age of 82. Her husband had been a doctor, and after his death, she apparently took matters into her own hands. "She was a worthy lady, prompt, cheerful and successful.…her obstetrical practice as late as 1810 surpassed that of any physician in this portion of

Pennsylvania." No matter how long or fatiguing the journey might be, "this sturdy and faithful woman charged one dollar for services rendered, although a larger fee was never refused if any one was able or rich enough to offer it." Older people spoke of "Granny Sprague" not only as a successful midwife but as a practitioner of "the healing art among children." She had no formal training, but was known as Mrs. Doctor Sprague.

Although the first medical schools in the United States were founded in the 18th century in large urban centers like Philadelphia and Boston, young men living in Western Pennsylvania who wanted to study medicine usually apprenticed themselves to a practicing physician. This was a mutually agreeable arrangement, since the physicians were overworked and the apprentice not only learned about medicine but about surgery and dentistry as well. He also blacked boots, cared for the physician's horses, chopped wood, learned the ways of bleeding and applying leeches, followed the doctor on his rounds, and read whatever medical books were available. After a suitable period, he traveled to the East to attend a series of lectures at a medical school, and when these were completed, he could hang out his shingle and accept patients.

The life of a doctor could be grueling: long hours, difficult journeys through the forests in rain and snow, across flooded creeks, with no guarantee that he could help the patient at the end of his journey. An early frontier doctor wrote:

> When I commenced my practice I had to ride on horseback. My field extended all through and over Jefferson, Forest, Elk and the western part of Clearfield counties. I have traveled a circuit of one hunded miles a day....remedies were crude and drastic; instruments few, imperfect, and clumsy; yet I tied arteries, set broken bones, amputated limbs, saved lives. [Fletcher, pp. 429-30]

Despite the difficulties of practicing medicine in late-18th-century frontier towns and villages, some physicians managed to live very comfortably indeed. Nathaniel Bedford, for example, the first doctor to settle permanently in Pittsburgh around 1765, owned a beautiful house on Liberty Avenue. He lived like an English lord, with servants, hunting dogs, and other luxuries. He married Jane Ormsby, daughter of one of Pittsburgh's most successful merchants, and was active in civic and church affairs. When his wife died, he withdrew from practice and married her lady's maid.

Peter Mowry, born in Pittsburgh in 1770, was apprenticed to Dr. Bedford at age 14 "to be taught the Science and Art of Medicine and Surgery." He spent his entire life in Pittsburgh and was renowned as a man of distinction. He advised other would-be practitioners to gain hospital experience. "God help the quack," he wrote, "who with little knowledge and much impudence rushes in where conscientious men fear to enter."

Andrew Richardson began practicing in Pittsburgh in 1798, and was active in many civic matters, including the delivery of the Fourth of July Oration in 1801.

He was known for his excellent medical library, his high collar, stock (a neck-cloth), and gold-headed cane.

Physicians often took out advertisements in the newspapers, some in the form of modest cards, others, more elaborate, extolling their extensive experience. The *Pittsburgh Gazette* of December 7, 1810, for example, carried the following:

> F. Pennington, Physician, surgeon and accoucher from old England. Near forty years extensive practice, 12 of which was spent in London with all the advantages to be derived from attending the different hospitals and the lectures of the first men of the ages, encourage F. Pennington to hope that he may render himself helpful to those persons who may make choice of his services. The accouchment of females and a strict attention to the diseases peculiar to the sex, have employed a great part of his studies for many years.

Most settlers believed that they could not afford to pay a doctor and this, coupled with their profound distrust of medicine and surgery, meant that many physicians were paid very little or nothing at all. Traveler Johann David Schoepf, who visited Bedford in 1783, wrote that:

> Dr. Peters....boasted that he had on his book for a year's praxix almost 200 Pd. Pennsylv. Current, but unfortunately cannot collect any money from the people, that being a scarce article in the mountains, and he had no use for what they bring in kind. [Harpster, pp. 137-38]

One early practitioner announced his fees as 25 to 50 cents for a city visit; a country visit, 25 cents a mile; and a fee of $5.00 for an obstetrics visit. Letters from Dr. Malthus A. Ward, one of Kittanning's first doctors, reveal his anxiety not only about money but about his ability to adequately serve his patients.

> I have been here just one month & although there is another physician (truly a poor one) in the place, I find that not-withstanding my want of many necessary articles of medicine and medical apparatus (I have not yet so much as a mortar) I have taken in cash for small jobs as extracting dent, etc. $5.68, and charged on book $37. My business is daily increasing. It is indeed wonderful how highly the "wee Yankee doctor" is esteemed. I fear nothing so much as their high expectations of his skill will be suddenly cut short & his real ignorance betrayed. [Barlow, p. 19]

Several months later he wrote that he had treated a young man who broke both thighs, which ought to have brought a good sum, "but his father is poor and I shall hardly get much." As the year progressed, he informed his friend he has done about $700 in business for the year, but "The times have been so hard that I have been able to collect very little money." He had decided to remain in Pennsylvania, however, since "here I am pretty sure of making a living tho' not a fortune quickly."

Professional dentistry was slow to arrive on the frontier, and do-it-yourself tooth care was the popular method of dealing with painful toothaches. Liwwät Böke wrote,"I have extracted many teeth with string and pliers. St. John (her village) is almost toothless." According to an old settler, heroic methods were endured by some, including the practice of "shooting it out."

> One end of a strong hempen string was tied to the aching tooth, and the other end to a notched bullet, which was placed in the barrel of a flint-lock musket loaded with an extra charge of powder. When all was ready, the desperate man caught hold of the gun and pulled the trigger. Out flew the tooth from the bleeding jaw and away bounded the musket several feet. [Fletcher, p. 432]

Slowly dentists began to set up practice in the towns and cities, and in 1825, one E. Merritt advertised in the *Pittsburgh Gazette* of July 15, 1825, that all operations on the teeth would be performed with the greatest care. "From his experience in setting Artificial Teeth," his ad explained, "he flatters himself that he will receive a reasonable share of public patronage." He also sold a "celebrated dentifrice" of his own making, guaranteed to polish the teeth and harden the gums when spongy.

Many doctors and dentists owned apothecary shops, mixing and dispensing their own medicines. Dr. Andrew Richardson had "medical stores" in his office, stocking Asthmatic Elixir, Glauber's Salts, liquorice [*sic*] juice and Mercurial Pills. By the beginning of the 19th century, dozens of advertisements crowded the newspapers, extolling the virtues of a bewildering array of patent medicines. In 1809 you could buy Sing's Patent Itch Ointment and Dr. Robertson's Patent Wine Bitters ("recommended for restoring weak constitutions, cleansing and strengthening the stomach, and increasing the appetite"). By 1810 someone named Lee advertised "a sovereign ointment to cure the itch" as well as anti-bilious pills "for headache, foul stomach and removing superfluous bile." By 1812 his same anti-bilious pills were also taking care of pains in the back and lassitude; indeed, the list of medicines Lee advertised was a full column long, including worm-destroying lozenges, Indian Vegetable Specific for venereal ailments, essence and extract of mustard for rheumatism, Infallible Ague and Fever drops, eye water, corn plaster, and, as some merchants were wont to say, many other items too tedious to mention.

In 1813 Dr. Robertson ("grandson of the late Dr. Robertson of Edinburg") took out virtual full page ads, not only listing his medicines but describing symptoms and suggesting courses of treatment—all, of course, involving his medications. Vegetable Nervous Cordial "is confidently recommended, as the most efficacious medicine, for the speedy relief and cure of all nervous complaints....hysteric fits...various complaints resulting from secret impropiety of youth and dissipated habits, residence in warm climates, the immoderate use of tea....disease peculiar to females at a certain period of life...barrenness, etc." Most of these medicines were worthless, and it is easy to visualize cabinets stacked with expensive and useless medicines, purchased in the ever-elusive search for cures and reassurance that the next one would indeed be infallible.

Until the first hospitals were built in the mid-19th century, the sick were nursed at home, almost always by the women of the house, and well into the century commercial cookbooks included a section on invalid cookery. Mrs. Child, writing in *The American Frugal Housewife,* recommended gruel, made with boiling water and Indian [corn] meal; arrow-root jelly, beef tea, made by broiling a tender steak and pouring hot water over it and letting it stand "to soak the goodness out of it," and calf's foot jelly ("boil four feet in a gallon of water"). Apple water, made by pouring boiling water on roasted apples, was recommended when "the stomach is too weak to bear broth."

Catharine Beecher, author of the *Domestic Receipt-Book* (1850), cautioned the bedside attendant to "have everything you use very sweet and clean.... Always have a shawl in hand, also a clean towel, [and] a clean handkerchief." She also provided directions for a variety of jellies and gruels, but her invalids could count on a more interesting choice of foods, with recipes for cranberry tea, spiced chocolate, codfish relish, and "A Great Favorite with Invalids" calling for "brisk cider" with sugar, nutmeg, and toasted bread.

Perhaps the most provocative observation about the settlers' health came from Johann David Schoepf, who found that "the country is healthy and supports no Doctor, because the people are not often sick; and they are sick less because they have no doctor." [Harpster, pp. 131-32] §

Mourning Art Sampler, signed and dated by Harriett Lenfesty (age ten), 1823. HSWP Collection. Mourning art was very popular in the early 19th century and the death of George Washington in 1799 is credited with initiating the vogue in America. This design was based on the print "Lived Respected & Fear'd—Died Lamented & Rever'd," published in 1800.

Log Cabin Meeting House.

A Meeting House of 2nd Class.

A Meeting House of 3d Class.

First Presbyterian Church, Pittsburg, Pa.

From Joseph Smith's Old Redstone: Historical Sketches of Western Presbyterianism, *1854.*

MIND & SPIRIT

Margaret Bunyan Morgan recorded her recipes in a firm and legible hand, but her spelling tended to be both phonetic and idiosyncratic. For pumpkin she wrote "pumcan," "surip" for syrup, "eaquil" for equal, "neight" for night, "drean" for drain, etc. This was hardly surprising, since in the late 18th century most parents believed that it was a waste of time and money to educate their daughters beyond the simplest of skills in reading, writing, and arithmetic, and some considered even those accomplishments of little value, since the girls were to become wives and mothers and would not even need that much formal education. Everything a woman needed to know, they believed, could be learned at home.

This was, of course, partially true, as youngsters in rural communities—both boys and girls—began to help with household and farm chores at an early age. The older children tended the younger ones while mother and father worked at their own tasks, and each child had other duties as well—chopping and splitting wood, carrying water, grating and pounding corn, driving the cows, and helping with milking. Even four- and five-year-old girls were taught to hold a needle and to knit, and responsibilities could increase quickly. Susan Blunt recalled that when she was around ten, her mother let her go about a mile away for a week to help out a neighbor's family which included twin girls and an elderly invalid. She had complete charge of the household, getting up at five o'clock to bring water from a distant well, then she "boiled potatoes, fried pork and made coffee" for breakfast, helped the girls off to school, took care of the old man, then "cleered away…put on some stew for dinner…made some biscuits and baked them in the tin baker before the fire." In return she received about 15 cents which she used "to buy a calico apron."[Larkin, pp. 33-34]

"You are training young minds whose plastic texture will receive and retain every impression you make…to pass again to the next generation."
—Catharine Beecher

Girls enjoyed some freedom from gender restraints in their early years. A significant number of autobiographies of Americans from different regions of the country record their memories of boys and girls playing together as children, and girls being allowed the freedom to fish and trap, dam streams, swim in the rivers in summer and skate in the winter. "I often climbed trees and tore my clothes," wrote an Iowa farm girl, reminiscing about her youth. She recalls playing "I Spy" and mumblety-peg, and "[we] skinned up trees...climbed on and jumped off the stable roof."[MacLeod, p. 100] Daniel Drake remembered that in his Kentucky boyhood, boys and girls "mingled together....Swinging by grape vines was, in general, a joint amusement, as was hunting nuts, haws, paw-paws, & other fruits, when in season."[Drake, p. 148]

But as adolescence approached, the door to freedom slammed shut, and young ladies were expected to learn the household skills that would enable them to manage their own home and keep their husbands and children in healthful comfort. On her way westward, Mary Ellen Todd exulted in learning a new skill when her father taught her to drive the family wagon.

> How my heart bounded a few days later, when I chanced to hear my father say to my mother, "Do you know that Mary Ellen is beginning to crack the whip?" And how it fell again, when mother replied, "I'm afraid it isn't a very lady-like thing for a girl to do." After this, while I felt a secret joy in being able to have the power that sets things going, there also was a sense of shame over this new accomplishment. [West, p. 142]

A young Indiana girl recalled "that most trying and uncomfortable age, when physicially I was almost a woman, but at heart, was still a child." Another wrote that her "happy-go-lucky, carefree childhood ended at 13. In memory's book, that leaf wears a margin of black."[MacLeod, p. 105]

In rural areas girls attended school for a few years whenever one was available. Schools were established either by parents who understood the importance of education and banded together with like-minded families to find a school teacher, or by religious groups hoping to combine secular and religious instruction for their pupils. Children living on isolated farms or in small communities were sent off to school only when there was one within reasonable walking distance, and if they could be spared from home chores and farm duties. Consequently, most schools were in session during the winter months, but rarely during the spring and summer when farm work was heavy. Since not all children were able to attend classes, some parents provided whatever instruction they could at home, but large numbers of youngsters failed to receive formal instruction of any sort.

The schoolhouse was usually a duplicate of a simple settler's cabin—logs, rough spaces for windows covered with oiled paper, puncheon floors, and crude desks. Books and materials were scarce and students made do with whatever was at hand. Standard texts included *Dilworth's Spelling Book,* a *New System of Mercantile Arithmetic, The New England Primer,* and the Bible. Many settlers were able to read, but writing was of less importance to them—except for learning to sign their own name. Penmanship was a luxury few schools provided.

Paper was expensive and making goose quill pens and tree bark ink was time-consuming, so that lessons were often written with charcoal on smooth shingles.

The competence of the teachers varied widely. The most knowledgeable were provided by the church, usually ministers or young men studying for that profession, beneficiaries of an education superior to that of the average schoolmaster. Often an itinerant young man would arrive in a community, offer his services as a schoolmaster, stay a few months and drift away. Daniel Drake was taught by "a Yankee!....He might have done me considerable good; but in the midst of business he perpetrated a crime and ran away!"[Drake, pp. 146-52] As a result of the practical problems involved in attending classes regularly, many students were forced to postpone their schooling until their teens or even beyond. It was not unusual to find 5- and 6-year-old girls sharing the classroom with strapping boys of 19 or 20. If a young man decided to proceed further in his studies, he usually left home for boarding school or, if he were fortunate, a nearby private academy, where he could pursue Latin and Greek or advanced mathematics. If he chose law or medicine as his profession, he apprenticed himself to a lawyer or doctor for a period of several years. Meanwhile his sisters and female friends remained at home and pursued their daily tasks, which, judging by this excerpt from the diary of a young girl in the 1790s, grew increasingly arduous.

> Fix'd gown for Prude,—Mend Mother's Riding-hood, Spun short thread,—Fix'd two gowns for Welsh's girls,—Carded tow,—Spun linen,—Worked on Cheesebasket,—Hatchel'd flax with Hannah, we did 51 lbs, apiece,—Pleated and ironed,—Read a sermon of Dodridge's,—Spooled a piece—Milked the cows,—Spun linen, did 50 knots,—Made a broom of Guinea wheat straw,—Spun thread to whiten,—Set a Red dye,—Had two scholars from Mrs. Taylor's.... Spun harness twine,—Scoured the pewter,—Ague in my face. [Holliday, p. 116]

As the new century approached, more attention was paid to the need to educate women—not so that they could take their place beside men in the world of business, medicine or law, but rather to ensure that the next generation of children would be adequately prepared for life. Dr. Benjamin Rush set the tone in his *Thoughts*

Frontispiece to a popular primary reader,
The Child's Guide, *published in 1833.*

on Female Education, in a speech he delivered in Philadelphia in 1787, when he called for women to direct their education toward their obligations as wives and mothers, nurturing young minds and bodies toward their full potential in the expanding republic. His suggestions were practical: who better to raise healthy, morally responsible children, he asked, than the one person who was always there—mother—while father was off conducting the business of the world. To be an effective guardian of the family, he reasoned, a woman must prepare herself to be agreeable, and a worthy companion for her husband. Among other things, this required learning to run a proper household, and above all, setting an example of Christian charity for the entire family.

Advice books and articles dwelt heavily upon this theme, with such influential people as Sarah Josepha Hale, the editor of Godey's *The Lady's Book*, suggesting that "the more real knowledge she possesses of the great principles of morals, philosophy and human happiness, the more importance she will attach to her station, and the name of a 'good housekeeper.'"[Hale, p. 127] Lydia Maria Child declared, "The difficulty is, education does not usually point the female heart to its only true resting place…" which she believed was "that dear English word '*home.*'"[Child, p. 96] And Catharine Beecher eloquently described the influence women can exert in the lives of their children.

> You are training young minds whose plastic texture will receive and retain every impression you make, who will imitate your feelings, taste, habits, and opinions, and will transmit what they receive from you to their children, to pass again to the next generation, and then to the next, until a *whole nation* will have received its character and destiny from your hands! [Beecher, p. 279]

On November 11, 1786, the following detailed advertisement appeared in the *Pittsburgh Gazette.*

A Boarding Day School for Young Ladies will be opened on Wednesday the 15th instant by Mrs. PRIDE, in the house where John Wilson formerly lived, behind his stone house. Where they will be taught the following branches of needle work, viz.

Plain work	Fringing
Coloured ditto	Dresden
Flowering	Tabouring and
Lace, both by the	Embroidery
bobin and needle	

Also reading, English, and knitting required.

Illustration from Jenkins's Art of Writing, *1813.*

Pennsylvania legislators had wrangled over providing public education to all children beginning in 1776, but did not reach a satisfactory resolution until 1834. However, while increasing educational opportunities became available in towns and cities, the same pattern of private and/or church schools prevailed until the public education law was finally implemented.

By 1817 the advertisements for schools devoted to the education and social development of young ladies filled the pages of the *Pittsburgh Gazette*. Mrs. Gazzam opened the Western Seminary where young ladies could be assured of proper instruction in needlework, orthography, reading, writing, arithmetic, English grammar, composition, history, geography, and the use of globes and maps. Boarding students were taught music and drawing. The Harmony Seminary for the Education of Young Ladies, established by Luthern pastor Jacob Schnee in 1817 on the premises vacated by George Rapp's Harmonist commune, offered a "common English education," including German, French, and the fine arts, as well as botanical and landscape drawing. Mrs. Moody, "late from Europe," offered herself as an experienced teacher for a limited number of young ladies and hoped "to merit a share of public patronage and favor." Brevost's, esconced in "a large and commodious house...on Scotch Hill," boasted a talented lady and gentleman who would offer instruction on the harp and the guitar. St. Clare's Seminary, with a new building unsurpassed "in situation, spaciousness and convenience," charged $100 per annum, with extra fees for music and fancywork instruction.

Perhaps the best known of the female seminaries in the Pittsburgh area was Edgeworth's, established in 1826 in Braddock's Field and later moved to Sewickley. The course of study was unremarkable—mathematics, history, botany, French, geography, elocution—but also included theology and chemistry. Each session ran 22 weeks at $66 per term, with drawing, painting, and mezzotinto extra. Laundry cost $1 per month and stationery was charged "according to the amount required." A student list shows young women attending from Ohio, Tennessee, Kentucky, New York, Virginia, and Maryland, as well as from Philadelphia, Lancaster, and Erie, Pennsylvania. The catalogue stated very clearly the credo of schools devoted to the education of well-bred young ladies in the early 19th century. The emphasis was, above all, on "right feelings."

> Besides all that may be done to improve the understanding and give the accomplishments to manners, it is designed always that systematic regard shall be given to health and the cultivation of right affections in the heart...It may well be asked, of what account all other advantages can be, where the social and moral feelings have been suffered to run wild and grow waste by reason of neglect....Music, painting and drawing are poor *accomplishments* in comparison with right sentiments and right feelings in the soul.

"One evil passion subdued or prevented," the catalogue summarized, "is of greater account than a system of geography laid up in the memory."

In 1845 a Pennsylvania physician wrote to his daughter at her boarding school, where she was studying grammar, writing, geography, and other usual subjects, stressing the importance of attaining good principles and "substantial, useful learning....To be good and to be wise is the sum and aim of human pursuit. Cherish the kind and generous affections of the heart, and next to that, cultivate the faculties of your understanding." [Reed Papers, April 11, 1845]

Clearly the frontier attitudes toward educating women for the roles of wives and mothers changed little in the transition to an urban environment. These roles were, if anything, strongly reinforced by the emphasis on genteel accomplishments—music, art, embroidery, foreign languages. "St Paul knew what was best for women when he advised them to be domestic," wrote Mrs. Sanford in Godey's *The Lady's Book* in 1831.

The writer of the following letter may well have agreed with her, the satirical tone notwithstanding. Reprinted from the *Freemasons' Magazine* in Pittsburgh's *Republican Compiler*, it pointed to the perils of women becoming too learned:

> I am one of those unfortunate tradesmen who are plagued with a reading wife, who, according to my notion, is a very great evil in a house. My wife does hardly any one earthly thing, but read, read, read, almost from the time that she gets up, to the time that she goes to bed....For my part, I read only the papers in order to see how the nation goes on, and what chance there is for pushing business. But the worse of the affair is to come. My wife has lately been very fond of a book full of hard words, and will persist in reading out of it to me whenever she can catch me....We had a terrible brush t'other day, Sir: upon her coming out with a plagued hard word.... "I should be glad to know," says I, "what language are you reading?"
>
> "Why English, to be sure," says she, looking fiercely at me as if she would eat me.... "[Y]our want of erudition is insupportable—I pity from my heart the paucity of your ideas; you are the lowest form of terrestrial beings, and it shocks me to death to find you so incapable of relishing the compositions of a man, who for the universality of his genius, the vivacious ebullitions of his fancy, and the exuberance of his imagination; for the diversity of his matter, the subtilty of his reasoning, and the melody of his diction, is uncontrovertibly one of the brightest luminaries in the literary world...."
>
> My wrongheaded wife, not contented with talking herself...brings up her daughter to have a taste for the same kind of language. which, I am sure, is not fit for common use....Polly has already lost a good match, a very good match, by her nonsensical behavior; and if she takes after her mother, will never get a husband worth hanging....I hope all unmarried tradesmen....will take special care how they venture on a bookish woman.

While most women were too busy running their households and taking care of their families to engage in philosophical arguments about education and opportunities for women, they clearly understood the importance of raising their children to love and fear God. Living a pious life was especially difficult on the frontier, however, since in the 18th century churches were virtually non-existent outside of towns like Pittsburgh and Washington. Devout settlers made do with

Western Theological Seminary at Allegheny City, *engraving by Sherman Day, 1843. Founded in 1825, this was only one of several seminaries and colleges established for male students in Western Pennsylvania in the early decades of the 19th century. The first college for women, Pennsylvania Female College (now Chatham College), was founded in 1869.*

itinerant pastors who passed through the small settlements and were prevailed upon to stay for a few weeks. Some denominations, notably the Methodists and Presbyterians, sent out circuit riders, who traveled many miles to minister to their flocks. The Reverend John Cuthbertson, the first Presbyterian minister in America, arrived around the mid-century, and immediately took to the road. His diary records trips of 8 and 10 miles almost daily, and he estimated that in the 39 years of his circuit-riding, he had traveled 69,255 miles and preached on 12,452 days.

On Sundays some families seized the opportunity for a day of rest and socializing, which included card-playing, hunting, and visiting. The majority, however, attended church services, whether they were held in the nearest schoolhouse in a cabin built primarily as a chapel, or in the open air under the trees. Families often rose at first light to begin the long walk to the meeting place. It was a time to socialize as well as to pray, as Daniel Drake recalled:

> Horses hitched along the fence, and men and women on foot or on horse back, arriving from all quarters; within the enclosure, neighbors shaking hands and inquiring after each other's families; a little group leaning against the fence in conversation; another seated on a bench talking…another little party strolling among the graves; and squads of children sitting or lying on the grass to rest themselves. [Drake, p. 192]

Sermons were long, usually lasting for several hours. After a brief recess for the lunch brought from home, the preaching resumed. Hymn-singing was an important part of the service, with a church elder "lining" out the hymns—intoning one line, then waiting for the congregation to repeat it. The quality of the

In *The Fields,* the second novel in his trilogy *The Awakening Land,* Conrad Richter describes a backwoods church service, a rare occurence in the life of Sayward and her children. The circuit rider, called the "dominie," preaches in the local sawmill, where a primitive arrangement of seats and a pulpit are quickly put together for the congregation.

Today a short, square-faced log had been set up on end to lay the Good Book on, and the platform that the [lumber] slabs dropped on was the pulpit. Why, Sayward hadn't laid eyes on a pulpit or the hide and hair of a dominie for nigh onto fifteen years!....Green ash plank was laid at one end for the women of the congregation to sit on. At the other end the men could make out on the skids and saw carriage. The dominie stood in the middle. He had to turn his head one way to preach to the women, and the other way to the men. He only had to be careful when he made a flourish that he didn't cut his hand on the up-down-saw....The sawmill had a a roof against the rain, but no sidewalls. You could sit in meeting and look right out into the woods, for the mill had hardly scratched them yet. The big butts stood mighty still like this was something they couldn't make out. They'd never seen white folks sit together so quiet and sober. And when the dominie prayed, those heathen green trees hardly moved a leaf.

Sacramental Scene in a Western Forest, *from Joseph Smith's* Old Redstone: Historical Sketches of Western Presbyterianism, *1854.*

sermons and the speakers varied greatly, but the content was predictably about hellfire, eternal punishment, and a vengeful God.

Christiana Tillson, a well-born lady from the East, found her first church service in the Illinois wilderness quite different from the services of her own New England tradition.

> The preaching had commenced at ten A.M., and it was not until between four and five o'clock that we were released from the rant....The order of preaching was for the first speaker to be somewhat logical, and to show forth to the listening audience his great learning and wisdom; for the last speaker was left the sensation. He would "get happy," clap his hands, froth at the mouth; the congregation responding, some groaning, some crying loudly, "Amen," some calling "glory, glory, glory to God!"

She describes the mothers and babies seated together, with the "young'uns" huddled on the floor, while the "lords of creation" occupied the back benches. At the luncheon recess:

> [T]he good mamas who had babies...had been giving them their lunch during the service [and] now lit their pipes and looked so happy and satisfied as the clouds of smoke curled out from under their sunbonnets, meanwhile the sterner sex paying suit to the water bucket...there being but one gourd shell for the whole congregation...each man would walk up to the bucket and while another was drinking would relieve his mouth of a heavy quid, holding it in one hand, would take the gourd of water, rinse his mouth, spitting the washing on the floor, then take his drink, and while passing the gourd to the next would throw his "bacca" in his mouth and be ready for a chat. [Tillson, pp. 79-80]

Church buildings were unheated in winter, and even though some women brought small footstoves along, for most of the congregation the bitter cold and penetrating dampness made concentration difficult. One church member recorded that "the Sacramental Bread was frozen pretty hard and rattled sadly as broken into the Plates."[Fletcher, p. 525]

Rural settlers were predominantly Protestant—Presbyterians in the majority, with substantial numbers of Baptists, Methodists, Lutherans, and German Protestant Reformers. Catholic representation was small. Priests were among the earliest clergymen in Western Pennsylvania, arriving with the French military establishment in the 1750s and departing when the French withdrew, but no permanent church was established until 1789. Within a decade, however, Father Demetrius Gallitzin was presiding over a growing Catholic enclave in Cambria County.

No matter what denomination the settlers professed, most of them were God-fearing people who missed the formality of a church service and the comforting presence of a pastor or priest. In the most remote areas, many months or even years could pass without a visit from an itinerant minister, and women particularly missed the opportunities for traditional Sunday meetings, christenings, weddings, and funerals.

Denominations differed widely in their educational requirements for ministers. Presbyterians were among the earliest settlers and remained highly influential in the region for many years. They were alone in requiring that only educated men be called as ministers, and their attitude toward life was uncompromisingly stern. Baptist and Methodist pastors were judged more on their oratorical ability than on their formal education, but they too preached that life must be lived piously and without frivolous amusements. Churches imposed strict rules on their members, and violations were punished severely. Chronic intoxication, malicious gossiping, and "dancing and frolickin'" were frowned on by all denominations, and members who were found guilty of these transgressions could be suspended from the church or totally excluded—but they could also be forgiven. At Friends' monthly meeting, members of the Quaker community could be separated from the church if found guilty of playing cards, attending cockfights or horse races, lying, cheating, or exhibiting vanity in dress. A Presbyterian who allowed his son to make sugar on the Sabbath was severely reprimanded by the congregation, as were two brothers who drove their teams too long a distance on Sunday.

Church governance was almost exclusively in the hands of male elders. Presbyterians were adamantly opposed to female participation in ecclesiastical affairs, and women dared not speak out in church. The Friends, on the other hand, gave women complete equality. Preachers often had to eke out a living by farming or teaching, since salaries were even lower than schoolmasters' and were rarely paid on time. An annual salary of $200 was considered good pay, and usually half of it was in the form of produce or flour. As late as 1846, Jacob Zimmerman, whose territory included Greensburg, Export, Leechburg, and half a dozen other villages, noted in his diary, "Having preached 8 years in this congregation, the reason why I quit is this: they never as a congregation payed me for my labor." Nine years later his situation was only slightly better at Frantz.

> On the 3rd, there was a congregation meeting, where it was resolved to pay the balance due me of the last 4 years, viz., $146.87, within 4 months and also to continue my services as formerly. [Zimmerman ms., p. 20]

In 1797 the religious movement known as the Great Revival swept through Kentucky, Tennessee, Virginia, and North Carolina, finally reaching Western Pennsylvania in 1802. Primarily a rural movement, the Revival brought thousands of settlers to camp meetings which could last 10 and even 20 days, reaching a fevered pitch by the close of worship. One of the largest gatherings was held in Upper Buffalo, Pennsylvania, in 1802, when, as writer John Dinsmore described it, "There gathered together in the wilderness a concourse of above ten thousand people within a radius of a hundred miles" who brought provisions with them and set up camp grounds "tarrying for many days." John Hamilton, a Centre County resident, reported that "The preaching was of the most uncompromising character. Heaven as a reward and Hell as a punishment were preached with all the vigor that intense conviction of their reality could supply."[Fletcher, p. 521]

In their expressions of religious fervor, worshipers were often "taken by the Spirit" and fell to the ground in a trance. The Reverend Elisha Macurdy from Washington County, renowned for his emotional delivery and passionate sermons, reportedly "popped them down like pigeons." Many ordinarily quiet and conservative people, both men and women, were victims of "falling work." One witness reported:

> Some hundreds were....convinced of their sin and misery; many of them sunk down and cried bitterly and incessantly for several hours. Some fell suddenly; some lost their strength gradually; some lay quiet and silent; some were violently agitated; and many sat silently weeping. [Buck, p. 425]

Some pastors were upset by these manifestations of salvation and tried to tone down their sermons by preaching about salvation through Christ rather than hellfire and certain damnation, but "falling work" actually increased. As Elisha Macurdy observed, "There it was and we could do nothing with it."

However bizarre these mass conversions may have seemed to a dubious secular observer, in rural Western Pennsylvania the results were lasting and impressive. Church membership increased and denominational administrators, though dubious about the methods of some evangelists, rejoiced in the strengthening of church bonds. Since the earliest days of settlement, religion had been a strong influence on the lives of rural settlers. A pastor from Redstone (now Brownsville) observed:

> Had a traveler...confined his visits to towns and villages he might have inferred that he had got into a heathenish land. Had some one on the other hand, carried him round the country churches...he would have thought that he had got into an earthly Canaan! [McKinney, p. 66]

ANSICHT DES VON PENN'S ERBEN 1787. GESCHENKTEN PLATZES MIT DEM VERSAMMLUNGSHAUS

The German caption translates, "View of the square donated by Penn's heirs with the meetinghouse." This German Evangelical Protestant Church, 1791-1814, was the first of five churches built on the same site in Pittsburgh.

Barbara Winebiddle Negley, 1778-1867

Born in the frontier village of Pittsburgh on the Allegheny River about two miles from the Point, Barbara Winebiddle was one of the most prominent young ladies in Pitt Township, mingling with the merchants, itinerant businessmen, and officers in the Continental Army who patronized her father's tannery.

At the age of 16 she married Jacob Negley of Negleystown. The couple lived in a log cabin near the center of their 2,000-acre farm, located in what is now the East Liberty and Highland Park area of Pittsburgh. They had six sons and six daughters.

Both of the Negley's German ancestors had followed the teachings of Swiss Protestant religious reformer Huldreich Zwingli. To maintain their religious observances, the Negleys invited a traveling preacher to preach in their house every Sunday for all of the remote area's residents. In 1819 Barbara Negley donated land for the East Liberty Presbyterian Church to serve the growing population. She did so only with the consent of her husband, since women were forbidden to transfer property ownership.

Although young women were presumably still taught to be God-fearing and pious when families moved from a rural environment to the city, the opportunites for formal worship were often as difficult to come by as were those on the frontier. Pittsburgh's organized churches were slow to develop. Presbyterians, the strongest denomination, erected their own log meeting house in 1786, but only a few years later the building fell into disrepair from lack of use. There was no regular pastor, and services were held sporadically and, finally, not at all. Not until 1802 was a permanent minister in residence. Even then there was dissatisfaction among the members, some of whom withdrew and formed a Second Presbyterian Church. By 1810 the First Church had only 65 members, the Second Church but 30, although by now the population of Pittsburgh was 4,786.

Other denominations fared no better. A Methodist church was established in 1796, and services were held in the Presbyterian Meeting House until a padlock was placed on the door to prevent those "offspring of the Devil" from using the church. Baptists met in one anothers' houses and counted on traveling missionaries to bring them the Word of God. There were few Catholics until 1808, and Lutheran and Reformed denominations worshiped on alternate Sundays in a small building with part-time ministers.

One of the reasons advanced for this lack of concern with organized religion was the absence of strong and effective leadership. Despite the impact of the Great Revival on the rural areas surrounding Pittsburgh, the city was left virtually untouched, "spiritually isolated, morally degraded, and destitute of ministerial leadership." [McKinney, p. 98] Ministers were poorly paid, lacked permanent quarters for religious services, and had great difficulty attracting members. One writer noted that church goers were more apt to interest themselves in horse racing than in contributing money to build a church. Samuel Barr, who served briefly as a Presbyterian minister in 1785, withdrew from the society of those playing cards, but one gentleman retorted that he "would not give up a hand of whist for the company of Sir Isaac Newton or the greatest man of the age." [McKinney, p. 84]

Pittsburgh was a gateway city, a transportation center where travelers might stop briefly to restock their wagons and boats and, after days on the trail or the river, indulge in some lusty recreation. An early history of Allegheny County declared that until 1810, the town was filled with rowdies, travelers on their way to the West, boatmen, wagon drivers, soldiers, and speculators. Heavy drinking was the norm and a day at the race track involved not only betting on the horses, but fighting, swearing, buying, selling, eating, and drinking. Among the affluent citizens, parties were large and frequent, while the poorer citizens enjoyed wrestling, boxing, and "coarse amusements." [Lambing, p. 87]

Although the acerbic traveler Ann Royal pointed out that there were more taverns than churches in Pittsburgh in 1828, town residents were beginning to come to terms with social and moral issues which they felt only the churches could successfully address. Indeed, 12 churches were well established in Pittsburgh by 1830. While some historians point to the city's preoccupation with business and expanding industrial opportunities at the expense of religious and cultural development as antithetical to the growth of religious institutions, others note that the "surging regional economy with attendant population growth and optimism about future expansion" contributed to the building of congregations. [Pritchard, p. 332] After a rocky beginning, the future of Pittsburgh's religious institutions seemed assured. §

Bridal Dress for the Marriage Ceremony from Harper's New Monthly Magazine, *1850. "Robe of white poult de soie [sic]. The skirt very full, and ornamented in the front with five rows of lace, finished at each end with bows of white satin....The hair in waved bandeaux on the forehead, and the back hair partly plaited and partly curled, two long ringlets dropping on each side of the neck. Wreath of orange blossom, jasmine, and white roses. Long bridal vail of Brussels net."*

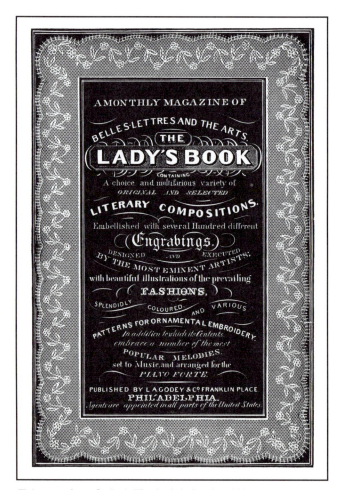

Title page from Godey's The Lady's Book, *1833.*

LOVE & MARRIAGE

In 1797 the English novelist Jane Austen began her novel *Pride and Prejudice* with the following words: "It is a truth universally acknowledged, that a single man in possession of a good fortune must be in want of a wife." What she did not add was the equally universal assumption that the only proper role for a woman was to be a wife and mother. Females unfortunate enough not to attain that state were usually doomed to lives of dependency on the goodwill of relatives. Nevertheless, both in England and America, a number of 19th-century women did achieve success and distinction as writers, artists, social workers, nurses, teachers, and political activists. The titles of the books that tell us about the American women, however, signal the fact that—married or not—they were exceptional: *Daughters of Genius; Eminent Women of Our Century*; and *Biographies of Distinguished Women*. It is easy to impose 20th-century sensibilities on 18th- and 19th-century lives. Why didn't women rebel? There are dozens of answers. But it is important to view the world of American women of an earlier era through *their* eyes and times, not ours. Every young girl was raised to believe that marriage and motherhood were the norm. To be a wife was to affirm woman's highest calling.

When a man decided to leave Europe or the Eastern United States to seek his fortune in the West, he had several options. If he was married, he could go on ahead of his family, establish a home, and return to fetch his wife and children. Or he could take his family when he first set out West, as many did. If he was unmarried, he could choose his future wife, become officially or unofficially betrothed, take off for the West and return in due course to complete marriage arrangements. Or he could look for a wife whenever he settled. But there were few single women over 16 on the frontier. Men diligently sought first wives, and most widowers quickly remarried. Unless a man was a real loner, a trapper and hunter always on the move, life without a wife was almost unthinkable. A man needed help in developing his land as well as in running a household. And he needed strong sons and daughters to help as well. Marriage was a partnership,

> *"The young couple are now also an individual household, with their own rules, regulations, and love for the entire life they will be together with one another."*
>
> —*Liwwät Böke*

a spiritual and physical union, an economic necessity, and if the couple were lucky, a love match as well.

Young people in Western Pennsylvania were less constrained about whom they could marry than their counterparts in Europe. There were far fewer arranged marriages and more opportunities for eligible young men and women to make their own choices. A French visitor observed:

> The youth of both sexes here enjoy a freedom of intercourse unknown in the older and more formal nations of Europe. They dance, sing, walk and "run in sleighs" together in sunshine and moonshine without the occurrence or even the apprehension of any impropriety. [D'Arusmont, p. 28]

Courtship on the frontier followed the pattern of courtship everywhere in the world, with changes only in the degree of formality and style. Boys met girls at parties—corn huskings, weddings, flax scutchings, and Sunday services, where they conducted adolescent mating rituals. Boys teased the girls, the girls flirted back. There were kissing parties, where each girl had to be kissed at least once. At corn huskings, a red ear allowed the husker to kiss the girl of his choice. At dances girls were as afraid of being a wallflower as in any generation. Boys hung around quilting bees and spinning bees, waiting to escort their girls home. And Sabbath meetings, whether in log churches or under the trees, were considered appropriate occasions on which to conduct courtships.

The custom of bundling is the subject of much mythology, but like most frontier activities, it was born of necessity. Bundling generally meant that an unmarried couple would go to bed with one another, but keep their clothes on. The practice was most common among already betrothed couples, but circumstances often dictated otherwise. Young men might ride several miles to visit their sweethearts, and if it was cold and the hour late, parents retired and left the two alone to bundle with parental approval. This custom was not confined to courting couples, however, as the arrival of unexpected travelers and guests could strain the facilities of a modest cabin, and sometimes they too were invited to share the same bed, on the assumption that basic decency would prevail. With courting couples, some parents took special precautions, like tying up the daughter's feet in a large stocking. But as Johann David Schoepf reported in 1783, the need "is commonly superfluous, the circumstance having rarely any other consequence than regular betrothal, which is the object had in view in allowing the meeting."

Although at the time the most conservative of families believed that bundling was an appropriate way to conduct a courtship, later writers were highly critical of the practice. Carl Holliday, author of *Women's Life in Colonial Days*, published in 1922, referred to it as a "curious and certainly outrageous custom" and considered it the worst of "all the immoral acts sanctioned by conventional opinion of any time." Despite attempts to explain the reasons for bundling, he wrote, it was true that "the custom led to deplorable results."

Bundling may have begun, as one anonymous writer noted in 1828, as "the shared understanding that innocent endearments should not be exceeded," but as a means of allowing young people the freedom to conduct a courtship without the fear of sexual consequences, the custom was not entirely successful. Birth and marriage records in many communities show that the number of pregnant brides rose during the 18th century. In the 1780s and 1790s in New England nearly one out of every three brides, was with child. The numbers began to decline in the early 19th century; by 1840 the rate was one in five or six. [Larkin, pp. 193-95]

As America moved into the Victorian age, women were increasingly viewed as the representatives and guardians of purity and morality, spiritual beings who would not give in to sexual passion before—and not too enthusiastically after—marriage. And even though everyone knew that men were sensual beasts, they were urged to temper this rage within and as "Christian gentlemen" show restraint and control.

Patterns of Embroidery For Ladies' Fancy Work, from Godey's The Lady's Book, *1833.*

Every girl began preparing for marriage when she was still a child, learning to spin, weave, and sew items for her dowry—bed ticks, blankets, sheets, and linens. As her wedding day approached, her parents might provide feathers to be stuffed into the ticks to make pillows and comforters, a cow or chickens, a few pieces of furniture, and tableware. The groom's father might give him a piece of land, some basic farm implements, perhaps some livestock.

But first, the wedding. The only celebration that did not require participatory manual labor on the part of the guests, a wedding was an opportunity for dancing and feasting, practical jokes, heavy drinking, tears, and laughter. The bride was married either at home or at the groom's home, depending on the ethnic origin and religious persuasion of the couple. In either case, members of the bridal party started toward their goal at an early hour and were usually met by felled trees or grapevines tied across their path, impediments considered hilarious by the groom's friends. At some point, bottles of whiskey appeared and everyone who was thirsty got a swallow "to quiet the nerves and to bring on a good appetite."

The wedding ceremony itself might be performed either inside or outside the house by a circuit riding preacher or the community priest. Liwwät Böke reported that "When there was no pastor, then three witnesses testified to the promises between the bridal couple. Later on, when the cleric visited the neighborhood again, he consecrated the two with God's blessings."

After the ceremony there was a magnificent feast, with each family bringing a contribution, Liwwät recalled, including, "bread, soup peas...pickled meat, sauerkraut....cabbage, potatoes, side meat, pork, chicken, berries, cherries, carrots....cornbread, venison....geese, hazelnuts." Joseph Doddridge reminisced about the dancing at such weddings:

> [There were] three and four handed reels, or squares and sets and jigs....The jigs were often accompanied with what was called cutting out; that is when either of the parties became tired of the dance...the place was supplied by some one of the company without any interruption of the dance. In this way a dance was often continued till the musician was heartily tired of his situation. Toward the latter part of the night, if any of the company, through weariness, attempted to conceal themselves for the purpose of sleeping, they were hunted up, paraded on the floor, and the fiddler ordered to play "Hang on till to-morrow morning."
> [Doddridge, p. 104]

Preparation for weddings included anticipating the presence of large numbers of dogs. Liwwät Böke reported that every family had at least two dogs, and when 30 or 40 families attended a wedding, so did the dogs, which could mean 100 or so animals and plenty of noise and dirt.

> So a week before the wedding, a neighbor or two catch a hundred live rabbits in traps or snares, and when it is eleven o'clock, they let the rabbits loose in the forest, and the dogs search and hunt for the rabbits until nearly time to go home.
> [Böke, p. 77]

If the couple had already built their own home, which was the usual practice, the bride's friends stole her away and put her to bed, usually in the cabin's loft. At the same time, the groom's friends made off with him and planted him firmly beside her. For the remainder of the night, whiskey and food were passed upstairs to them, musicians serenaded them, drunken young men yelled outside the cabin and generally made themselves obnoxious, while the dancing continued.

If the cabin was yet to be built, the bride or groom's family home served the purpose, and several days after the celebration, guests gathered for a cabin raising for the young people. When it was completed, another party commenced, and when it was finally over, the newlyweds were allowed to begin their lives in their own home.

Liwwät Böke was a German Roman Catholic, and her community's customs required that the house be finished prior to the wedding and that after the ceremony,

> [N]o one in the community goes by their house for three days, and then the four parents visit the young pair and bring vegetables and meat and bread. Everyone knows that the new housewife doesn't know how to cook yet, and also has not the time!....The young couple are now also an individual household, with their own rules, regulations, and love for the entire life they will be together with one another. [Böke, p. 78]

The progress of love and marriage in the towns and cities was less carefree and more formal. Samuel Jones deplored the passing of the old ways, as he was wont to do, and declared that young men could no longer call upon a young lady without being looked upon with suspicion or:

> [S]landered by gossiping trollops....belles are so anxious, on the third visit at farthest, to discover the real intention of their gallants, that they deter them from a fourth call, by their "side-long looks" and indirect inquiries, as to the object which they have in view....[He added] Talk six times with the same single lady, and you may get the wedding dresses ready. [Jones, p. 44]

Upper-class women especially seemed to delight in keeping their beaux dangling. They pretended to be surprised by an expected proposal and always refused the first time, playing the game as long as they thought they could get away with it, presumably because consent stopped the fun and required fidelity and obedience from that day forward.

Sevin Bell, a magistrate in Washington, who wrote gossipy letters to his niece Madelaine LeMoyne in Ohio, reported of one couple:

> It is still said that the good Mr. Carson and the sweet little Miss C. are to be married....I should say, from appearances at least, they were both old enough to know their minds, and when once determined on, I should say, in all cases, the sooner the better, and in their case neither had much time to lose.

Betrothal Tumblers, c. 1835, designed by glassblower James Lee as an engagement gift for Charlotte Barker. The white rose engraved on the tumblers represents Charlotte's birthplace in Yorkshire, England; the thistle, James's Scottish background. The shield and pair of doves bind them together. HSWP Collection.

A later letter reported:

> The business of the good Mr. Carson and Miss C. remains pretty much as you left it. The Town is divided in its opinion—as old as I am, I do not think any Lady could keep me off so long. I have never heard a single reason opined for its delay except they are too cold to be in a hurry. I should myself think there was not much time to spare.

He described a young lady he had recently met, a "most superior girl," who would soon marry the parson:

> There never were two people who appeared to suit each other better, but they are both as poor as Church Mice, and you know it is generally the luck of Parsons to be very rich in children....We barely support him while single, and I am very much afraid that while times last as they are, his four hundred dollars a year will not be much added to. [LeMoyne Papers, ALS, January 27, July 13, 1824]

The *Pittsburgh Gazette* carried formal and stylized marriage announcements like the following, which appeared in 1801:

> Married on 22nd instant by the Rev. Francis RENO, Doctor John DICKEY, of Beaver Town, to the agreeable Miss Mary HART, of the vicinity. Pittsburgh, Oct. 30.

But some people's marriages were of greater interest than others'. Pittsburgh society apparently was just as smitten with celebrities and new brides as are contemporary readers of gossip magazines. Mrs. Judge Wilkins, née Dallas, was married in 1819, at the same time that the first bridge over the Monongahela opened at Smithfield Street. "A great crowd turned out that day, and 'twas said as many came to see the new bride and famous beauty as the handsome structure."

The author of the *Social Mirror,* an account of Pittsburgh society at the turn of the 18th century, lauded the city's beautiful women. "The Scotch-Irish blood [that]...has so strongly impregnated our physical characters, together with the peculiar atmosphere which floats between our hills, seems to have been most benefical in perfecting womanly charms."

Magazines, newspapers, and books were full of advice for women on how to be a good wife and for men on how to find one. "Seek a good wife of thy God," men were told, "for she is the best gift of her providence." They were warned not to be taken in by superficial charms or talents, since:

> The Harp and the voice may thrill thee, sound may enchant thy ear,
> But consider thou,—the hand will wither, and the sweet notes turn to discord,
> The eye, so brilliant at even, may turn red with sorrow in the morning,
> And the sylph-like form of elegance must writhe in the cramping of pain.
> [Tupper, p. 156]

They were to make certain that their wife-to-be was healthy and "springeth of a wholesome stock, that thy little ones perish not before thee," and cautioned that "many a fair skin hath covered a mining disease, and many a laughing cheek bright with the glare of madness." In addition to good health and sanity, the gentleman searching for a wife must make certain that his future partner had wisdom, but "beware that thou exceed; For woman must be subject, and the true mastery is of the mind."

In 1814 John P. Brace wrote in his journal, "To be sure—I shall choose a wife, but it must be a matter of calculation and regularly composed like an Apothecary's bill—ten grains of neatness, two of industry and two of amiability, a teacup full of 'brains'—acquired knowledge, talents to be immersed in a silver cup—with a handful of flowers of beauty flung in."[Bank, p. 50]

In 1780 the following ad appeared in the *Pennsylvania Packet*. This apparent advertisement for a housekeeper may well have masked a search for a prospective wife.

> Wanted at a Seat about a half a day's journey from Philadelphia, on which are good improvements and domestics, A single Woman of unsullied Reputation, an affable, cheerful, active and amiable Disposition; cleanly, industrious, perfectly qualified to direct and manage the female Concerns of country business, as raising small stock, dairying, marketing, combing, carding, spinning, knitting, sewing, pickling, preserving, etc., and occasionally to instruct two Young Ladies in those Branchs of Oeconomy, who with their father, compose the Family. Such a person will be treated with respect and esteem, and meet with every encouragement due to such a character. [Holliday, p. 109]

"The Duties of Married Females," appearing in *Patterson's Pittsburgh Town and Country Magazine Almanac for 1820,* instructed wives not to neglect the little endearments, "but let the charm which captivated the *lover*, secure the attachment of the *husband*." Stay within your own sphere and be charming, they were told, for "A woman in politics is like a monkey in a china shop; she *can* do no good and *may* do a great deal of harm." Colesworth Pickney cautioned women to keep a cheerful countenance in the face of adversity, since "A man's perplexities and gloominess are increased tenfold, when his better half moves about with a continued scowl upon her brow." They were further warned not to be untidy in dress and to remember the promises they gave, even though they "may be the injured, not the injuring one—the forgotten, not the forgetful wife." One has to search diligently to find advice to husbands, and in one instance, it is preceded by what his expectations should be. "A man's house should be his earthly paradise….And in order that it may be so, it should be his daily task to provide everything convenient and comfortable for his wife….Generally every shilling expended by the husband for the accommodation of his wife in her domestic operations, is returned upon him four-fold—if not precisely in pecuniary advantage, though this is often true, it will be found in the order, peace, and happiness of his family."

This advice was in keeping with the prevailing view of men's and women's roles. Man was the provider, woman the keeper of the family's values. Before 1750 and well into the 1800s, a woman entered marriage knowing full well what was expected of her. She gave up all of her legal rights and property when she took her husband's name: she could not enter into contracts; sue or be sued; leave anything to her heirs except that which she could prove belonged to her before her marriage, such as clothing and some household items; she could not vote or run for office, but if she did own property, she was subject to taxation. Women who expected a smooth and felicitous married life would have done well to follow the guidance of Dr. Benjamin Rush, when he advised a young woman about to be married, "from the day you marry you must have no will of your own....if he [the intended husband] is like others of his sex, [he] will often require unreasonable sacrifices of your will to his....The happiest marriages I have known have been those when the subordination I have recommended has been most complete." Some women must have wondered why marriage appeared to be designed for the happiness of men. But the only alternative, the spinster state, was not a desirable one, since unmarried ladies, so the prevailing wisdom would have us believe, were probably too ugly or bad-tempered to snare a husband.

> Old Maid's Last Prayer
> Come gentle, come simple, come foolish, come witty—
> Come don't let me die a maid, take me out of pitty.
> I have a sister Sally, she's younger than I am—
> She has so many sweethearts she's oblig'd to deny them.
> I never was guilty of denying any;
> You all know my heart, I'd be thankful for any. [De Pauw, p. 12]

Visitors to the United States often remarked on the degree of independence enjoyed by young people, particularly in choosing a mate, but there was a danger in this for the woman. Alexis de Tocqueville wrote that "In America the independence of woman is irrecoverably lost in the bonds of marriage." When a woman married, she submitted her future life totally into the hands of her husband. This is the paradox of domesticity in America, Nancy Cott tells us, since "women were expected to make a voluntary choice amounting to self-abnegation." She quotes the diary of George Younglove Cutler, a young law student who wrote in 1820:

> The contract is so much more important in its consequences to females than to males for besides leaving everything else to unite themselves to one man they subject themselves to his authority....he is their all—their only relative—their only hope—but as for him, business leads him out of doors, far from the company of his wife....& then it is upon his employment that he depends almost entirely for the happiness of his life. [Cott, p. 79]

Women rarely discussed sex—never with their friends, rarely with their mothers. References to sex in women's diaries is unusual, which makes Liwwät Böke's writings all the more singular. She was happily married to her childhood sweetheart, and the pages of her journal are filled with references to "eating and laughing, and a little kiss, when we go to bed we are not too tired. That is rejuvenation from God." In a remarkable document, given the times, she wrote to the Catholic Bishop in Cincinnati on behalf of one hundred women in the small

Ohio hamlet of St. John and surrounding areas, complaining because the local priest had told them that they were committing a mortal sin if they had sex with their husbands more than twice a year. She was outraged by his interference, and in a long refutation of his views to the bishop, called the priest, among other things, a silly fool. Condemning his ideas as "at best bizarre, eccentric, and at worst unhealthy," she explained to him that "Sex is powerfully important to people…this need of freedom to express, as husband and wife, their *love* for one another, *in, by and through sex.*" She went on to say:

> Today, here in the forest, in our hectic, short, active life, men and women often are alone a long time, and often they are tired, they sleep, they are exhausted from work. Sex is sometimes the only way it is possible to hold love together. *For a great many it is the only way.* [Böke, pp. 81-83]

She chastized the clergy for their want of understanding, and implied that they also lacked feeling. "In sex" she went on, "one can feel. In the surge of sexual desires and pleasures, one comes alive with strong feelings. One does not often find strong emotions in this forest, and therefore, they are precious and welcome." In a final burst of eloquence, she wrote, "Husband and wife come to this stage in their relationship when the desire to touch one another springs up wildly throughout their consciousness. 'It doesn't matter' what they are doing, they must get their clothes off! Sex is perhaps the only way they are together with one another."

Unlike Böke, most women were very reticent about discussing sex and pregnancy, and even though they were expected to produce children as soon as possible, there is little information about how they felt during pregnancy. Even in intimate and gossipy letters to her family, Nancy Swearingen said very little except that she looked forward to her confinement "with uneasiness and anxiety."

"On the way home in winter, January 1838, at St. John, Marion (Tp.), Mercer County, Natz Boke, my treasure, my beloved whom I love more than the whole world. He is carrying three skins with the traps. The gun is new." From Liwwät Böke's Pioneer. *Drawn 1842.*

In the course of a pregnancy 11 years later she wrote nothing until she announced "We call our babe James."

It is clear from an unusually frank letter from Sevin Bell to his niece that references to pregnancy were veiled in talk about the wearing of shawls. "Mrs. Claypoole has been wearing *the shawl* for some time, but poor Mrs. Ward I am afraid will never want one except to keep her warm. Our Parson's Lady will certainly increase the number of our congregation as soon as law and decency will permit, but she is so far from wearing a shawl that she appears to make a boast of it. Her sister has no symptoms yet, but on the whole our town is increasing very rapidly." In another letter he tells her, "We have scarcely a wife in town who is not either minding an infant or waddling about with the rotundity of a beer barrel. As wonders are never to cease, there is Mrs. Wood, who will in a short time be thicker than she is long."[LeMoyne Papers, ALS, July 13, September 10, 1824]

Large families were desirable since infant mortality was high, and it was not uncommon for a mother to bear 10 or 12 children and see only 3 or 4 live to adulthood. Children were needed to share the endless tasks falling to their parents and were put to work as soon as they were able to understand responsibility—girls learned to sew, knit and cook, while boys learned to fetch wood, care for livestock, and hunt. But even if a mother loved each child dearly, there was undoubtedly a time when she said, either aloud or to herself, "No more."

Some historians believe women settlers may have learned a great deal about pregnancy and childbirth from Native-American women, including ways of inducing abortion by using various roots and fungi. Women of several tribes believed abstinence for an indeterminate period following childbirth was necessary both to prevent immediate pregnancy and to ensure a good milk supply for

After bearing eight children, Sayward, in Conrad Richter's *The Fields,* decided there was a time to begin and a time to end.

O, she couldn't expect Portius to fall in line with her....It was just hard on a man, Sayward reckoned, when his woman stopped being a wife to him. He didn't stop to figure out he'd had a mighty easy time of it, making trouble whenever he wanted and then going about his business. The woman was the one who had to pay the fiddler. She had to give her flesh and blood before the baby was born, and her milk and tending afterward. You might as well say she was mammy and pappy both. The man was just the one who didn't know what he was doing when he dropped the seed, like a squirrel hiding a nut or acorn in the ground.

the newborn. In 1828 Dr. Jonas Rishel published *The Indian Physician*, a little manual discussing a variety of diseases and their cures by use of herbs and other medicinal plants. His chapter on the causes of miscarriages may well have served, though unwittingly, as a manual for ending a pregnancy.

Childbirth was accomplished with the help of family and friends, and when available, the services of a midwife. These women were in great demand, and many of them were very skilled, having studied with physicians in Europe or the Eastern United States. But there were also the less skilled, those who relied on superstition and intuition and were not always right in their decisions. Liwwät Böke trained as a midwife in Germany and was in great demand in her new country, almost too much so, as she complained that people called on her for all kinds of medical advice. "I am a midwife, not a body or mind doctor," she lamented, but this did not prevent her from laying down rules of general health for the community.

An early manual described the perfect midwife: "She should be young and vigorous, learned in her art, able to take all-night vigils, strong of arms and hands for difficult cases of turning and extraction….She must have slender hands, long fingers, tender feelings, sympathy, be hopeful, and above all, silent." By the beginning of the 19th century, midwifery was gradually being taken over by men. The professionalization of medicine and the exclusion of women from medical schools led to a decline in midwifery, except in the most isolated wilderness areas and among the urban poor.

Single women were a rarity on the frontier. If they were young and unmarried, there were always plenty of suitors. And if their husband died, widows almost always married again in a very short time. Sarah Rist rejected a proposal by a young widower, even though he wrote her "stating how nicely he and his wife had gotten along, and what a nice home he had, and how many peach trees he had on his farm." After she turned him down, he married another girl and Sarah reported that he was apparently a very good husband. A year or so later her own widowed father went courting "the widow Stauffer."

> I then went to work and made his wedding shirt attached to pleats in the bosom like machine stitching as near as I could….There was snow on the ground, and Conrad Walker had taken father in his sleigh, and by noon he came back with the bride and groom. I had a fat turkey roasted and had some neighbors in to greet them. That evening my brothers got some neighbor boys to come, and they serenaded them with horns and tin pans. [Galley, p. 347]

Left with children, widows found marriage an economic necessity, since their futures depended entirely on the provisions of their husbands' wills. They received only what husbands chose to leave them, and if they married again, they frequently lost that as well.

For a woman in Pennsylvania, having an estate in her own right was more the exception than the rule. Until 1843 the state abided by English common law, so that a wife had no legal separate existence from her spouse, unless she had committed a crime. She could not determine the disposition of her personal possessions after her death unless they had been hers prior to marriage, so that her worldly goods passed automatically to her husband and children. Although her husband owned everything, and upon marriage became responsible for her debts, this provision excluded "superfluities and extravagances," as defined, presumably, by the courts. In 1820 Supreme Court Justice John Bannister Gibson noted, "In no country where the blessings of the common law are felt and acknowledged, are the interest and estates of married women so entirely at the mercy of their husbands, as in Pennsylvania." Improvements in the laws were made from time to time. For instance, until 1853 the earnings of a married woman were not considered property and still belonged to her husband. Judge George W. Woodward, commenting on the law, stated that although the legislature had done much to change marriage legal relations, "it has not yet extinguished quite all of the material rights of a husband. He is still entitled to the person and labor of his wife, and the benefits of her industry and economy." Not until 1893 was a woman given the sole right to own her own property outright and to distribute it as she pleased in her will.

Jane Swisshelm, editor of the Pittsburgh paper *The Saturday Visitor*, worked indefatigably to change the laws concerning women and property. She spoke in public, editorialized in her paper, and generally made herself very visible—some would say obnoxious—until in 1847 the state legislature began to modify the law. A well-known lawyer told her, "We hold you responsible for that law, and I tell you now, you will live to rue the day when you opened such a Pandora's box in your native state, and cast such an apple of discord into every family in it." In the latter half of the 19th century, it was ruled that a husband could open and read any mail belonging to his wife. In response, Swisshelm announced that the marriage bond was "made for Saxon swine-herds, who ate boar's heads, lived in unchinked houses and wore brass collars, in the days when Alfred the Great was king."

A husband could bequeath property to his wife at his death, and many did that or made arrangements to provide for her care. It was important that he be specific, however, since a slip of the pen could deprive her of what she considered to be her own. When David Strawbridge drew up his will, for example, he bequeathed his wife Ann "all of her wearing apparel to use during her life and dispose of at her death according to her pleasure." He made certain, however, as did most men, that the "use of my dwelling house, bed, and household furnishings" and indeed he meant "use," was hers only during her widowhood, and if she remarried, the deal was off.

When John Morgan left his wife the "free and undisturbed possession of the dwelling house...during her natural life," the catch was that "natural life" meant widowhood in the legal sense. If she remarried, her legacy was voided. Wills abounded in phrases referring to the length of time a widow could retain the legacy—"the above privileges only during her widowhood"—"during such times as she may remain my widow"—"if my wife should marry whilst my son is a minor....she is to withdraw from the premises instantly."

Peter Kalm, author of *Travels in North America, 1748–1750*, described what was known as a "shift wedding," which demonstrates the degree to which the early laws deprived a woman of control over her personal possessions. His account concerned a widow who took a new husband but because she was unable to pay her deceased husband's debts was stripped by his creditors of everything in the house, including her clothes, and thus was forced to marry in her shift. Kalm notes that "as soon as she has married, and she no longer belongs to her deceased husband, she puts on the clothes which the second husband has given her."

In making their wills, the fathers of single daughters faced the problem of how to provide for them in case they did not marry. Thomas Mallarson in 1812 left his four daughters the "privilege of washing in the kitchen, the privileges of garden, firewood; and each of them one row of apple trees on the north side of the orchard." Patrick Cavitt in 1820 either didn't want his daughter to marry or else knew that she never would, since he decreed she should live in her mother's house all her life, and if she did so, she would receive $40, a young mare, a cow, and two sheep.

The initial reaction to these stern bequests is to assume that the men who wrote them were punitive and uncaring. However, the law was rigid, and most women did not expect more than they received. Most husbands and fathers probably viewed their meager bequests as protecting their widows and daughters against fortune hunters, more interested in marrying the women for their money and material goods than for their sterling characters.

Pennsylvania was unique in that the state denied a widow any part of her husband's estate—even that to which she was legally entitled—until the man's creditors had been paid off. Other states, and indeed the generally harsh English common law, allowed her to receive her share first, before the creditors made their claims. The Pennsylvania interpretation created many indigent widows dependent on children, other family members, or public relief.

However, if a man bequeathed property to his wife, that property belonged to her outright and she could dispose of it as she wished in her will. As Chalfant points out, there is a poignancy in the wills of women in this period and a sharply focused view of what was important. The first woman's will recorded in Allegheny County in 1790 is of special interest, since although Jennat Fraizor was illiterate —her will is signed with a "mark"—her prized possessions bequeathed to her children were books on religious subjects, including two to be sent to her daughter in "Kaintuckey." Daughter Elizabeth also received "one Callico short gound, one flanning Shift....one Spinning Wheele, one pewter dish....the bed I ly on, one blue and white kiverlid, One pair fier tongs and my Cow."

Clothes were important in women's wills, since of all possessions, they were the most personal. Clothing was expensive as well, and thrifty homemakers wanted to make sure they were put to good use. In 1812 Hannah McRoberts left to her daughters her "spotted dress, green dress, black silk dress, black shall, yellow shall, and all the other shalls [*sic*]" along with yard goods to make a riding coat and an "Umbrel."

Prized possessions were carefully allotted, and it is clear that a great deal of thought went into these bequests. Margaret Harrah gave her sons money, farming utensils, a clock, and some furniture. To her daughter Sarah she left "my Spinning Wheels, Chears and the count reel and cupboard....to my daughter Mary Long....fifty dollars and my largest Looking Glass. To my granddaughter Margaret Long, my second Looking Glass. To my granddaughter, Margaret Baldwin, my silver Tea Spoons."

Eleanor Elliott's 1819 will was unique on two counts. First, she left everything to her three grandchildren "for the benefit of their educations," and she appointed a woman, "the mother of my grandchildren" as executrix. Also concerned with her children's education, Ann Plumer in 1815 directed that her estate be sold and the proceeds go to educate and maintain her children, four boys and two girls.

Last Will and Testament of William Maxwell

In the name of God, amen. I, William MAXWELL, of the Township of Unity, County of Westmoreland in the State of Pennsylvania, tanner, being in my usual health of body and of sound mind, memory, and understanding...do make and publish this, my Last Will and Testament, in manner and form following, viz: ...the whole of my estate that I may be possessed of at my death, real and personal, land and movables, be sold as soon as conveniently can be done after my decease, that money arising from said sale and all other money that may belong to me be divided into sixteen equal shares. And I do give and bequeath unto my dear wife Jane MAXWELL four of said shares, being one-fourth of my estate. I do declare it to be in lieu and instead of her dower at common law. And to my son William MAXWELL I give and bequeath four of the said shares, being one-fourth of my estate.

And to my sons Robert MAXWELL, John L. MAXWELL, and my daughters Sally MAXWELL and Betsy MAXWELL, to each of them one of the aforesaid shares. And to my sons James MAXWELL and Adam MAXWELL I give and bequeath to each of them two of the said shares....

And I do hereby appoint Jane MAXWELL my wife and my son William MAXWELL and Benjamin ALSWORTH sole executors of this my Last Will and Testament...8th of July 1815.

Inventory and Appraisement of the Estate of William Maxwell

1 (malt ?) mare	$ 50.00
1 colt	20.00
1 jack horse	50.00
1 snip mare	37.00
1 nel mare	35.00
1 lightfoot mare	32.00
The hogs	23.00
1 brocked cow	16.00
1 crummy cow	12.00
1 broken horn steer	10.00
1 fleckled steer	10.00
1 chub	7.50
1 fleck cow	12.00
1 spreckled cow	9.00
1 broke horn cow	12.00
1 red cow	13.00
1 little cow	7.00
1 bell cow	16.00
2 yearling steers	10.00
1 big horn steer	12.00
2 yearling heifers	13.00
4 spring calves	13.00
12 sheep	33.00
33 sheep (second lot)	66.00
1 wagon	30.00
The big plough and double-tree	9.00
The little plough and doubletree	4.50
1 harrow and (?) horsetree	2.00
1 old plough	.50
The hay in the barn	30.00
Oats in the barn	24.00
1 cuting box	2.50
One half bushel	1.00
1 (greap?) & Pitch fork	1.00
2 set of gears, 3 collars	6.00
2 ditto	8.00

2 barrels and flaxseed	3.00
The unbroke flax	2.50
1 break	.75
2 mattocks	1.50
2 scaps of bees & 4 boxes	2.50
Mail, wedge, and ax	2.00
14 acres of rye	42.00
16 acres of wheat	48.00
1 hay stack at the foot of the long meadow	10.00
1 hay stack at the head of the meadow	10.00
1 hay stack in the west meadow	15.00
3 (curling?) (kives?)	3.00
1 lot of old barrels	1.50
1 lot of tanning tools and whetstones	1.50
Hoes and spade	.67
1 lot of vessels in the cellar	2.00
1 tar can	.50
1 loom and taklings	10.00
1 whiskey barrel	.65
1 hackle and bench	1.50
1 bedstead	1.50
1 wheelbarrow wheel	1.50
1 big wheel	.50
1 (chack?) reel	.75
2 old wheels and winning swifts	1.00
1 lot of old scythes and (hems?)	1.00
2 hogsheads	1.00
1 bed and bedstead (upstairs)	20.00
2 spinning wheels	4.00
2 bedsteads and cords	3.00

1 old chest	.06
1 new bedstead with posts and cords	2.00
2 side saddles	8.00
1 mans saddle	4.00
1 creadle	.75
1 lot of books	4.00
1 pair of stilyards	2.00
1 bureau	10.00
1 bed clothes and bedstead	30.00
1 table	5.00
1 chest of drawers	16.00
1 small looking glass	.25
1 bed clothes, bedstead, and cord	35.00
Cupboard furniture	3.30
1 dining table	5.50
6 windsor chairs	3.00
4 old chairs	1.00
1 arm chair	1.00
1 (se?ver)	.50
1 candlestick & snuffers	.25
First lot of kitchen furniture	4.50
Second lot of kitchen furniture	3.50
1 lot of tinware	1.00
The kitchen table	.75
1 saw and barrel auger	.37
1 fire lot	1.50
1 lot of old bridles	.12 1/2
Twenty dollars in cash	20.00
1 lot of old yokes, (stradle?), and churn	1.50
1 box of old irons	.75
1 grindstone	1.00
By bank account	19.96

Total: $1,022.59 1/2

(facing page and above) From Old Westmoreland: the History and Genealogy of Westmoreland County, Pennsylvania, *Vol. 4, No. 1, August 1983.*

Women tended to favor their sons in making out wills, but this was often because they were carrying out the wishes spelled out in their husbands' wills. The law held that money was the rightful inheritance of the son, unless the mother could prove that she had owned it prior to her marriage.

Even the most happily married women on the frontier must have experienced enormous difficulties in their marriages. Anxieties about crop failures, wild animals, attacks by Native Americans, illness, poverty and relentless fatigue do not contribute to an idyllic family life. Some men were naturally restless and had to roam, leaving their women at home alone for long periods. And some had little or no understanding of the loneliness their wives endured.

Liwwät Böke offered advice to husbands based on her encounters with the many women she served as a midwife. A man, she explained, achieved self-esteem through his work; a woman had no work other than what she performed in the home. "She can cook good food, but, when it is once swallowed, her family forget to thank her. Her housework brings no respect to her from the community, and it is not likely she shall have praise for the suitableness of her cleaning methods." No, she continued, a husband has to be the one person who provides her with self-respect, self-confidence and well-being. In other words, "*women feel themselves worthy when they are loved.*" Husbands do not understand their wives' needs, she explained. "I have never before seen so many wives mentally ill. They now cannot speak out or talk things over. They say they are tired, feel alone, afraid and also homesick. They are so spiritless; they cannot produce any outburst."

She pointed out to the husbands that they spent more time with the livestock than with their wives. "It is disgraceful, for God's sake; you see your wife the least of all!" She told the men that pregnancy is a difficult time and wives need special understanding. "Help the wife by listening! Talk things over with patience, with tenderness. Say to her, 'I love you!' That will please any woman, any time." Her advice could have been given to urban men as well, since their total immersion in the business of a burgeoning city surely led to the same kind of neglect. (For livestock, read iron and coal.)

Physical abuse and battered women were subjects no one talked about. Given the heavy drinking that took place on the frontier and in polite urban society, there was bound to be violence. In 1824 magistrate Sevin Bell wrote to his niece:

> I have a complaint this morning against a clergyman for whipping his wife last night, he is a rigid Covenanter all the way from *ould* Ireland, and altho a very young and handsome man he is very fond of *whiskey*—and his good and prudent wife thinking and perhaps knowing he had drank enough and a little more, hid the bottle and he took up his horse whip—. When the neighbors went in to her relief they found her entirely naked and he pouring water on her. Miss Deibler states that when she was assisting her on with her shirt she discovered her back very

> much striped. It is so scandalous a thing I have, for the honor of the clergy, advised it may be hushed up. I hope they will follow my advice for I feel too indignant to be a proper judge of the punishment. [LeMoyne Papers, ALS, July 14, 1824]

In *The Lady's Token*, "Directions for the Ladies" exhorts women to behave obligingly when a man is out of temper. "If he is abusive, never retort—and never prevail over him to humble himself."

Among the staple items in the *Pittsburgh Gazette* were husbands' announcements about wives who had left their husbands' bed and board. The very first issue of the paper to carry advertisments on the front page in 1787 included a statement by John Clevedance that he would no longer be responsible for the debts of his wife Catherine, who "for some time past behaved in an unbecoming manner." Abraham Morgan of Washington County announced that his wife Susanna had "eloped from my bed and board and behaved in a very scandalous manner." Even more explicit was J. C. of Pittsburgh.

> Whereas my wife, Isabella Culbertson, has gone off with one John Deary, alias Rouney, and [they] have carried off some valuable property belonging to me, I hereby offer a reward of FIVE DOLLARS to any person or persons who will secure the said John Deary. And I hereby advertise that no person credit the said Isabella Culbertson, as I will pay no debts on her account. It is said they stole a canoe and went down the river. —J.C., Pittsburgh, March 23, 1787.
>
> N.B. Said Deary has taken with him the subscriber's certificate of the oath of allegiance to this state, and may pass himself by my name.

Surely there is a plot for a novel here. Did Isabella marry Culbertson for security? Was he many years older than she was? And was John Deary, a handsome young hired hand, full of blarney, ready to comfort her. Did they take everything they could lay their hands on, including a certificate which would lend credence to their story, steal a canoe and flee into the wilderness never to be heard from again? Perhaps they drowned in the river, or were captured by Indians, or died of snakebite. Is there a chance that they lived happily ever after? The odds are against it.

Sometimes the woman who had left her husband fought back. In 1800 James Hilliard, a farrier, published an advertisement refusing to pay debts for his wife. Mrs. Hilliard, who had inherited property in her own right from her father, immediately responded in the same newspaper. She noted that her husband had requested her to take the children and call on a friend, and while she was gone, he had sold all of her household effects, including her clothing. Since all her rightfully owned articles were now gone, she had no bed and board to go to. She countered by stating that no credit should be given to *him* on the strength of her estate, and in the future, her estate "shall not be expended in paying his tavern bills."

Divorce in Pennsylvania was legally possible in the late 18th century, but in fact virtually unknown. In 1785 divorces could be granted on the grounds of

Jane Grey Cannon Swisshelm, 1815-1884
Self-portrait, c. 1845. HSWP Collection.

Born in Pittsburgh, Jane Swisshelm became an advocate of abolition and women's legal rights, authoring numerous letters and articles which appeared in local newspapers. She fought for property rights for married women and began a weekly journal called *The Saturday Visitor*, in which she published numerous articles against slavery. In 1850 she ran for mayor of Pittsburgh and received three votes. She also became a contributor to the *New York Tribune*. During the Civil War she worked as a nurse in hospitals and camps. She lived most of her life in Pittsburgh, where she died in 1884.

adultery, willful desertion of four or more years, bigamy, and "knowledge of sexual incapacity before marriage." Pennsylvania was considered liberal in comparison with the New England states, especially in regard to provisions for separation. As long as women remained married, they had claims on their husbands for financial support, even if they were separated. As soon as a divorce was made final, however, husbands had no legal obligation whatsoever to support the woman.

Jane Swisshelm's marriage was a stormy one, and after 21 years of conflict, she took the couple's child and left. Three years later her husband filed for divorce and was granted one on the grounds of desertion. But such cases took many years of litigation, all the way to the Supreme Court in one instance, before they were finally resolved.

There were, of course, many happy marriages, but one rarely hears of the couples who lived together devotedly. One young man wrote to his friend in 1786, "The moment you taste the happiness of the marriage union, you will curse yourself for a fool, that you have lived so long without it." At the death of her husband in 1818, Sarah Ripley Stearns wrote, "I did love him, alas but too tenderly—we lived together on such terms as man and wife ought to live, placing perfect confidence in each other, bearing one another's burdens and making due allowances for human imperfections." On the frontier, men and women needed each other, and even the most difficult circumstances required that they reach an accommodation in order to survive and prosper. The lucky ones, like Liwwät Böke, could say of their husbands:

> He loved me, I him. As two we were in all things one, in work, viewpoint, suffering. At the table, at prayer, with the children, with everything. Our relationship, experiences and sexuality delighted us both in the same way. That was to us another gift from God. [Böke, p. 134]

The ambivalence with which both men and women approached marriage is understandable. Women were expected to give up any expectations of power, status, and personal achievement, and surrender their futures to their husbands. Men took on the complete responsibility for the financial support and well-being of their wives and children. As Nancy Cott notes, women in the 19th century were exalted by their roles as wives and mothers, but at the same time, society restricted these roles by refusing to grant them the freedom to be anything else. A Chicago businessman wrote:

> Nature made woman weaker, physically and mentally, than man, and also better and more refined. Man, compared with her is coarse, strong and aggressive. By confining themselves to the duties for which nature has prepared them, respectively, the better they will harmonize. Let her stay in; let him go out. [Dewhurst, p. 39]

Women were permitted to venture into the wider world only to help make society better for their families through teaching, charitable endeavors, and reform movements. Yet even the most conservative members of society conceded that the influence "a good woman" wielded over her husband and children was of the utmost importance. Her role as a wife and mother was to nurture, to educate, to dispense warmth, love, and tenderness. Her moral superiority was recognized as a civilizing influence on the family, and thus, on the wider world.

The early 19th century was a time of rapid political, social, and economic change, and women particularly had difficulty in adhering to the roles prescribed for them by previous generations. As the century progressed, these roles were questioned and re-examined, but the importance of maintaining a happy home and educating young children for the future was rarely called into question. Men concerned with the business of making money were increasingly absent from the home, and women were expected to maintain the spiritual and moral strength of the family. Sarah Josepha Hale, the influential editor of Godey's *The Lady's Book*, wrote, "Our men are sufficiently [*sic*] money making….Let us keep our women and children from the contagion as long as possible." §

Bedford Springs, *engraving by Sherman Day, 1843. Leisure activity could be found here, a bucolic setting with good food and wine, and the comforting knowledge that you were in the company of the "right" people.*

Early Christmas Card by W. M. Egley, c. 1845.

Fun & Games

Considering the amount of work necessary to survive on the frontier, it would not be surprising if recreation and relaxation had been unknown words in the pioneers' vocabulary. As it turned out, however, the settlers found ingenious ways to combine work and play by using every opportunity to join with their neighbors to accomplish major projects like raising barns, happily followed by the consumption of large quantities of food and a little hell-raising. These gatherings were not only productive but also offered participants an important respite from the anxieties and frustrations of frontier life.

Every record we have of life in the wilderness emphasizes the importance of cooperation among neighbors. If there *were* no close neighbors, people were willing to travel long distances to participate in cabin building, field clearing, butchering, flax scutching, barn raising, cornhusking, quilting, weddings, and a vast array of other crucial activities. And, like the everyday lives of the settlers, parties and celebrations tended to be seasonal. There was less free time during the summer because of farm chores, and there was more leisure in the early spring and late fall before planting and after the harvest.

To many of us, some of these "frolics" may seem too stereotypical to be taken seriously. Since grade school we have heard tales of quilting bees and corn huskings among the happy pioneers. Actually, stereotypes tend to have substantial nuggets of truth in them, which is, of course, why they have become stereotypes. Settlers soon learned that their families often were not large enough to supply all the labor they needed. Collaborating with neighbors in a combination of work and play served both utilitarian and social ends. The family in need of help became host for the day and whatever else they had to do as well, the women of the household faced the unrelenting task of providing food and drink for the hungry and thirsty volunteer workers.

Shucking a harvest of corn was an onerous and uncomfortable task, but ingenious farmers discovered several ways to accomplish it. Corn could be

> "I have never heard a woman speak of this diversion but with rapture. In sleighing weather the tavern and innkeepers are up all night.... "
>
> —a European visitor

husked out of the shock in the fields by the men, while the women cooked, spun, or quilted. The more popular method, however, was to cut the shocks, haul them to the barn, and pile them in a circle with a middle space in which to toss the husked cobs. Captains were chosen and teams lined up. An old-time settler looking back on his youth remembered the fun as well as the work load.

> Then came the liveliest, noisiest contest you ever saw, to see which side would husk through to the goal first, the losing side to pay forfeits to the "winners"…. How the boys did work while the girls on each side urged them on, and did their full share of the fun-making as well as some of the husking.

Whether or not the girls helped in the husking, they joined their mothers in preparing the food which rewarded the workers.

> This cornhuskers' supper was no ordinary affair. In quantity, quality and variety, that old table was spread with the best the season could afford and was the result of no small amount of work on the part of the hostess and her daughters. As one good old grandmother used to express it, "It took longer to get the supper than it did to husk the corn." [Galley, pp. 327-28]

When supper had been cleared away, guests were invited to stay for dancing, unless they were the strictest of Presbyterians. Most communities had at least one fiddler, but if not, the dancers sang and clapped their hands. Everyone took part in square sets and three- and four-handed reels, while the younger and more vigorous guests stamped their way through Irish jigs or impromptu figures of their own design.

Cabin and barn raisings were another task to be combined with fun and games. A farmer could cut his own logs but could not put them in place without help. On the appointed day families from miles around gathered at the homestead and the men notched the logs, split others to make the puncheon floor, and with substantial effort raised the logs into place. After an abundant noon dinner prepared by the women, the roof was laid on and the cracks chinked with mud. As with every community party, dancing followed well into the night.

One task, always performed by women, that also lent itself to cooperative effort was spinning. Although all women had to spin in their own homes to make thread for family clothing and bedding, they lost no opportunity to come together and hold spinning contests, where they might operate as many as 60 spinning wheels. The contest was won by the woman who not only spun the most skeins during the long day but who also produced the best quality of thread. One wonders who prepared the meals on those days.

After cloth had been woven, the material had to be "fulled," or softened. This was men's work and took the form of what were known as "kicking bees." Barefoot men sat in a circle on benches surrounding the cloth. Hot soap suds were poured over the cloth and the men then kicked at it for several hours—with appropriate rest periods and drinking intermissions—until the homespun was soft and shrunken. And, unsurprisingly, they ate a huge supper and walked home with clean feet.

Just as girls sometimes urged their male friends on to husk more corn, men often hung around outside a cabin in which a quilting bee was in progress. In Kentucky, when young unmarried women were at work on a quilt, the boys roamed around outside "plaguin' the girls" in a kind of primitive courtship ritual. When the work was over, they were invited inside to eat and later to dance. This activity moved westward with the frontier, as we know from similar accounts of quilting bees from such far-flung places as Texas, Oklahoma, and the Far West.

In preparation for quilting women saved scraps of worn-out clothing, and then cut them out and pieced them together in various designs. When three or four tops were ready to be quilted, their owner invited her friends over for a day to finish off the coverlets. Her husband set up a large quilting frame, and the women stitched the pieced top to a padded lining with the tiniest of stitches. (Observers of present-day Mennonite women, who still make a prodigious number of quilts, notice that the older women supervise the younger ones very carefully indeed. And if a young woman's stitches are too large or haphazard, she is banished from the quilt frame and assigned another task.)

Quilting served several purposes. It put scraps of cloth to good use and created a product that kept family members warm. Piecing the cloth into patterns gave the women a chance to express their creativity, an opportunity not often provided by the nature of their daily chores. There was an added bonus of friendly gatherings, gossip, and exchange of information among women who were frequently isolated from female companionship for long periods. And for all members of the family, quilts offered an evocative record of their history, as in the case of the small boy who pointed to a tiny quilt square and proudly proclaimed, 'Them's me pants."

Quilting patterns were passed down within families and exchanged with neighbors. Just because a pattern was traditional and popular, like Log Cabin or Double Wedding Ring, did not mean that the woman making it could not use her own ingenuity, and the kinds of materials used, especially the colors, were the result of an individual's taste and talent and the materials at hand. As one quilter wrote:

> [Y]ou're just given so much to work with in a life and you have to do the best you can with what you got. That's what piecing is. The material is passed on to you or is all you can afford to buy....that's just what's given to you. Your fate. But the way you put it together is your business. [Myres, p. 15]

Frontier social life occasionally allowed for just plain parties, where no work was expected to be accomplished. The legendary kissing parties enabled young men and women to conduct adolescent courtship in the company of their peers and have fun while doing it. To the accompaniment of loud and boisterous reels and jigs and usually accompanied by a fiddle, boys and girls danced and sang folk songs, ending each verse with a kiss. Every girl had to be kissed at least once before a new verse could be started, but the earliest receivers of kisses were undoubtedly the belles of the community, and they must have felt a special triumph at being selected.

Almost every community occasion—weddings, work parties, and political gatherings—offered an opportunity for men and boys to display certain skills that separated them from the women. The Reverend James Finley wrote, "The men then went some to shooting at a mark, some to throwing the tomahawk, others to hopping and jumping, throwing the rail or shoulder-stone, others to running footraces; the women were employed in cooking."

Short winter evenings offered little opportunity for leisure. If the family was not working—spinning, weaving, and knitting for the women, whittling, mending tools, cleaning guns for the men, shelling corn, cracking nuts, sewing rags for carpets for the children—there was little to do except go to bed. But if someone in the family could read and there was sufficient light, they might read aloud for everyone's pleasure. An anonymous writer recalled that in his youth:

We had....the Bible, George Fox's Journal, Barkeley's Apology, and a number of books, all much better than much of the fashionable reading of the present day....To our stock of books were soon after added a borrowed copy of Pilgrim's Progress, which we read twice through without stopping. ["Our Cabin," p. 443]

One of the few winter pleasures on the frontier was sleighing. A visitor from Europe observed in 1802, "I have never heard a woman speak of this diversion but with rapture. In sleighing weather the tavern and innkeepers are up all night and the whole country is in motion." Individual couples would visit friends, but a procession of sleighs with a fiddler in the lead was the most fun. The traveler noted that at every tavern, all the couples alighted and danced. Another writer reminisced:

How everybody kept open house, as it were, even into the night, when sleigh-bells were heard in the crisp cold winter air. How the joyous party would stop where any young folks lived; how there would be a rush of girls and boys with red noses and cheeks into the house; how the metheglin [a honey and hard cider drink] and mince pies, and doughnuts, and apples, and nuts were brought out and eaten and drunk; and how they rushed off with shouts and laughter and tumbled into the sleigh or sled among quilts and comforters and coverlets and straw and sped away, laughing and singing, to the next house. [Fletcher, pp. 449-50]

Amusements in the town, especially in Pittsburgh, were more sophisticated, but sleighing seems to have carried over its charm to the big city. Thomas Ashe, visiting from England, wrote:

> All young men of a certain condition provide themselves with handsome carioles [*sic*] and good horses, and take out their favorite female friends, whom with much dexterity they drive through the streets; calling on every acquaintance and taking refreshment at many an open house. For the night, an appointment is generally made by a large party (for instance, the company of twenty or thirty carioles) to meet at a tavern several miles distant; to which they go by torchlight, and accompanied by music. On arriving there, the ladies cast off their fur pelisses, assume all their beauties, and with the men commence the mazy dance. [Ashe, p. 23]

The wearing of a "fur pelisse" would indicate that the upper classes enjoyed sleighing as much as their wilderness contemporaries, but in an urban environment class differences were more marked than in the countryside.

Successful businessmen and professionals—the doctors and lawyers—comprised the upper crust, and their wives kept the cultural and social torches burning. Looking back, a social arbiter in 1888 suggested that in 1788 Pittsburgh society consisted of only a few families, and:

> [T]hese, while of sturdy stock and sterling honesty, could be looked on as comparatively lacking in culture, and somewhat deficient in the refinements which are the distinguishing characteristics of the society today. [Nevin, p. 121]

The wives of James O'Hara and General Wilkeson, who gave lavish balls and parties, would surely have taken issue with this assessment.

Hugh Henry Brackenridge, jurist and author, noted that after the Revolutionary War, a number of army officers, "families of the first respectability," returned to Pittsburgh and provided "a degree of refinement, elegance of manners and polished society, not often found in the extreme frontier."

In 1813, Nancy Swearingen, the well-born Virginian wife of Captain James Swearingen assigned to the quartermaster corps at Fort Pitt, displayed somewhat ambivalent feelings about Pittsburgh when she followed her husband to take up residence in the garrison. Although she thought Pittsburgh "a very pretty place," she was disappointed in her reception there. "The society in this place," she wrote to her family, "is very indifferent, the people not

An elegant, winter ball costume, from Harper's New Monthly Magazine, *1851.*

more attentive to Strangers than other parts of Pennsylvania." She was not impressed with the married daughter of General Neville, "who is, I have been told," she wrote, "quite bloated and disfigured with the ardent [alcohol], the case with many other ladies of this place, so says common report, but I do not wish this repeated. I am determined to live in harmony with them all." Despite her resolution, in the same letter she mentions the wife of a Fort Pitt lieutenant who was to attend a party, "but she might as well stay home as she will not be noticed." Another "friend" called Morrow "is not respected, keeps a scrub tavern, was once respectable, nobody visits them." The next year, however, she wrote of:

> [A] splendid dance party given by Mrs. Beltzhoover. Everyone in Town. She is a charming, pretty woman. Daughter of Judge Wallace, worth about $20,000 or more. Quite young, 17 or 18, married about 18 months. Her husband a very gentlemanly little fellow. Mrs. Mason's youngest brother, always invited in the first company here. He has a glass-works and is getting very wealthy. [Dandridge Papers, ALS, January 19, 1814]

During the war years, military balls and entertainments had enlivened the social scene in town, and even though the number of active troops at Fort Pitt was greatly reduced after the war, the opening of Fort Fayette took up some of the slack and allowed the social life of the town to shine once again. Women were fond of reminiscing about the varied colors of the officers' uniforms, the ball gowns of silk and brocade, and the elaborate powdered hairdos. Balls given by the Duquesne Grays and the Pittsburgh Blues vied in popularity with "hops" held in the Exchange Hotel or the Monongahela House. An elderly lady remembered a glimpse of an elaborate refreshment table when she was a child, and was allowed to peek at her elders. "Pyramids of maccaroons, buttressed with barley sugar, reaching almost to the chandelier," she wrote. "Ice cream in ravishing shapes....a pyramid of calves-foot jelly glasses, alternating pink and yellow, high openwork china dishes heaped with almonds"—a far cry from the squirrel potpies of the wilderness frolics. [Buck, p. 260]

The work-oriented socializing that formed the backbone of frontier society had little place in an urban environment where the well-to-do could hire or buy various services that frontier dwellers had to do for themselves. This was especially true of women of some means, who might attempt to recapture that aspect of frontier life but were hardly convincing in their efforts to do so. Sevin Bell of Washington, Pennsylvania, wrote his niece:

> They have what they pretend to call the social working parties. They meet after supper, each with their work bag, and they sometimes collect around the candle, but generally, the evening is spent in eating cakes, fruit, and talking and laughing, every one at the same time, and of course, you know there would be but few listeners and but little work. [LeMoyne Papers, ALS, 1824]

Many members of what one might broadly define as the middle class—clerks, merchants with small businesses, skilled craftsmen, managers, and overseers, often people with excellent educations—shared the aspirations of their "betters." Following the American ethos of self-improvement and upward striving, they intended to get rich, and many of them did.

On the lower rungs of society were the laborers in the mills and glass factories who faced relentless 12- and 14-hour work days; river roustabouts; and, among the women, domestic servants of various levels. Lengthy working days and scarce resources put severe limits on the social life of this segment of society.

Roistering in the taverns, however, seemed to cut across all class lines. Nevertheless tavernkeepers catered to the "more refined" classes in special ways. In 1799 William Irwin kept a tavern where, in addition to selling the usual spirits, he also handled a few dry goods and rented out assembly rooms for dancing classes for ladies "at three o' clock in the afternoon" and for gentlemen "at six o'clock in the evening." (In 1801, Irwin named his race horse "Dancing Master.") Tavern owners liked to refer to their establishments as "Houses of Entertainment," and the taverns named "The Sign of the General Butler" and "The Sign of the Waggon" each boasted a ballroom.

Dancing was popular with all levels of society, and Pittsburgh saw an influx of dancing masters in the late 18th and early 19th centuries. In 1798 B. Holdich advertised his intention of teaching country dances, the Scotch minuet, and the City Cotillion as taught in Philadelphia and New York. The same year another dancing master sold tickets for a ball at one dollar a couple and suggested that "The company of his Pupils Parents will be very agreeable to him, as they will have the opportunity of witnessing the improvement of their Children." In1802 Blondel D. St. Hilaire advertised that he intended to open a dancing school, "and hopes to give entire satisfaction to those who favor him with their attendance. He will teach minuets, *minuet de la cour* and every French and English new dance." By 1816 some masters found it necessary to spell out rules of decorum and

From Godey's The Lady's Book, *1849. Musicians of the era found ready employment playing for balls and parties.*

decreed that no gentleman might be admitted unless he had been introduced by a lady known to the dance master, nor would dancing in boots be permitted.

Separate dancing classes were held for ladies, as were classes in music instruction, but concerts were open to all. Pittsburgh evinced an early interest in music and in 1786, a newspaper advertised for a singing master.

> Wanted, a man who understands Vocal Music, and can teach it with propriety; such a person will meet with good encouragement from the inhabitants of Pittsburgh. [*Pittsburgh Gazette,* November 25, 1786]

We don't know if anyone answered the ad, but the following year, Peter Declary and Miss Sophia Weidner gave a public concert in one of the assembly rooms of a tavern, and in 1801 Mr. Declary, describing himself as a "Music Master," gave a concert at the courthouse featuring his pupils. Selections included the *President's March,* later to be called *Hail, Columbia,* and a rendition of Kotzwara's *The Battle of Prague* by an eight-year-old. However, Mr. Declary was either out-classed by other music teachers or dismayed by the quality of the available talent, as he later opened a dry goods store.

In 1808 Fortescue Cuming met a gentleman named Mr. Tyler at a musicale and was impressed with the 60-year-old's skill at teaching sacred music and with his personal story of hardship and sacrifice. The social event that evening was "a numerous party of young people of both sexes," but the Apollonian Society, which he also visited, presented "instrumental musick performed by about a dozen gentlemen of the town, with a degree of taste and execution I would not have expected in so remote a town."

A local store sold instruments and sheet music in 1819 and, by 1841, a business directory listed four music stores. Pianofortes, the instrument of the upper- and middle-class female, were being manufactured in Pittsburgh by 1813, but some musicians preferred to get theirs from Philadelphia if money was not an issue. In 1824 Sarah Claypoole wrote from Philadelphia to Madelaine LeMoyne

in Washington, Pennsylvania, that she had completed her assignment and purchased an imported instrument for her friend.

> I hope your piano will suit you in every particular, as I adhered as strictly as possible to your directions. The Tone is to me, and some excellent judges whom I took to see it, very delightful and remarkable for sweetness, melody....The exterior though not much ornamented is handsome....Yours is made by Gunther and Horwood (London) whose pianos are considered very fine and are remarkable for keeping in tune for a long time. [LeMoyne Papers, ALS, November 12, 1824]

She also sent strings and tuning hammers, along with a stool "covered with light blue Damask and you may think it will be easily soiled." She had preferred crimson but couldn't get it. She sent, as well, a large collection of music and a bill: $308 for the piano and $10.50 for packing.

Amateur theatricals—for men—were popular, but the professional theater got off to a slow start. This was probably due, in part, to the influence of the Presbyterians who formed the preponderant part of the city's population and who considered the theater and everything connected with it immoral. But the absence of a sizeable community of culturally sophisticated people undoubtedly also played a role.

In February of 1803 the "young gentlemen of the town," it was reported, performed a comic opera by John O'Keefe, called *The Poor Soldier*, followed by Arthur Murphy's farce, *The Apprentice*. Earlier the same year two professional actors named Bromley and Arnold arrived to produce several weeks of theatricals, presumably with the aid of the young gentlemen.

> This evening at 7 o'clock will be performed at the Court House, the comedy of "Trick Upon Trick"; also the farce of "The Jealous Husband, or the Lawyer in the Sack," the whole to conclude with the pantomine of "The Sailor's Landlady, or Jack in Distress," with songs, etc., etc., etc. [*Pittsburgh Gazette*, January 20, 1803]

Women were not included in the amateur efforts, though Fortescue Cuming observed that, "The female characters

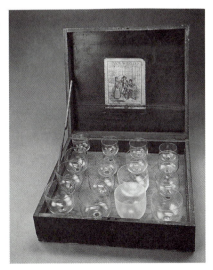

(facing page) Pianoforte, c. 1795. Manufactured by Charles Taws of Philadelphia, this instrument was purchased by Major General Richard Butler for his daughter Mary and transported to Pittsburgh by pack mules. (right) New World Harmonicom, c. 1830. A popular household instrument, it was played by wetting one's fingers and rapidly rubbing the edges of the glasses, with each producing a different note. HSWP Collection.

being sustained by young men, are deficient of that grace and modest vivacity, which are natural to the fair sex, and which their grosser lords and masters vainly attempt to copy." Women were sought after as an audience, however, since their presence lent some tone to the production and suggested that the institution of the theater was refined and respectable—even if this was not always the case.

The first commercial theater in Pittsburgh was erected in 1812 by William Turner, whose wife was a singer and actress "of some local fame." It opened the following year with a performance of a play by Mrs. Inchbald, *To Marry or Not to Marry,* but there is no indication of whether Mrs. Turner had prevailed on her husband to let her appear in this production. Although most of the performers were male, the practice of putting men into female roles seems to have been discontinued once the professionals took over. In 1817 the editor of the *Pittsburgh Gazette,* John Scull, waxed rhapsodic over the new season. He remembered when the town was no more than a village, "when the only circumstances that attended to chase the gnome of dullness....were the occasional visits of an awkward itinerant slight of hand man, or the war dances of our red brethren on their periodical visits to their great father in Washington," and he believed that the appearance of the actress "Mrs. Entwhisle [*sic*] on the Pittsburgh boards will constitute an important era in the annals of western taste and improvement." He made an eloquent plea to "the fair sex in particular to step forward on this occasion and, with their presence as well as praises, prove that taste is not confined to the [Eastern] seaboard."

Dramatic performances remained scarce until 1833, when The Pittsburgh Theater was built on Fifth Avenue. The directors engaged Francis Courtney Weymss, a well-known manager and former actor, to supervise the building and decoration of the theater. He arrived in Pittsburgh with his family on July 10 to find only a shell of a building, although the opening was set for September 1. But all turned out well. The elegant two-story theater accommodated an audience of 1,200 people:

> There were five entrances....two tiers of boxes, rose colored and ornamented with gold, and each bearing the arms of the United States. The seats were covered with crimson and edged with velvet and brass nails, and the auditorium was lighted by eighteen chandeliers. [Baldwin, pp. 263-64]

Second from right in Charles Glenn's 1840 drawing of Fifth Avenue is the ornate facade of The Pittsburgh Theater, popularly known as "Old Drury."

The dressing rooms were carpeted and furnished, and the green room was designed to replicate a "modern drawing room," with pianos, chairs, mirrors, and ottomans. The interior of the theater alone was reputed to have cost upwards of $1,000.

For patrons box seats cost 50 cents and seats in the pit cost 25 cents. The second tier of box patrons were charged 37 1/2 cents, while the gallery seats, two sections of which were reserved for African Americans, cost 12 1/2 cents. There were three bars and a tavern next door.

When the building was completed, the stockholders honored Mr. Weymss's herculean efforts with a dinner at the Shakespeare House tavern, where 60 gentlemen guests dined well and toasted dozens of people and institutions, including the contractors, Mr. Weymss, the press, and the new theater, "not surpassed by any city in the Union." They also toasted education, Shakespeare, Western drama, the march of Refinement and Liberality—"We hail those lovely harbingers of a 'new Era,' even amid clouds of smoke and the fulminations of intolerance"—and finally, the [absent] "Ladies of Pittsburgh—Where they take the lead, who will fear to follow."[Weymss, pp. 221-22]

Despite the elegance of the theater, the audience bordered on the rowdy. Men removed their coats but kept on their tall beaver hats. In 1838 a newspaper commented that "The babel, confusion and uproar, the yelling and cursing— swearing and tearing—the friendly interchange of commodities—apples, pignuts, etc., between the tenants of the upper boxes and pit, have become intolerable."

Manager Francis Weymss engaged the best actors he could find, including Tyrone Power and Junius Brutus Booth (father of Edwin). The playbill usually included one "serious" drama and ended with a farce, but soon the producers offered fewer and fewer serious dramas in favor of more entertaining fare. Since the audiences were not drawn entirely from the intellectual elite of the city, this included a certain amount of slapstick.

Some of Mr. Weymss's famous actors let him down badly, one appearing on stage too drunk to stand and requiring an understudy and the manager himself to fill in. "The theatre was filled with ladies," he wrote, "which I need scarcely add, did not occur again during the season. It was a death-blow to our reputation, and resented as every similar exhibition should be, by every respectable citizen absenting himself from the theatre."

By 1840 Weymss found he could not make the theater profitable even though he had raised the price of box seats to $5 and of gallery seats to 20 cents. The theater fell into disuse and decay but was briefly reopened in 1841 by an English actress, a Miss Clarendon. She distinguished herself by taking a horsewhip to someone who had insulted her, meting out the punishment in the lobby of the theater. In 1844 two men who were rafting down the Allegheny and Ohio rivers buying and selling lumber stopped off in Pittsburgh to attend the theater. "They have a pretty good theater here," one reported, "and quite a good band of music, but they appear to be hard up for performers." The theater was used sporadically until 1870, when it closed for the last time.

The constantly improving Turnpike and National Road made it possible for troops of actors and other performers to visit Pittsburgh as well as Washington and Westmoreland counties. Itinerant showmen brought wild animals, magicians, ventriloquists, sword swallowers, rope-dancers, acrobats, and jugglers to the country as well as the city. Pepin's Circus was the first such show to appear in Pittsburgh in 1814, and in 1819 wild animals were exhibited in the Diamond, the public square on Market Street. By 1840 brightly decorated wagons began to make their appearance on the roads, as Raymond, Waring and Company's Philadelphia Circus turned up in Western Pennsylvania with horses, bands, and Burmese ponies. The shows prided themselves on their decorum, and although they included female equestrians, the ladies were not permitted to wear tights. The show's management took great pains to inform the public that the reputation and behavior of each female performer was impeccable. As one advertisement stated in remarkably oblique prose:

> No females shall in the smallest degree be connected with the performances or travelling of the Exhibition, but that the reputation of their Amphitheatre shall be advanced beyond the slightest possible shadow of obloquy, by the probity and upright conduct of the performers in private, and chaste, talented and astonishing performances in public. [Jordan, p. 334]

Pittsburgh's tastes in entertainment were eclectic, since the town was also favored with appearances by the Albino Lady and the Irish Giant in 1836, and two South Sea Islander brothers with "long claws on both wrists and ancles" [*sic*] in 1844, to be viewed for only 12 1/2 cents. There were displays of waxworks portraying famous people, and other attractions included a display of "philosophical entertainments" as well as "illusions in ventriloquism."

In 1786 the *Gazette* advertised that the Jockey Club would commence races on October 19, with "3-mile heats," an entrance fee of $5, and a purse of $120. The same year the club decreed that "no jockey will be permitted to ride unless he has some genteel Jockey Habit," perhaps a hint that female sensibilities were being bruised by the riders' uncouth attire. Race days took on the atmosphere of a carnival, with performing animals, acrobats, and other exciting entertainments in evidence, along with many booths selling food and drink. Brackenridge, describing the race days of his youth, claimed that the entire town turned out for them,

"many of all ages and sexes as spectators." Although an effort was made to keep the races out of the hands of "the criminal element," not everyone thought that they were conducted honestly. William Irwin took out an ad in the *Pittsburgh Gazette* to express his displeasure:

> Let no one hereafter expect either justice or pleasure from the Races at McKee's Port if under the direction of the Jockey Club or Judges who preside over the last. [*Pittsburgh Gazette*, October 2, 1801]

Zadok Cramer's bookstore and circulating library, which flourished during the first half of the 19th century, offered both men and women excellent opportunities to catch up on the latest literary works. Books of moral and religious significance, as well as scientific treatises, made up the bulk of the shop and library stock, but there were also romantic novels with tales of bygone days. "Ladies were the principal readers" of works by such writers as Mrs. Ann Ward Radcliffe and Charles Brockden Brown. Other works whose provocative titles suggest adventure or romance novels have sunk without a trace, including: *The Silver Devil, Being the Adventures of an Evil Spirit; The Wanderings of William, or the Inconstancy of Youth; Julia and the Illuminated Baron;* and *The Rebel, Being a Memoir of Anthony 4th Earl of Sherwell, Including an Account of the Rising at Taunton in 1684, Compiled and Set Forth by his Cousin, Sir Hilary Mace.*

Cramer also operated a small printing and publishing business and his success encouraged others to open similar estabishments. By 1816 more than 100 titles had been published in the city, including the third volume of local resident Hugh Henry Brackenridge's novel *Modern Chivalry*. In 1801 Cramer ran a self-congratulatory ad in the newspaper:

> It is observed with pleasure that the number of readers has doubled since its commencement, which is only about six months. It would seem to justify a conclusion, that an enlightened and observing public scarcely ever fail in advancing an institution whose sole principle is the public good. [*Pittsburgh Gazette*, December 18, 1801]

As one would expect, the "old-timers" decried the increasingly sophisticated entertainments and longed for the simpler good old days. Samuel Jones asked:

> Where are our pleasant social tea-drinkings? our sturdy blind-man's bluff; our evening chit-chat, in which both sexes participated, without a thought of visiting cards…? Where are the strawberry huntings; the unclassed balls; the charming promenades, of which all partook with light hearts, and careless of fashionable ceremonies? [Jones, pp. 52-53]

He admitted, however, that "the days of simple happiness, which were once enjoyed upon the banks of our two, aye, three pleasant streams, are gone, and it would be very silly to mourn over them."

Pittsburgh was somewhat inhospitable to art and artists, except for the occasional exhibition of a famous painting on tour. Portrait painters were the exception, and several of them made good livings painting the likenesses of Pittsburgh's rich and famous, among them Hugh Henry Brackenridge; his son Henry Marie Brackenridge; Ebenezer Denny, the city's first mayor and captain of industry; and historian Neville B. Craig. For public display, biblical subjects were popular, as were representations of foreign antiquities.

A review of 100 years of progress in Allegheny County offers the tersest of comments about art.

> Of the early artists, if such there were who were native to the locality, they have left no impress on the times, either by works or in memories. Among the older features are family portraits, but they are the work of occasional artists, either imported from the East, to do a special portrait, or on an accidental tour, staying in Pittsburgh a while to pick up a few dollars with a "pot boiler." [Thurston, p. 307]

A French artist exhibited paintings of Mount Etna and Mount Vesuvius, and Mr. Parmly, a dentist, advertised that he would see patients from "9 until 2," and then would display a painting of the Capuchin Chapel at Rome for a few days from "3 until 9," admittance 12 1/2 cents. *The Temptation of Adam and Eve* and *The Expulsion from Paradise* were shown for two weeks, as was a painting of Cain meditating on the death of his brother Abel. A French painter passing through the city summed up the feelings of many Easterners when he observed, after taking a suspicious sniff of the carbonized air, "There could not be any art worth mentioning in a city where the whole gamut of the artist's palette could be represented by cork black and flake white." [Nevin, p. 97]

There is little evidence of the development of important local talent of either sex, and certainly an "artistic" woman would have been encouraged to pursue her interests only for the edification of her family and friends. Journalist Jane Gray Swisshelm, for example, needed to support her family after her father died in 1823, so she sold her lacework and paintings on velvet for additional income. Despite the interest of a possible patron who offered to pay for her to have further training in art, her family would not permit this. She later declared that it was not possible to have "had an artistic education, or any other education....for a Western Pennsylvania girl in that dark age—the first half of the nineteenth century."

The exclusionary behavior of males was both the written and the unwritten law at this period. Men formed debating clubs, classical literary societies, choirs, political clubs, drinking and dining clubs, amateur theatrical groups, and fraternal lodges like the Masons. Women were sometimes invited to musical and theatrical entertainments, but only as observers, never as participants. Men went hunting, fishing, rode to hounds, attended the race track, participated in military musters and drills, played billiards, spent leisurely hours drinking in taverns and talking politics, visited beer cellars and brothels, played in bands, and marched in parades. A good wife kept the house in order, provided meals, entertained her husband's friends as needed, raised the children, ministered to the poor, attended church, and participated in such leisure activities as her husband deemed appropriate.

The elite and affluent classes of women called upon one another, took carriage rides, planned lavish parties, entertained at tea, and went shopping. Some of them undoubtedly felt the way Sarah Eve of Philadelphia did when engaged in a seemingly endless round of calls and tea parties. Visiting an acquaintance for dinner, she observed:

> [D]are I call it the *shallow* elegance of my surroundings and the more shallow compliments and conversation of the greatest part of the company....We drank Tea at candlelight, the silver candle sticks very handsome and much admired. As soon as possible I bade the company goodnight...I came home thanking fate that I had so little to do with high life and its attendants! [Eve, p. 202]

Middle-class ladies participated in charitable fairs and sewing circles and did their large-scale entertaining in public facilities, since their homes were not large enough to accommodate many guests.

Both groups of women enjoyed promenades with their husbands in the evenings, and Grant's Hill was often crowded with strolling couples. In the summer the hill was covered with grass and bushes, with level open spaces for walking. Judge Henry M. Brackenridge looked back fondly on the time when "it was pleasing to see the line of well-dressed ladies and gentlemen and children. ...repairing to the beautiful green eminence."

The wives of workers and laborers occasionally continued the frontier tradition of work-oriented leisure, and bees of various sorts offered an opportunity for socializing without the expenditure of much money. The absence of servants in most of their homes meant less time available for recreation, and working-class women tended to see one another infrequently except for marketing trips and other task-oriented occasions.

As roads and transportation improved, excursions into the country offered another option for leisure activity. Working-class families could not afford anything but brief day trips, but their needs were served by places such as Saxe-Hall Gardens, a pleasant rural space just outside the smoky city, or Greenwood and Rosedale Gardens, a mile or so from Pittsburgh on the Monongahela River, where a

Carriage costume, from Harper's New Monthly Magazine, *1850.*

small admission charge offered the chance to stroll, picnic, and participate in outdoor sports. Hotels and taverns in Allegheny or Point Breeze offered upscale accommodations and activities for those with more money and leisure, including riding and sports for the men and needlework and conversation for the women.

For the most affluent the choices were very attractive. One of the spots favored by the elite was Bedford Springs, which offered a bucolic setting, good food and wine, and the comforting knowledge that you were in the company of the "right" people. The diversions for the ladies were similar to those available in the city—needlework and chatting with friends. The young unmarried girls thought about the eligible men and hoped they would be noticed. Men indulged their pleasure in field sports while women waited for the return of the hunters—and waited, and waited. A lady from Bedford recalled:

> How the girls waited in their rooms until midnight for the delicate dishes of fried trout, sure to be sent up to them with compliments of friends and admirers who had caught them. Oh, the glory of having several dishes of such tribute....We were a simpler-minded set of feminines in those days, fond of the good things in this life, which we took when offered without troublesome introspection. [Martin, p. 190]

There was some mingling of the sexes on special occasions—weddings, funerals, holidays, especially on the Fourth of July, but even then women took a passive role, watching the fireworks, cheering the parade of militia men, and listening to political speeches, though rarely discussing their content. "A female politician," warned *The Female Friend*, a handbook of appropriate behavior for women, "is only less disgusting than a female infidel." But the author was careful to distinguish a female politician from a female patriot, which is what "every American woman should study to be."

Political rallies were great social occasions, but only for men. Since women could not vote, there was no need to court their favor, and elected officials and aspiring officeholders limited their bonfire rallies and generous distribution of hard liquors to men. When David Porter ran for governor of Pennsylvania in 1830, he advertised a Pittsburgh rally and barbecue by scattering handbills throughout the Western Pennsylvania counties.

> When the great day came around, the jubilant host assembled on a large sandbar in the Monogahela River about opposite the mouth of Wood Street, and there, having erected a spit and kindled a fire, they roasted an ox; and all present were invited to partake of the feast....A bridge of flatboats afforded a highway for passing to and fro. [Johnson, p. 50]

We know from letters and diaries that many women were concerned about politics and the state of the world. Although they may have been loathe to express their opinions publicly, they were not reluctant to let family and friends know how they felt. Nancy Swearingen's letters to her family in Virginia are full of political pronouncements and opinions, particularly about the military. "The attack on Macinaw was badly planned," she wrote in 1814. "Nothing but blunders and disasters, except Brown's command which has been glorious though at the expense of many, many lives." The same year she wrote with disgust that she had never seen so much "waste, destruction and loss of public property in any country than by the Northwestern Army. I have heard 20 officers say so! $50 for a barrel of flour, $30 a bushel for corn. We must have it, said the General. Spare no expenses. The treasury is open to me." By 1829, living in Ohio, she had not mellowed:

> General Jackson is doing all the mischief he can. I begin to think Democracy and equal rights are very pretty things on paper. In theory but the Practice of late I deplore. No man should vote unless he is a freeholder, here [in Ohio] the most ignorant, low creatures....can be bought for 1 pint of whiskey, the vote of such is as good as the best man in Ohio, this cannot be right, our country is in a fair way to go as all republics [that] fall into the hands of a military chief. Tis a most dangerous precedent. [Dandridge Papers, ALS, April, 1829]

On lavish public occasions, such as the visit of General LaFayette to Western Pennsylvania in 1825, female patriots stood in the streets alongside school children and strewed flowers in the street as the hero's procession made its way to his headquarters at the Mansion House. The evening's banquet was a stag affair, but presumably the "magnificent ball at the Pittsburgh Hotel" which followed the dinner included the ladies.

The presence of women was often sought for educational and cultural events, as the organizers apparently believed that this added a stamp of gentility to the affair. In Washington in 1843, a hotel owner exhibited a night-blooming Ceres plant, and "a throng of citizens of both sexes, and troops of the more juvenile classes" stopped by to see the flowers bloom and die at dawn. At an 1836 lecture on phrenology, the expert was pleased to see most of Pittsburgh's "literati" in the hall, but "what is better than them all, the Ladies, those bright luminaries which light up the otherwise dark horizon of man's existence, turned out almost en masse."

The idea of woman lighting up man's existence was embodied in the 19th-century cult of true womanhood. Since women were considered morally superior to men and were charged with the responsibility of civilizing the home, it was small wonder that theater managers and lecturers sought their attendance to add an aura of respectability to the event.

Whatever cultural aspirations a society might have, it was clearly women's responsibility to make them work. Denied a traditional and classical education, they formed self-improvement groups and encouraged their husbands to participate in the intellectual and cultural events available to them. Difficulties arose only when, perhaps as a result of all that culture, women did indeed become involved in "troublesome introspection." §

AFTERWORD

At noon on April 10, 1845, a small fire broke out in a laundry shed near the center of Pittsburgh, and within an hour the blaze was roaring through the city. High winds fanned the flames, which spread eastward across the business district, destroying glass factories, iron works, churches, cotton factories, retail stores, bridges, the luxurious Monongahela House and other hotels, and more than 1,100 dwellings. Before the fire burned itself out, more than 60 acres of the city—one-third of its total area—had been destroyed and property damage was estimated to amount to more than six million dollars.

· Families huddled together in church basements and other hastily constructed shelters, while businessmen sadly surveyed what little remained of their establishments. But despite the confusion and despair, there were acts of bravery and compassion. The *Pittsburgh Gazette* reported that, "The sufferers bore their calamities with manly firmness, and as soon as they had unavailingly tried to save their own property, they put forth their exertions to save their neighbor's."

Much needed contributions poured in from all over the country and Europe—money, clothing, household articles, and food—since even those fortunate enough to have insurance discovered that the insurance companies had also suffered losses and would pay only a few cents on the dollar in compensation. Town meetings were held, and relief efforts organized, as Pittsburgers made plans to rebuild their city. And rebuild they did. New stores sprang up and factories began to function again, and the new Monongahela House was even more elegant than its predecessor. And wives and mothers began to put their lives back together again.

A woman who had arrived in Pittsburgh at the turn of the 19th century and had spent 50 or more years in the city, would have been able to document the small miracles of indoor plumbing, adequate heating, improved lighting, paved streets, and access to a cornucopia of goods now manufactured west of the Alleghenies. But because some changes take longer than others, her life would still have been circumscribed by her traditional role as wife and mother.

Many years would pass before expectations for women changed substantially. Indeed, while American proponents of women's right to vote began their struggle in 1848, this basic goal was not achieved until 1920. But despite only small gains in legal rights and professional and educational opportunities in the early 19th century, American women exhibited extraordinary determination and resourcefulness in establishing new lives for themselves and their families in the wilderness and towns of Western Pennsylvania.

Virginia K. Bartlett

SOURCES & SUGGESTED READINGS

*Allegheny County Sesquicentennial Review. Pittsburgh: Allegheny County Sesquicentennial Committee, 1938.

*Anderson, Edward Park. "Intellectual Life of Pittsburgh 1786-1836."Western Pennsylvania Historical Magazine. Pittsburgh: Historical Society of Western Pennsylvania, 1913.

*Armstrong, John. Patterson's Pittsburgh Town and Country Magazine for 1819. Pittsburgh: Patterson and Lambdin, 1819.

*Ashe, Thomas. Travels in America, London: Richard Phillips, 1809.

Bailey, Francis. Journal of a Tour in Unsettled Parts of North America in 1796 and 1797. London: Baily Brothers, 1856.

*Baldwin, Leland. Pittsburgh, The Story of a City. Pittsburgh: University of Pittsburgh Press, 1937.

*Bank, Mirra. Anonymous Was a Woman. New York: St. Martin's Press, 1979.

*Barlow, William and David O. Powell, "Frontier Medicine and Life." Western Pennsylvania Historical Magazine. Pittsburgh: Historical Society of Western Pennsylvania, 1978.

*Bausman, Reverend Joseph H. History of Beaver County, Pa. and Its Centennial Celebration. Vol. 1. New York: Knickerbocker Press, 1904.

*Baxter, Francis. "Rafting on the Allegheny and Ohio in 1844." Pennsylvania Magazine of History and Biography. Philadelphia: Historical Society of Pennsylvania, 1927.

Beecher, Catharine E. Treatise on Domestic Economy. New York: Harper and Brothers, 1846.

*____Miss Beecher's Domestic Receipt-Book. New York: Harper and Brothers, 1854.

*Böke, Liwwät, Luke B. Knapke, ed. Liwwät Böke 1807-1882 Pioneer. Minster, Ohio: Minster Historical Society, 1987.

*Brackenridge, Henry Marie. Recollections of Persons and Places in the West. Philadelphia: James Kay, Jr., and Brother, 1834.

Bryce, Charles C. "The Backwoodsman Era in Western Pennsylvania." Western Pennsylvania Historical Society Magazine. Pittsburgh: Historical Society of Western Pennsylvania, 1941.

*Buck, Solon and Elizabeth Buck. The Planting of Civilization in Western Pennsylvania. Pittsburgh: University of Pittsburgh Press, 1971.

*Burland, Rebecca. A True Story of Immigration. Chicago: Lakeside Press, 1936.

Caley, Percy B. "Child Life in Colonial Western Pennsylvania." Western Pennsylvania Historical Magazine. Pittsburgh: Historical Society of Western Pennsylvania, 1926.

*Carlo, Joyce. Trammels, Trenchers and Tartlets. Old Saybrook, Conn.: Peregrine Press, 1986.

*Century of Population Growth 1790-1900, A. Washington, D.C.: Government Printing Office, 1909.

*Chalfant, Ella. A Goodly Heritage. Pittsburgh: University of Pittsburgh Press, 1955.

*Cheesman, Abiah Herrick. White Servitude in Pennsylvania. Philadelphia: John Joseph McVey, 1926.

*Child, Lydia Maria. The American Frugal Housewife. Boston: Carter, Hindee and Co., 1833.

*Cooper, James Fenimore. The Chainbearer. New York: G.P. Putnam and Son, 1896.

*Cott, Nancy. The Bonds of Womanhood: Women's Sphere in New England 1780-1835. New Haven, Conn.: Yale University Press, 1977.

*Craig, Neville B. A History of Pittsburgh. Pittsburgh: John Mellor, 1851.

Cramer, Zadok. Cramer's Almanac 1816. Pittsburgh, 1816.

____Cramer's Almanac 1821. Pittsburgh, 1821.

____Cramer's Almanac 1822. Pittsburgh, 1822.

*Cramer, Zadok, Karl Yost, ed. The Navigator. Madison, Ill.: Karl Yost, 1987.

*Cuming, Fortescue. Sketches of a Tour to the Western Country. Pittsburgh: Cramer, Spear and Michlaum, 1810.

*Cummings, Richard Osborn. The American and His Food. New York: Arno Press, 1970.

*D'Arusmont, Frances Wright. Views of Society and Manners in America. New York: E. Bliss and E. White, 1821.

*Dahlinger, Charles W. Pittsburgh: A Sketch of Its Early Social Life. New York: G.P. Putnam, 1916.

Darlington, Mrs. M. Carson. Fort Pitt and Letters from the Frontier. Pittsburgh: J.R. Weldin and Co., 1892.

*De Pauw, Linda Grant and Conover Hunt. Remember the Ladies: Women in America 1750-1815. New York: Viking Press, 1976.

*Dewhurst, C.K., Betty McDowell and Marsha McDowell. Artists in Aprons. New York: E.P. Dutton, 1979.

*"Diary of 1822, A." Pennsylvania Magazine of Biography and History. Philadelphia: Historical Society of Pennsylvania, 1928.

*Diller, Theodore, M.D. Pioneer Medicine in Western Pennsylvania. New York: Paul B. Hoeber, 1927.

---

* Cited in this volume.

*Doddridge, Joseph. *Notes on the Settlement and Indian Wars of West Virginia and Pennsylvania.* Pittsburgh: John C. Rittenour and William T. Lindsay, 1912.

*Douds, Howard Calvin. *Merchants and Merchandising in Pittsburgh, 1758-1800.* Ph.D. Dissertation. University of Pittsburgh, 1937.

*Drake, Daniel, M.D., Emmett Field Horine, M.D., ed. *Pioneer Life in Kentucky 1785-1800.* Mt. Vernon, N.Y.: Golden Eagle Press, 1948.

*Dwight, Margaret Van Horn, Max Farrand, ed. *A Journey to Ohio in 1810.* Yale University Press: New Haven, Conn., 1912.

*Earle, Alice Morse. *Home Life in Colonial Days.* New York: Grosset and Dunlap, 1898.

____*Two Centuries of Costume in America 1620-1820.* Vol. 2. New York: Dover Publications, 1970.

*Eve, Sarah. "Extracts from the Journal of Miss Sarah Eve." *Pennsylvania Magazine of History and Biography.* Philadelphia: Historical Society of Pennsylvania, 1881.

*Ewing, James Hunter, John C. Dann, ed. "An Account of Travel to Western Pennsylvania, Niagra [sic] Falls, and Return by Way of Erie Canal, 1826." *American Magazine and Historical Chronicle.* Ann Arbor, Mich.: University of Michigan, 1986-87.

Finley, James B., W.P. Strickland, ed. *Autobiography of James B. Finley or Pioneer Life in the West.* Cincinnati: Methodist Book Concern, 1855.

*Fletcher, Stevenson Whitcomb. *Pennsylvania Agriculture and Country Life.* Vol. 1. Harrisburg, Pa.: Pennsylvania Historic and Museum Commission, 1971.

Food of Our Fathers. Chicago: Institute of Food Technologists, 1976.

*Galley, Henrietta and J.O. Arnold. *History of the Galley Family.* Philadelphia: Philadelphia Printing and Publishing Co., 1908.

Geise, John. "Household Technology of the Western Frontier." *Western Pennsylvania Historical Magazine.* Pittsburgh: Historical Society of Western Pennsylvania, 1931.

*Gilpin, Joshua, Joseph E. Walker, ed. *The Journals of Joshua Gilpin. 1800.* Harrisburg, Pa.: Pennsylvania Historical and Museum Commission, 1975.

*Hale, Sarah Josepha. *The Good Housekeeper.* Boston: Otis Broaders and Co., 1841.

*Hall, Mrs. Basil, Una Pope-Hennessy, ed. *The Aristocratic Journey Being the Outspoken Letters of Mrs. Basil Hall During a Fourteen Month Sojurn in America 1827-1828.* New York: G.P. Putnam's Sons, 1931.

*Harper, R. Eugene. *The Transformation of Western Pennsylvania 1770-1800.* Pittsburgh: University of Pittsburgh Press, 1991.

*Harpster, John W., ed. *Crossroads: Descriptions of Western Pennsylvania.* Pittsburgh: University of Pittsburgh Press, 1938.

*Harris, Thaddeus Mason. *A Tour in the Country Northwest of the Allegheny Mountains 1805.* In Reuben Gold Thwaites, *Early Western Travels.* New York: AMS Press, 1966.

Hatch, Elizar. *Journal of a Vanished America.* Hammermill Paper Company. (n.p., n.d.)

*Hechtlinger, Adelaide. "Yesterday's Housekeeper." *Early American Life,* October 1974.

*Heckewelder, John, Paul A.W. Wallace, ed. *The Travels of John Heckewelder in Frontier America.* Pittsburgh: University of Pittsburgh Press, 1958.

*Hildreth, S.P. "Early Immigration." *American Pioneer.* Cincinnati: Logan Historical Society, 1843.

*Holliday, Carl. *A Woman's Life in Colonial Days.* Williamstown, Mass.: Corner House, 1968.

*Houston, Matilda Charlotte Jesse Fraser. *Hesperos, or Travels in the West.* London: J.W. Parker, 1850.

Jensen, Joan M. *Loosening the Bonds: Mid-Atlantic Farm Women 1750-1850.* New Haven, Conn.: Yale University Press, 1986.

*Johnson, Frederick C. Address, "Pioneer Women of Wyoming," before Wyoming Valley Chapter of the Daughters of the American Revolution. Wilkes-Barre, Pa.: 1901.

*Johnson, Laurence A. *Over the Counter and On the Shelf.* Rutland, Vt.: Charles S. Tuttle, 1961.

*Jones, Samuel. *Pittsburgh In the Year 1826.* Pittsburgh: Johnston and Stockton, 1826.

*Jordan, Philip D. *The National Road.* Indianapolis, Ind.: Bobbs-Merrill Co., 1948.

*Kirkland, Caroline. *A New Home Or Life in the Clearing.* New York: G.P. Putnam and Son, 1953.

*Lady, A. (Anonymous). *The Housekeeper's Book.* Philadelphia: William Marshall and Co., 1837.

*Lambing, Reverend A.A. *Allegheny County.* Pittsburgh: Snowden and Peterson, 1888.

*Larkin, Jack. *The Reshaping of Everyday Life 1790-1840.* New York: Harper and Row, 1988.

*Lathrop, Elise. *Early American Inns and Taverns.* New York: R.M. McBride, 1926.

*Lee, Alfred McClung. *Trends in Commercial Entertainment in Pittsburgh 1790-1860.* Ph.D. Thesis. University of Pittsburgh, 1931.

*Leslie, Eliza. *The House Book.* Philadelphia: Carey and Hart, 1849.

Lorant, Stefan. *Pittsburgh.* New York: Double-day, 1964.

*MacLeod, Anne Scott. "The *Caddie Woodlawn* Syndrome: American Girlhood in the Nineteenth Century." In *A Century of Childhood,* Mary Lynn Stevens Heininger. Rochester, N.Y.: Margaret Woodbury Strong Museum, 1964.

Sources

*Martin, Scott. *Leisure in Southwestern Pennsylvania 1800-1840*. Ph.D. Thesis. University of Pittsburgh, 1990.

*May, John, Dwight L. Smith, ed. *Journal and Letters Relative to Two Journeys in Ohio Country 1788-89*. Cincinnati: Historical and Philosophical Society of Ohio, 1961.

*McDermott, Robert W. "Early Furniture of Western Pennsylvania." *Western Pennsylvania Historical Magazine*. Pittsburgh: Historical Society of Western Pennsylvania, July 1970.

*McKinney, William Wilson. *Early Pittsburgh Presbyterianism*. Pittsburgh: Gibson Press, 1938.

*McKnight, Dr. W.J. *Pioneer Notes of Jefferson Country, Pennsylvania*. Brookville, Pa.,1900.

*Michaux, F.A. *Travels to the West of the Alleghany Mountains*. In Reuben Gold Thwaites, *Early Western Travels*. New York: AMS Press, 1966.

*Mills, Betty J. *Calico Chronicle*. Lubbock, Tex.: Texas Tech Press, 1985.

*Myres, Sandra L. *Westering Women and the Frontier Experience 1800-1915*. Albuquerque, N. Mex.: University of New Mexico Press, 1983.

*Nevin, Adelaide Mellier. *The Social Mirror: A Character Sketch*. Pittsburgh: T.W. Nevin, 1888.

*"Our Cabin." Anonymous. *American Pioneer*. Cincinnati: Logan Historical Society, 1843.

*Phipps, Frances. *Colonial Kitchens, Their Furnishings and Their Gardens*. New York: Hawthorn Books, Inc., 1972.

*Pickney, Coleworth, ed. *Lady's Token or Gift of Friendship*. Nashua, N.H.: J. Buffam, 1848.

The Pittsburgh Gazette, from July 29, 1786, on.

*Pritchard, Linda K. "The Soul of the City: A Social History of Religion in Pittsburgh." In *City At the Point*, Samuel P. Hays, ed. Pittsburgh: University of Pittsburgh Press, 1989.

Republican Compiler. Pittsburgh, 1818.

*Reynolds, William, Robert D. Ilisivich, ed. *Diary of William Reynolds 1841*. Meadville, Pa.: Crawford County Historical Society, 1981.

*Richter, Conrad. *The Fields*. New York: Alfred A. Knopf, 1945.

*____*The Town*. New York: Alfred A. Knopf, 1950.

*____*The Trees*. New York: Alfred A. Knopf, 1940.

*Riddle, J.M. and M.M. Murray. *Pittsburgh Directory 1815*. Pittsburgh, Pa.: James M. Riddle, 1815. Reprinted by the Duquesne Smelting Corporation, Pittsburgh, Pa., 1940.

*Rishel, Dr. Jonas. *The Indian Physician*. Joseph Miller: New Berlin, Pa., 1828.

*Rothman, Ellen K. *Hands and Hearts: The History of Courtship in America*. Cambridge, Mass.: Harvard University Press, 1987.

*Salmon, Marylynn. *Women and the Law of Property in Early America*. Chapel Hill, N.C.: University of North Carolina Press, 1986.

*Scott, Donald M. and Bernard Wishy, eds. *America's Families. A Documentary History*. New York: Harper and Row, 1982.

*Simmons, Amelia. *American Cookery*. Grand Rapids, Mich.: William B. Eerdmans Publishing Co., 1965.

Sterrett, Mary M. *Pioneer Women of Western Pennsylvania*. Ph.D. Thesis. University of Pittsburgh, 1931.

*Swetnam, George. *Pennsylvania Transportation*. Gettysburg: Pennsylvania Historical Association, 1964.

*Swisshelm, Jane G. *Half a Century*. Chicago: Jansen, McClurg and Co., 1880.

*Thurston, George H. *Allegheny County's Hundred Years*. Pittsburgh: A.A. Anderson and Sons, 1888.

*Tillson, Christiana Holmes. *A Woman's Story of Pioneer Illinois*. Chicago: Lakeside Press, 1919.

*Trollope, Mrs. Frances. *Domestic Manners of Americans*. Barre, Mass.: Imprint Society, 1969.

*Tupper, Martin Farquhar. *Proverbial Philosophy*. New York: Wiley and Putnam, 1847.

*Turnbull, Agnes Sligh. *The King's Orchard*. Boston: Houghton Mifflin, 1963.

*Van Horne, Elizabeth, Elizabeth Colette, ed. "Journey to the Promised Land: The Journal of Elizabeth Van Horne." *Western Pennsylvania Historical Magazine*. Pittsburgh: Historical Society of Western Pennsylvania, 1939.

Wade, Richard C. *The Urban Frontier. The Rise of Western Cities, 1790-1830*. Chicago: University of Chicago, 1972.

West, Elliott. *Growing Up with the Country: Childhood on the Far Western Frontier*. Albuquerque, N. Mex.: University of New Mexico Press, 1989.

*Weymss, Francis Courtney. *Twenty-six Years of the Life of an Actor and Manager*. New York: Burgess, Stringer and Co., 1827.

*Wharton, Anne H. *Social Life in the Early Republic*. Williamstown, Mass: Corner House, 1970.

*Wilkeson, Samuel. "Early Recollections of the West," *American Pioneer*. Cincinnati: Logan Historical Society, April 1841; April, 1843.

*Wright, Elijah, Vincent A. Carrafiello and Richard O. Curry, eds. "The Black City." *Western Pennsylvania Historical Magazine*. Pittsburgh: Historical Society of Western Pennsylvania, 1972.

*Wright, J.E. and Doris Corbett. *Pioneer Life in Western Pennsylvania*. Pittsburgh: University of Pittsburgh Press, 1968.

Wright, Louis B. *The Culture of the Moving Frontier*. Bloomington, Ind.: University of Indiana Press, 1955.

MANUSCRIPTS

*Dandridge Papers. Special Collections Department, William R. Perkins Library. Duke University, Durham, N. C.

*Key, F. "Receipts to Make Some of the Good Things of Life." 1800. Historical Society of Western Pennsylvania, Pittsburgh, Pa.

*LeMoyne Papers. Washington County Historical Society, Washington, Pa.

*Morgan, Margaret Bunyan. Recipe Book. 1790. Historical Society of Western Pennsylvania, Pittsburgh, Pa.

*Prescriptions and Recipes. 1840-50. Historical Society of Western Pennsylvania, Pittsburgh, Pa.

*Professional Diary of Jacob Zimmerman. 1841-1899. Westmoreland County Historical Society, Greensburg, Pa.

*Reed Papers. Historical Society of Western Pennsylvania, Pittsburgh, Pa.

*Thaw Papers. Historical Society of Western Pennsylvania, Pittsburgh, Pa.

INTRODUCTION ENDNOTES

[1] "General Braddock's Campaign," *Pennsylvania Magazine of History and Biography* 11 (1887), 93-97.

[2] Jack D. Warren, "A Young Woman's Vision of Western Pennsylvania: The Diary of Mary Ann Corwin, 1842-43," *Pittsburgh History* 75 (1992), 90-107.

[3] Alfred P. James, *The Ohio Company: Its Inner History* (Pittsburgh, 1959).

[4] Solon J. and Elizabeth H. Buck, *The Planting of Civilization in Western Pennsylvania* (Pittsburgh, 1939), 141-42.

[5] Donald Jackson and Dorothy Twohig, eds., *The Diaries of George Washington* (Charlottesville, Va., 1976-79), II, 316 [October 17, 1770].

[6] For a thorough discussion of the case, see the editorial note from Thomas Smith to GW, Feb. 9, 1785], in W.W. Abbott, ed., *The Papers of George Washington* (Charlottesville, Va., 1976-), Confederation Series, II, 338-358.

[7] The formation of these ethnic and religious communities can be traced mainly through land records and church histories; for an account of how women shared work within a community in a similar frontier setting, see Laurel Thatcher Ulrich, "'A Friendly Neighbor': Social Dimensions of Daily Work in Northern Colonial New England," *Feminist Studies* 6 (1980), 392-405.

[8] Mary Dewees, "Journey from Philadelphia to Kentucky, 1787-1788," *Pennsylvania Magazine of History and Biography* 28 (1904), 184-185. The argument that land ownership was declining among settlers in Western Pennsylvania and their economic position growing more grim is advanced in the following book and two doctoral dissertations: R. Eugene Harper, *The Transformation of Western Pennsylvania, 1770-1800*, (Pittsburgh, 1991); Andrew Cayton, "'The Best of All Possible Worlds': From Independence to Inter-dependence in the Settlement of the Ohio Country, 1780-1825," Ph.D. diss., Brown University, 1981; and James P. McClure, "The Ends of the American Earth: Pittsburgh and the Upper Ohio Valley to 1795," Ph.D. diss., University of Michigan, 1983. For a different interpretation, see Lee Soltow and Kenneth Keller, "Tenancy and Asset-Holding in Late Eighteenth-Century Washington County, Pennsylvania," *Western Pennsylvania Historical Magazine* 65 (1982), 1-15.

[9] Paul A. Wallace, ed., *The Travels of John Heckewelder in Frontier America* (Pittsburgh, 1958), 379.

[10] Buck, *Planting of Civilization in Western Pennsylvania*, 212.

[11] On the postwar depression and recovery in the region, see esp. Richard C. Wade, *The Urban Frontier: The Rise of the Western Cities, 1790-1830* (Cambridge, Mass., 1959).

[12] Joan M. Jenson, *Loosening the Bonds: Mid-Atlantic Farm Women, 1750-1850* (New Haven, Conn., 1986), esp. 79-113.

[13] W. J. McKnight, *A Pioneer Outline History of Northwestern Pennsylvania* (Philadelphia, 1905), 468-69.

[14] Suzanne Lesbock, *The Free Women of Petersburg: Status and Culture in a Southern Town* (New York, 1984).

[15] The best treatment of the importance of the idea of "separate spheres" in the formation of the American middle class is Mary P. Ryan, *Cradle of the Middle Class: The Family in Oneida County, New York, 1790-1865* (Cambridge, 1981); see also the treatment of Nancy F. Cott, *The Bonds of Womanhood: Woman's Sphere in New England, 1780-1835* (New Haven, 1977).

[16] Nancy Grey Osterud, *Bonds of Community: The Lives of Farm Women in Nineteenth Century New York* (Ithaca, N.Y., 1991); see also Glenda Riley, *The Female Frontier: A Comparative View of Women on the Prairie and the Plains* (Lawrence, Kan., 1988).

INDEX